NEW SEED AND OLD LAWS

*Regulatory reform and the
diversification of national seed systems*

Edited by

ROBERT TRIPP

Intermediate Technology Publications
on behalf of the
Overseas Development Institute
1997

Intermediate Technology Publications
103/105 Southampton Row   London   WC1B 4HH, UK

© Overseas Development Institute 1997

A CIP Catalogue record for this book is available from
the British Library

ISBN 185339 415 7

Typeset by Dorwyn Ltd, Rowlands Castle, Hants
Printed in the UK by SRP Exeter

Contents

Preface

THIS BOOK IS the result of a three-year project on seed regulatory reform. Seed provision in developing countries has been subjected to a number of important changes, including a reduction in public sector budgets for agricultural research and extension, the growth of commercial seed enterprises and voluntary organization seed projects, the continuing reduction of plant genetic diversity in farmers' fields and considerable uncertainties about the implications of intellectual property protection applied to plant varieties. The project was motivated by the concern that many national seed regulatory frameworks were not sufficiently flexible and innovative to meet these challenges. The project's goals included an assessment of the conduct of current regulatory frameworks and the development of guidelines and principles that would be broadly applicable for regulatory reform.

The project was managed by the Overseas Development Institute (ODI) and the Centre for Arid Zone Studies, University of Wales (CAZS). The work included literature reviews, a series of detailed country case studies and a workshop that brought together a very knowledgeable and diverse group of people to discuss and debate the project's tentative conclusions.

The research at CAZS focused on the regulatory implications of public plant breeding programmes, as well as seed regulatory frameworks in India. This work was managed by John Witcombe and Daljit Virk, and it was a pleasure to collaborate with them. ODI's task involved an examination of the organization of seed regulation. The initial conception and the development of the project at ODI were carried out by Elizabeth Cromwell and John Farrington.

The project involved two separate phases, both supported by the UK Overseas Development Administration (ODA) (Natural Resources Policy Research Programme). In addition, a separate country study in Nepal was supported by ODA's South East Asia Development Division. The usual disclaimers apply, but ODA's support for the project is gratefully acknowledged.

Many of the conclusions of the project are based on case study research, and we were fortunate to attract an excellent group of people to lead these studies. The researchers included: (Bolivia) Jorge Rosales, Gonzalo Romero, Iciar Pavez, Alan Bojanic, Guido Revollo; (India) S.K. Banerjee, B.G. Jaisani, Y.M. Upadhyaya, K.L. Vyas; (Kenya) Lydia Kimenye, Hezron Nyangito, Kiarie Njoroge, Jeremiah Kipligat; (Nepal) Krishna

Joshi, Kamalesh Rajbhandary, Bhuwon Sthapit; (Pakistan) Zahur Alam, A.R. Saleemi, Altaf-Ur-Rehman Rao; (Philippines) José Hernandez, Terrisita Borromeo, Manuel Logroño, (Zimbabwe) Nehemia Mashiringwani, Joseph Rusike, Temba Musa and Christmas Pasipanodya.

The Pakistan and Philippines case studies were managed by John Nelson and the Bolivia case study was organized and managed by Jonathan Woolley. P.S. Sodhi provided invaluable support for the case studies in India. Andrew Packwood and A.G.B. Raj contributed to the case study analysis at CAZS. Paul Balogun developed an economic analysis of regulatory failure, with input from Paul Heisey.

The project's results and hypotheses were discussed, debated and reformulated during a three-day workshop in London in May 1996. While perhaps few of the workshop participants will agree with all of the conclusions of this book, they are responsible for having advanced the analysis to a higher level. The participants are listed in Appendix 1. The organization of the workshop profited greatly from the leadership of Michael Hayward, Niels Louwaars and W. Joost van der Burg. Additional support was provided by Paul Balogun and John Nelson.

Most of the chapters in this book are the product of the debates of the workshop. Many of the chapters have also benefited from suggestions made by the following people who kindly took time to provide reviews: Sam Bockari-Kugbei, Bees Butler, Niels Louwaars, Michael Morris, Ortwin Neuendorf, Victor Ocran, Cadmo Rosell, Louise Sperling, Bhuwon Sthapit and Michael Turner.

Sue Squire cheerfully and competently prepared more drafts of these chapters than she will care to remember and Margaret Cornell provided her usual precise editorial supervision.

It is the hope of everyone associated with the project that the material presented in this book will contribute to the development of more responsive and imaginative regulatory frameworks to support the growth and diversification of national seed systems.

Robert Tripp
Overseas Development Institute
London

Acronyms

AASCO	Association of American Seed Control Officials
AIC	Agricultural Input Corporation (Nepal)
AICCIP	All India Co-ordinated Crop Improvement Programme
AKRSP	Aga Khan Rural Support Programme (Pakistan)
AMSAC	Mexican Seed Producers Association
AOSCA	Association of Official Seed Certifying Agencies (US and Canada)
ARPOV	Argentinean Association for Plant Variety Protection
ASSINSEL	International Association of Plant Breeders for the Protection of Plant Varieties
ASTA	American Seed Trade Association
AVT	Advanced Variety Trial (India)
AYT	Advanced Yield Trial (Kenya, The Philippines)
BPI	Bureau of Plant Industry (The Philippines)
BRAC	Bangladesh Rural Advancement Committee
CAZS	Centre For Arid Zone Studies (University of Wales)
CDR	complex, diverse and risk-prone
CESA	Ecuadoran Centre for Agricultural Services
CGIAR	Consultative Group on International Agricultural Research
CIAL	Committees for Local Agricultural Research (Colombia)
CIAT	International Centre for Tropical Agriculture
CIMMYT	International Maize and Wheat Improvement Centre
CSVIG	Corn and Sorghum Varietal Improvement Group (The Philippines)
CV	coefficient of error variation
CVT	Co-ordinated Variety Trial (Nepal)
CYT	Comparative Yield Trial (Bolivia)
DADO	District Agriculture Development Office (Nepal)
DLG	German Agricultural Society
DOA	Department of Agriculture
DUS	distinct, uniform and stable
EMBRAPA	Brazilian Agricultural Research Enterprise
EU	European Union
FAO	Food and Agriculture Organization
FFT	Farmers' Field Trial (Nepal)

FIS	International Seed Trade Federation
GATT	General Agreement on Tariffs and Trade
GIS	Geographic Information System
GLP	Good Laboratory Practices
HYV	High Yielding Variety
IBTA	Institute of Agricultural Technology (Bolivia)
ICA	Colombian Institute of Agriculture
ICAR	Indian Council of Agricultural Research
ICARDA	International Centre For Agricultural Research in the Dry Areas
ICRISAT	International Crops Research Institute for the Semi-Arid Tropics
IET	Initial Evaluation Trial (India, Nepal)
INASE	National Seed Institute (Argentina)
IPGRI	International Plant Genetic Resources Institute
IPR	intellectual property rights
IPRA	Participatory Research in Agriculture (Colombia)
IRRI	International Rice Research Institute
ISAR	National Agricultural Research Institute (Rwanda)
ISNAR	International Service for National Agricultural Research
ISTA	International Seed Testing Association
KARI	Kenya Agricultural Research Institute
KOSEPAN	Koshi Seed Entrepreneurs Association (Nepal)
KOSEVEG	Koshi Hills Seed and Vegetable Project (Nepal)
KRIBP	Krishak Bharati Co-operative Indo-British Rainfed Farming Project
KSC	Kenya Seed Company
LARC	Lumle Agricultural Research Centre (Nepal)
MAFF	Ministry of Agriculture, Fisheries and Food (UK)
MASIPAG	Farmer–Scientists Partnership For Agricultural Development (The Philippines)
MCC	Mennonite Central Committee
MV	modern variety
NARC	Nepalese Agricultural Research Council
NARS	National Agricultural Research System
NCT	National Co-operative Testing (The Philippines)
NGO	non-government organization
NPT	National Performance Trial (Kenya)
NRRP	National Rice Research Programme (Nepal)
NSQCS	National Seed Quality Control Service (Kenya)
NUYT	National Uniform Yield Trial (Pakistan)
ODA	Overseas Development Administration
ODI	Overseas Development Institute

OECD	Organization for Economic Co-operation and Development
OFT	On-Farm Trial (The Philippines)
OPV	open-pollinated variety
OYT	Observational Yield Trial (Pakistan)
PAC	Pakhribas Agricultural Centre (Nepal)
PBR	Plant Breeders' Rights
PGRC/E	The Plant Genetic Resources Centre/Ethiopia
PPA	Plant Patent Act (US)
PPB	Participatory Plant Breeding
PRONASE	National Seed Company (Mexico)
PVP	Plant Variety Protection
PVPA	Plant Variety Protection Act (US)
PVS	Participatory Varietal Selection
PYT	Preliminary Yield Trial (Kenya, Pakistan, The Philippines)
QDS	Quality Declared Seed
RT	Regional Trial (Bolivia)
RVIG	Rice Varietal Improvement Group (The Philippines)
RYT	Replicated Yield Trial (Pakistan)
SADC	Southern African Development Community
SANSOR	South African National Seed Organization
SCCI	Seed Control and Certification Institute (Zambia)
SD	standard deviation
SEAN	Seed Entrepreneurs Association of Nepal
ShBR	Sheath Brown Rot
SNICS	National Seed Inspection and Certification Service (Mexico)
STU	Seed Technology Unit (The Gambia)
SVRC	Specialist Variety Release Committee (Kenya)
TRIP	Trade-Related Intellectual Property Rights
UNIMILHO	an association of maize seed producers (Brazil)
UPLB	University of the Philippines at Los Baños
UPOV	International Union for the Protection of New Varieties of Plants
USDA	US Department of Agriculture
USAID	US Agency for International Development
VAT	value added tax
VCU	value for cultivation and use
VT	Validation Trial (Bolivia)
WTO	World Trade Organization

List of contributors

Jaqueline Ashby	Director of Research, Natural Resources, International Centre for Tropical Agriculture (CIAT), Cali, Colombia
Elizabeth Cromwell	Research Fellow, Overseas Development Institute
David Gisselquist	Consultant, International Economics Department, World Bank, Washington, DC
Niels Louwaars	Seed Systems Specialist, Centre for Plant Breeding and Reproduction Research, Wageningen, The Netherlands
Louise Sperling	Visiting Research Fellow, Overseas Development Institute
Robert Tripp	Research Fellow, Overseas Development Institute
W. Joost van der Burg	Senior Seed Technologist, Centre for Plant Breeding and Reproduction Research, Wageningen, The Netherlands
Daljit S. Virk	Research Fellow, Centre for Arid Zone Studies, University of Wales, Bangor
Jeroen van Wijk	Research Fellow, University of Amsterdam, The Netherlands
John R. Witcombe	Senior Research Fellow, Centre for Arid Zone Studies, University of Wales, Bangor

PART 1

SEEDS AND REGULATION

1 Introduction

THIS BOOK IS concerned with the regulation of national seed systems. The attempt to address simultaneously the subjects of seed and government regulation must begin by acknowledging a tremendous gulf in imagery. 'Seed' is commonly utilized as a symbol for renewal and diversity in agriculture. The contrast with the barren, routinized and uninspiring character of government bureaucracy is sharply drawn. But these two seemingly disparate themes are brought together by the realities of agricultural change in developing countries. Seed is no longer a subject of universal optimism. There is ample evidence of inequities in access to seed between rich and poor farmers; concerns are expressed about the declining diversity in farmers' fields; and there are signs of increasing concentration in the private control of seed supply. It is the principal thesis of this book that a thorough re-examination of public regulatory responsibilities will help to restore optimism to national seed systems and at the same time rejuvenate an interest in the public role in agricultural development.

The state and agricultural development

State responsibilities for agricultural development may seem an unpromising place to begin addressing the challenge of strengthening national seed systems. The public sector role in agriculture is, after all, in disarray and disrepute. Perhaps the most common perception is that government research and input systems have provided so-called Green Revolution technology to farmers in the more favoured environments but have neither served the majority of resource-poor farmers nor sufficiently protected the genetic diversity on which all farming depends. In addition, popular opinion increasingly regards government seed activities as irrelevant, and attention shifts to the growing influence of transnational corporations and their ability to control seed supply through intellectual property protection and genetic engineering.

This book contends that the scenario is not nearly as starkly conceived nor as inevitably determined as popular perceptions might indicate. There is considerable justification for believing that national seed systems can be developed that are responsive to the needs of farmers, supportive of rural diversity and capable of change and evolution. The key to taking control of seed system development, however, is renewed attention to public sector

3

responsibilities, and in particular the potential contribution of innovative regulation.

Until recently, the direction of agricultural development in most countries was almost exclusively in the hands of the state. There is now a widespread feeling that the state has not performed adequately in this role and that other institutions should be given a chance. Donor demands for the adoption of structural adjustment policies have led many governments to reduce their support for agricultural research and extension and to remove subsidies for agricultural inputs and marketing.

The increasing scepticism about the state's role in agriculture has been partially responsible for the emergence of alternative strategies. Private initiatives are now common, as the commercial sector takes more responsibility for agricultural marketing and input supply, especially to serve the needs of better-off farmers. There is increasing private investment in agricultural research, and even instances of private extension services, often employing former staff of state institutions who have been retrenched or lured away by more attractive salaries.

While these private sector endeavours address the state's failure to meet effectively the demands of commercially oriented farmers for inputs and services, another movement is addressing the state's failure to address the needs of more economically disadvantaged farmers. A wide range of community-based efforts at strengthening local farming systems have been organized by NGOs and other groups. These efforts seek to strengthen local capacity to develop improved farming practices, to support and augment the flow of local knowledge in agriculture and to design more sustainable and self-sufficient local agricultural systems.

This participation of commercial and voluntary institutions in agricultural development should be seen as a positive move towards diversifying the agricultural sector. There is the danger, however, that a rush to embrace more attractive and fashionable strategies may leave the state and its potential contributions completely neglected. There is a distinction between addressing the undeniable failures of state policies for agricultural development, on the one hand, and abandoning any interest in state roles or responsibilities, on the other. As Lipton and Paarlberg (1990:134) caution: 'Neither the market as such nor indigenous non-governmental organizations represent a well-formulated answer; rather they are too often hopeful or idealized models that contrast with past, rejected, perhaps exaggerated muddles of parastatal misbehaviour.'

Much 'parastatal misbehaviour' can indeed be addressed through commercial and voluntary alternatives, but it is also necessary to re-examine the legitimate contributions of the state in supporting agricultural development. In most industrialized countries the state still plays a significant role in agricultural research and extension, for instance. Also, effective and responsive markets do not simply emerge, but must be fostered and developed.

4

Perhaps most important, the state has a leading role in determining the direction of agricultural change. Agriculture is the most important source of livelihood for the rural poor, and improvements in rural income translate to wider growth in the economy; the state must be a guarantor for equitable agricultural development and help strengthen the integrity of diverse rural societies. The choice of agricultural development strategy also has significant environmental consequences for which neither commercial nor voluntary efforts can be expected to take complete responsibility; the state must guide the protection and enhancement of the nation's natural resources.

There is thus much work to be done in specifying the precise contributions that the state should make to agricultural development in a complex and dynamic environment of institutional change. Both commercial enterprise and community-led initiatives offer considerable strengths. In this sense, the state is but one potential supplier of services, and must prove its worth. But the state should also be a mediator, an enabler and a conscience. Any examination of current practices of state agencies reveals a huge gap between promise and performance, indicating the seriousness of the challenge. The potential of a rapidly evolving institutional landscape in agriculture must be matched by a careful identification of the strengths, limitations and responsibilities of state, commercial and community contributions to a coherent agricultural development strategy.

Regulation

The subject of regulation is a particularly appropriate focus for specifying institutional responsibilities in agricultural development. At first sight, public perceptions of regulation would seem to belie its potential for contributing to our understanding of institutional change. On the one hand, a common view of regulation is that of a dry, technical subject, characterized by arcane rules and bureaucratic red tape. On the other hand, we recognize the role of regulation in the rhetoric of political debate, where frustration with unjust practices leads to calls for government 'regulation', and (more frequently) attempts to reduce government intrusion are represented by demands for 'deregulation'.

The breadth of these unflattering associations with the subject of regulation indicates, however, that it may indeed be a particularly useful entry point for thinking about institutional responsibilities in agriculture. Regulation, and agricultural development itself, encompasses technical and political issues, and both must be addressed. Regulation includes scientific concerns that direct farmers and consumers to safe and productive technologies; and it represents the political compromises made between competing interests for access to resources. It embraces everything from the technical details of environmental protection to the negotiation of the rules that structure the agricultural economy.

Regulation addresses issues that are at the core of economic development. Some regulation is concerned with protecting society from the unintended consequences of actions that may jeopardize public safety or welfare. But equally important, regulation seeks to structure the interactions among individuals and organizations to foster the growth of productive relationships that are in the public interest. The basic regulatory scenario can be reduced to the interaction between the provider and the user of a service or commodity, such as seed. How is this interaction to be organized so that there is trust between the parties and incentives to continue the relationship? There are only three possible answers, and they provide the basis of all regulation.

The first possibility is to integrate provider and user so that they share a common purpose. In the case of seed, this is what happens when a farmer saves and uses his or her own seed, or when provision and utilization are managed within a community, a co-operative, or an enterprise. The second possibility is for provider and user to develop mechanisms that promote mutual trust and allow for negotiation and exchange of information. At the local level, examples are provided by relations developed between farmers or between partners in indigenous trade and markets. Further examples include the contracts, trading partnerships and investment in reputations that characterize much of modern commercial life. The final regulatory possibility is to rely on a third party to help structure the terms of a relationship; the third party may be an independent entity, or the responsibility may fall to the state.

It should be clear that the third-party option, the classic case of the government regulator, is only one option. Once we begin to examine the purposes of regulation we understand that regulatory responsibilities cannot reside only with the state. Regulation is not simply concerned with technical questions regarding the quality of interaction between provider and user, but also involves the integrity and the capacities of the parties in the relationship. Thus regulatory reform is part of larger questions concerning the appropriate institutional division of labour to promote a productive and equitable agriculture.

This book examines regulation and regulatory reform as it relates to the development of national seed systems. The treatment involves both the technical, operational side of seed regulation, which is the theme of Part 2, and the institutional side of seed regulation, which is addressed in Part 3.

The focus of seed

If we wish to look at changing institutional responsibilities in agriculture, there is no better place to start than with seed, the most essential agricultural input. It is universally required, the object of intense care and selection, the source of hopes for future seasons and lessons from previous ones, at once an important item of commerce and a symbol of self-sufficiency.

Seed is a unique input in terms of the breadth of management and expertise that it attracts. In the hands of resource-poor farmers, who struggle against difficult and uncertain conditions, seed is the most precious of resources. It is carefully stored and selected, the repository of knowledge passed from generation to generation, and the result of continual adaptation and innovation in the face of ever greater challenges for survival. In the hands of some of the world's largest corporations, seed is a focus of investment that attracts advanced biotechnological research and sophisticated marketing techniques. And in between these extremes are countless farmers, seed producers, traders, community groups and plant breeders, all of whom depend upon seed and respect its singular role in agriculture.

All of these actors are drawn together by their common dependence on seed, by the fact that seed can be exchanged or traded among them, and by the fact that seed can be modified and improved in the most modern laboratory or in the most remote hillside field. It is impossible to treat community-level seed activities, the commercial seed sector or public plant breeding and seed production, in isolation. They are increasingly interdependent parts of national seed systems and they are all affected by national seed regulation. If we wish to understand how regulation has the potential to promote or to impede the development of the agricultural sector, there is no better example than seed.

National seed systems are changing rapidly. The traditional public sector roles in plant breeding and seed production are being reshaped, but often with no clear idea of what alternatives might replace them. Both public and private efforts have provided an increasing selection of new varieties, but many farmers must still rely entirely on their own resources. There are more varieties in the market but fewer varieties in farmers' fields, as genetic diversity is jeopardized by the structure of current incentives for plant breeding. There are increasing debates about what types of new varieties should be developed and how access to them is to be controlled. And there is considerable uncertainty about who will be allowed to produce seed and how its quality will be assured, as the state continues to guard its regulatory prerogative in the face of growing commercial and voluntary sector innovation. All of these issues are the subject of national seed regulation, and they affect all participants in the seed system, from the most isolated farming village to the most powerful corporation.

The organization of seed regulation

Seed is a special commodity and its regulation involves particular challenges. It is both an essential agricultural input that is widely traded, and a living organism that requires particular care. Farmers have quite specific requirements for crop varieties, thus seed supply must be carefully planned and targeted. The qualities of the seed purchased by the farmer may not be evident until after planting, or even until harvest; hence the farmer seeks some assurance about the integrity of the seller. Seed is often a profitable item of commerce, yet because farmers can easily multiply and distribute many types of seed, it has some of the characteristics of a public rather than a private good, and incentives for commercial seed production will develop only under specific conditions.

The seed regulations of developing countries exhibit considerable variability in scope and design, but they tend to share several characteristics. First, they were usually established at a time when virtually all plant breeding and seed production was in the hands of government organizations. They were designed to regulate public sector activity, with little thought to commercial or community-level alternatives. Second, most seed regulatory frameworks in developing countries are borrowed from industrialized countries whose seed systems, economies and infrastructure may make them inappropriate models for regulatory design. Finally, a consensus that current seed regulations are inadequate is shared by a remarkable range of farmers, plant breeders, seed enterprises, voluntary agencies and regulators themselves. There is widespread belief that seed regulatory frameworks need to be redesigned if national seed systems are to achieve their potential.

This book describes the current status of national seed regulatory frameworks and suggests how they can be changed to support the development of diverse and equitable national seed systems. Three principal areas are addressed.

The first is the set of regulations that determines what crop varieties are available for sale or distribution. In many countries a variety must be registered before it can be made available. In addition, most public sector varieties and many private ones are required to pass a series of performance tests before release. We shall be interested in the relevance of these registration and performance-testing procedures for various types of farmers. We shall also ask who controls the variety release process, what incentives it provides for plant breeding, and what effect it has on farmers' own variety development.

A second regulatory theme is seed quality control. The seller of seed may know considerably more about its quality than the buyer, and seed sale is often subject to some type of control that provides a guarantee to the farmer. Most governments maintain a seed certification service that controls public sector seed supply, and often regulates private sector seed as well. Is the management of seed quality control by the state sufficient to protect farmers or, on the other hand, is it too restrictive and does it discourage innovative seed provision? As new alternatives for seed production appear, should the state continue to manage the quality control

8

system, and what responsibilities should the seed producer, the merchant and the farmer be encouraged to assume?

The third area addressed by our analysis is the organization of public plant breeding. Although this may seem to fall outside the conventional conception of seed regulation, it is extremely relevant for our purposes. National variety release and seed quality control regulations have a considerable influence on the way plant breeding is conducted; to be successful, a new variety must be compatible with regulatory standards. On the other hand, the priorities and conduct of public plant breeding systems have strong implications for the design of adequate regulatory systems. In particular, we shall be concerned with the questions of whether shifting more attention to the varietal needs of resource-poor farmers requires changes in the standards that are used to evaluate new varieties, and whether more decentralized plant breeding to meet farmers' diverse needs implies changes in the way seed production and quality control are structured.

The issue of intellectual property protection for plant varieties will also feature in our discussions of seed regulatory frameworks. Given the considerable public debate about various attempts to patent life forms, and the prominence of plant variety protection (PVP) in many debates about the future of national seed systems, the reader may be surprised that the subject is not given even more emphasis. There are several reasons for addressing PVP in the broader context of national seed regulatory systems. First, despite legitimate concerns about the possible effects of PVP on farmers' access to seed and the conservation of plant genetic diversity, it is not sufficiently appreciated that conventional national seed regulatory systems also have a strong impact on these same issues. Second, it is not likely that policy makers will be able to devise adequate national strategies for PVP before considering how to make their current seed regulatory system more responsive to the needs of farmers. In addition, it would be a mistake to give undue emphasis to PVP which, in most countries, will have an initial impact on a relatively few food crops grown by the more commercially oriented farmers, while ignoring current regulatory systems that affect the lives of countless farmers today.

Seed regulations and institutional change

It should be clear that regulation involves not only the organization of technical procedures and controls, but is also intimately linked to issues of institutional development. The potentially broad implications of regulation and regulatory change are nowhere more clearly illustrated than in national seed systems. Seed regulation has the capacity to influence significantly the direction of change for agricultural institutions.

It is impossible to compartmentalize national seed systems. The subject of seed confounds the facile classifications often applied to agricultural

9

development; the divisions of 'commercial' versus 'subsistence' or 'formal' versus 'local' are easily traversed by the flow and exchange of seed, and by its universal attraction for every class of farmer. Local-level variety development, for instance, has provided the basis of much formal plant breeding. Controls or privileges for the commercial seed industry, on the other hand, may have serious repercussions for the capacities and options available to community-level seed provision. Thus any discussion of seed regulation must be prepared to address the concerns of the entire national seed system.

The public, commercial, and voluntary sectors all have a vital role in national seed systems, and all have significant contributions to make in improving regulatory capacity. Again, sharp distinctions among these sectors are not always helpful. The dividing line between voluntary and commercial activity in national seed systems is not particularly clear, for instance, especially as NGOs place more emphasis on ensuring the economic viability of their seed activities. Similarly, discussions about options for regulation cannot be reduced to a debate about 'markets versus states'. We must realize that most national seed systems illustrate how important it is 'to strengthen both states and markets, [while currently] they often tend to weaken and undermine each other' (Streeten, 1995:31).

An open and realistic consideration of options for seed regulation requires an abandonment of the confrontational characterizations that often punctuate debates about the future of national seed systems. The commercial seed sector is not cradled by a benign invisible hand that unerringly moves to the side of public welfare, but neither is it composed of predatory entrepreneurs bent on the control and destruction of genetic and cultural diversity. Similarly, it must be acknowledged that relatively few voluntary sector seed initiatives are yet sustainable, and many are based on unrealistic premises, but the proven record of the voluntary sector in other endeavours promises significant potential contributions to seed sector development.

The principal institutional focus in any discussion of regulation however, must be the state. Much of the blame for current regulatory problems lies with the state, both through misguided carelessness and selfish protectionism. Once again, 'dogmatism here leads to error; . . . many governments are neither monolithic nor impervious to pressures for rational and altruistic policies' (ibid.:37). Any hope for useful regulatory change must be directed first to state agencies, which set the tone for regulatory management. We shall argue that, paradoxically, the state can gain regulatory authority in national seed systems only by ceding many of its responsibilities to other institutions. Much of this book is directed towards defining how that transition can be organized, contributing to the development of 'a strong state, with a limited agenda' (ibid.:20).

The search for a definition of the state's 'limited agenda' in seed regulation will be described here as regulatory reform. A well-defined role for the

10

state in national seed systems should set a complementary course of action for civil society and commercial interests. The state's role is to enable the diversification of the seed system, and its oversight is meant to direct attention to the interests of the disadvantaged and to ensure protection of the nation's plant genetic patrimony. Thus the juxtaposition of seeds and regulation is not as contradictory as this chapter's introduction implied, and regulatory reform may serve to return growth and diversity to both seed systems and public responsibility.

This book is not about the theory of regulation, nor is it concerned with the technical details of seed production. It is rather a summary of current experience and a set of practical suggestions about how regulatory reform can contribute to the growth of national seed systems. It is addressed to all those who have a stake in agricultural development, including policymakers, researchers, donors, voluntary agencies and commercial seed producers.

Because seed systems are broad and complex, any attempt to address regulatory reform must include the interests and experience of a wide range of actors. Seed regulation and regulatory reform involve a much wider set of participants than just state agencies and policymakers. The interests of all farming communities, commercial seed enterprises, and voluntary agencies must be considered. The strategy is to seek consensus rather than to promote confrontation. But this requires that all participants be realistic about their motives, capacities, and limitations. Regulatory options are rarely clear-cut, and most involve compromise, trial and evolution. More important, they require commitment from all participants to strengthen and diversify the national seed system.

The organization of the book

The book is divided into three parts. The first part serves as an introduction to the subjects of national seed systems and regulation. Chapter 2 is an outline of national seed systems. It discusses how farmers' variety improvement and seed management practices, developed over centuries, have been complemented by the growth of formal plant breeding and the establishment of public and private seed production enterprises. It emphasizes the fact that seed may be both an input and a source of new genetic material, and that these two qualities help determine whether farmers save their own seed, rely on other local sources, or choose to use formal sector seed. The chapter also examines the current status of national seed systems, outlines the case for greater diversification and introduces the themes that are important for the subsequent examination of seed regulatory reform.

Chapter 3 is an introduction to the subject of regulation. A brief review of the literature examines the nature of regulation and the justifications for its establishment. This is followed by an analysis of the problems and dilemmas associated with reliance on government regulatory structures and an introduction to regulatory alternatives. Particular emphasis is placed on the fact that regulation consists of three separate responsibilities: setting standards, monitoring and supervision, and enforcement. Innovative regulatory options for national seed systems can take advantage of possibilities for dividing these responsibilities among different institutions. Options for seed regulatory reform must be designed to involve wide participation from various actors in the seed system, address the diverse needs of farmers and seed producers and be able to accommodate change and evolution in the seed system.

The second part of the book looks at the organization of seed regulation, focusing on variety testing, variety regulation and seed quality control. In each case, it combines an analysis of the problems of current regulatory systems with a thorough examination of options for reform. Chapter 4 focuses on public sector plant breeding in developing countries. It features a detailed and innovative analysis of data from public breeding systems that shows significant inefficiencies in the way variety testing is organized. It also questions the relevance for resource-poor farmers of many of the standards and protocols that are followed, and in particular it questions excessive reliance on the strategy of breeding for broad adaptation. A number of alternatives for the organization of public plant breeding are then discussed, and emphasis is placed on possibilities for decentralization, the development of greater farmer participation in the plant breeding process, and the implications for the management and mandate of public agricultural research.

Chapter 5 examines the regulations that govern the availability of new crop varieties. It reviews evidence from a number of countries on the organization of variety registration, performance testing and release. These procedures are responsible for significant delays in the delivery of new varieties, and the standards used are often inappropriate for the circumstances of many farmers. Variety regulation is also subject to national policies that may try to give undue protection to public sector research and seed production. The reform of variety regulation includes attention to simple registration strategies that are not confounded with the requirements of a PVP system and do not threaten the use and diffusion of local varieties. If more responsibility for performance testing is placed in the hands of farmers and plant breeders, increasingly responsive variety development can be expected.

Chapter 6 discusses seed quality control, which includes both seed certification (for genetic purity) and seed testing (for physical quality). Most countries have established some type of public certification service, and problems are evident in the efficiency of the service provided, the lack of attention to monitoring seed marketing and the possibilities for corruption when certification is rigidly applied. Three major options are discussed for reforming seed quality control. One is the possibility of improving the management of public regulatory agencies. The second option comprises several strategies for sharing quality control responsibilities between the public agency and seed producers. The third option assigns most responsibility for quality control to the seed producers themselves. The chapter discusses the factors that should influence the choice among these options.

The third part of the book addresses the institutional implications of seed regulatory reform. Chapter 7 argues that regulatory reform occupies a unique and important position between broad institutional change and specific organizational strategies. The options and principles discussed in the previous three chapters can be applied to seed systems. Because each national seed system is a unique combination of political, economic, technical, and historical forces, regulatory reform will naturally vary from country to country, and will reflect particular regulatory cultures. But implications can be drawn for specific organizational responsibilities, and the remainder of the chapter outlines conclusions for public agricultural research and extension, agricultural policy and public regulatory agencies.

The rest of the book examines the commercial and voluntary seed sectors in greater detail. Chapter 8 is a spirited appeal for governments to remove the barriers they have established against commercial seed production and trade. It argues for the opening of markets and presents justifications for eliminating many of the rules and regulations that have discouraged entrepreneurial activity in the seed sectors of developing countries.

Chapter 9 examines the issue of plant variety protection, which is increasingly associated with the growth of the commercial seed sector. It is based on research in Latin America, where the first evidence is becoming available on the impact of PVP in developing countries. The basic issues and options for PVP are described, and the likely outcomes for farmers are discussed. Emphasis is also given to the fact that PVP is not the only way that access to plant varieties may be restricted.

Chapter 10 reviews recent experience with farmer participation in plant breeding and variety selection. There are a growing number of endeavours that explore farmer contributions and responsibilities for productive partnerships with public plant breeding programmes. An assessment of such activities is vital for the consideration of the strategies discussed in Chapter 4.

Chapter 11 is based on the most complete review to date of NGO and other local-level seed activities. It describes the remarkable range of small-scale seed projects that have been developed in the past decade and provides an assessment of their strengths and weaknesses. It then goes on to describe the responsibilities of NGOs and public organizations if local-level seed production innovations are to play an important role in diversifying national seed systems.

2 The structure of national seed systems

ROBERT TRIPP

Seed systems

SEED SYSTEMS ARE as old as agriculture itself. They encompass the development, maintenance and diffusion of crop varieties and the production, storage and distribution of seed. The prehistoric transition from hunting and gathering to agriculture involved the development of skills in seed selection, cultivation and maintenance. The range of food crops available today, and the remarkable variability within it, is largely due to the increasing sophistication with which farmers have learned to manage their seed systems.

The resources available to early farmers were severely limited. Knowledge and skills were developed and exchanged within small communities, and the germplasm base from which seed could be selected and improved was drawn from the local area. Nevertheless, this process of domestication led to remarkable transformations in the character and productivity of food crops (Evans, 1993). As trade and exchange among communities developed there were increasing opportunities for access to new sources of germplasm and new ideas for its management. Conquest and trade brought ever-expanding cycles of seed and planting material of both familiar and exotic crops. The Song emperor Zhenzong promoted the cultivation of earlier-maturing rice varieties in the Lower Yangzi region by importing 30 000 bushels of seed from Fujian province in AD 1012; the varieties had originated far away in the state of Annam, but had been spread by farmer-to-farmer contact since at least the sixth century. The new varieties did not at first yield as well as the local ones, but peasant farmers quickly began to adapt them to their own farming conditions (Bray, 1986:22).

The expansion of European exploration in the fifteenth century was responsible for an expanded movement of crops. A number of authors point out that a large proportion of the food crops currently grown in industrialized countries originates in the South (e.g., Kloppenburg and Kleinman, 1988). New World crops such as potato and maize were introduced to Europe, and maize, cassava and groundnut were carried to Africa. European colonists and settlers brought their own crops with them to North America and adapted and selected them for the conditions they encountered; until 1930, for instance, the vast majority of the wheat grown in the US was based on germplasm that could trace its origin to the former

14

Soviet Union (Cox, 1991). In the mid-nineteenth century, the agricultural division of the US Patent Office was distributing as many as 60 000 seed packets a year to farmers as part of a campaign to collect useful varieties from all over the world and make them available to US farmers (Kloppenburg, 1988).

Although the movement of new crops greatly expanded farmers' range of possibilities, the work of adapting the germplasm to local conditions and selecting for improvements was still the responsibility of local farming communities and individual farmers. Sorghum varieties introduced from Africa to the USA flowered late and were not adapted to cool temperatures. It was farmer selection of dwarf and early mutants that converted the crop to the growing conditions of higher latitudes (Evans, 1993:127). This

---

Box 2.1   The maintenance of crop varietal diversity in highland Peru

The farmers in the Paucartambo region of Peru's southern Andes grow potatoes and maize as basic staples. For both crops, farmer selection techniques maintain a high degree of genetic diversity.

Potatoes are the most important crop in the region. Local potato varieties are classified by 'use category', divided among those appropriate for boiling, soup-making or freeze drying. Further subclassification is done on the basis of morphological differences. Farmers also classify the different production zones in which they plant potatoes, depending on altitude and planting season. Most farmers plant between three and six separate potato fields, each one devoted to a mixture of varieties of the same category of use. Women are responsible for selecting planting material. For a field of a particular use category, they generally select a few of the most important varieties and then make a representative selection of the remaining material to provide the desired diversity. Observations in a sample of 26 fields of the 'boiling-potato' category showed that women sowed a mean of 21.1 varieties per 225 plants.

Maize is also classified into use categories by the farmers of Paucartambo, who distinguish between maize for boiling and for parching; they recognize many other uses as well, such as beer-making, hominy and crushed maize. Twenty-seven local varieties, representing 11 different races of maize, are found in the region. Three different planting regimes are distinguished for maize, depending on altitude, planting date and type of maize to be sown. In contrast to potatoes, maize varieties of different use types may be planted in the same field. Because of the possibility of hybridization between types, women pay particular attention to eliminating ears of mixed types as possible sources of seed. The average number of varieties per field (2.9) is much lower than for potatoes, and the women who select the seed make more precise choices about which varieties will be planted in particular fields.

Source: Zimmerer, 1991

process is still in evidence today and is the source of continual innovation and change. Boster (1986) analyses how Jivaro women in the tropical forest of Peru exchange information and planting material for cassava varieties. Richards (1986) describes a rice farming community in Sierra Leone where as many as 70 different varieties are recognized. The principal sources of these varieties are: introductions from other communities and regions, fortuitous discoveries in the rice fields, and the conscious and continuous selection activities of the farmers. Box 2.1 describes how farmers in southern Peru maintain their maize and potato varieties and Box 2.2 presents evidence of the varietal diversity of rice in India.

It was only at the end of the eighteenth century that the selection and hybridization techniques characteristic of formal plant breeding began to be developed, although an understanding of the scientific basis of these techniques had to await the rediscovery in 1900 of the work Mendel had carried out in the 1860s. The organized selection of short-strawed, fertilizer-responsive rice varieties was carried out by farmer associations encouraged by the government in late nineteenth-century Japan (Francks, 1984). Wheat breeding in Europe was well established in the late nineteenth century; in some countries, such as France, private breeders took the lead and soon established commercial operations, while in other countries, such as the Netherlands, government institutions were responsible for

---

Box 2.2   The diversity of rice varieties in Orissa State, India

A study in Jajpur District, Orissa showed the rich diversity of rice varieties used by farmers during the *kharif* (rainy) season. Rice is the main crop during this season. Farmers plant a range of traditional varieties, and many farmers plant modern varieties as well. The following data illustrate the importance of traditional varieties and their diversity.

	Local varieties	Modern varieties
% farmers growing	100	38
No. of different varieties	33	11
% rice area	88	12

Farmers use three major land types: *dhipa zami* (upper terraces), *majhili zami* (middle terraces) and *khala zami* (lower terraces). Farmers with access to more land types tend to plant a wider range of rice varieties.

No. of land types used by farmers	Average no. of rice varieties grown
1	3.4
2	4.4
3	6.3

Source: Kshirsagar and Pandey, 1996

the early development of wheat varieties (Lupton, 1988). In the US, most plant breeding was carried out by the Department of Agriculture and the land grant agricultural universities (which were established in 1890), and the contribution of commercial plant breeding was negligible until the advent of hybrid maize in the 1930s (Kloppenburg, 1988). A wheat breeding programme was established at Pusa in north-eastern India in 1904, partly to stimulate wheat production that could be exported to the UK (Busch *et al.*, 1991).

The great increase in the availability of new varieties was a stimulus to the development of more formal seed production and distribution. In many cases, government research stations took responsibility for modest seed production and distribution efforts for their new varieties. In the US, state experimental stations helped establish crop improvement associations that multiplied and disseminated new varieties. The American Seed Trade Association (ASTA) was formed by 34 companies in 1883, and this growing private seed trade competed with (and complained about) public sector seed provision (Kloppenburg, 1988). Commercial seed operations came to replace most government seed production efforts in Europe and North America. In some countries, most notably France, much commercial seed production was initiated by co-operatives (McMullen, 1987). Until recently, the seed industry has been characterized by small, independent and often family-owned firms, but this pattern changed drastically in the 1970s with mergers and take-overs often involving companies with other interests, such as chemicals or food processing. Despite these changes, there are still many small family seed businesses in the US and other countries. Most large commercial seed companies have their own plant breeding capacity, although they often use the products of public sector breeding as well.

The transition to private seed production noted in Europe and North America has been less evident in developing countries, where public plant breeding tended to be accompanied by the establishment of public seed enterprises. In India, for instance, the National Seed Corporation was established in 1963, and was soon followed by the emergence of public sector seed companies in various Indian states, some of which used the proceeds of their sales to fund plant breeding research. Although private seed companies were allowed to operate, as long as they were domestically controlled, there was much evidence of discrimination (McMullen, 1987). Only since 1980 have changes in official attitudes and policy allowed private seed companies more scope to operate in India (Pray, 1990). Seed sale of crops such as wheat is still predominantly in the hands of the public sector, but private companies are playing an increasingly important role in seed supply of many other crops such as maize, sorghum and oilseeds. In Kenya, a small group of farmers established the Kenya Seed Company in 1955 (McMullen, 1987). This became a partially government-owned enterprise and, although it produces seed of several crops, its success has been

17

based on hybrid maize varieties. Until very recently the company enjoyed monopoly rights to the production and sale of maize seed in Kenya.

In some countries in Latin America, the move to private sector seed production took place more rapidly. Mexico began to allow private maize research and seed production in the mid-1960s (Echeverria, 1990), but also established a public seed company (PRONASE). PRONASE's fortunes rose and fell in response to government policies; in the late 1970s it accounted for about 40 per cent of seed sales in Mexico, but government rural development programmes and subsidies increased its share to 60 per cent of the market by 1982, before it fell again when structural adjustment policies were introduced (McMullen, 1987). In Brazil, government policy promoted an interaction between public plant breeding and private or co-operative seed production (ibid.).

Seeds and varieties

Thus, the initiatives in scientific plant breeding and organized seed production that began little more than a century ago have led to what may be characterized as two distinct seed supply sectors. The first is that of local seed supply, where the farming community manages variety selection, seed production and storage under local conditions (Almekinders *et al.*, 1994). In contrast, formal seed supply is a chain of activities, extending from breeding to marketing and distribution, managed by specialists (Louwaars, 1996).

Before analysing the future role of the formal seed sector in national seed systems, it will be useful to review the rationale behind formal seed supply. Policy pronouncements too often assume that a shift to complete farmer dependence on the formal seed sector is inevitable, and that it is a priority to encourage farmers to use formal (public or private) seed sources in preference to their own seed. This message is transmitted through extension bulletins, rural development programmes and a myriad of subsidies, incentives and initiatives associated with agricultural development policy.

The contributions of the formal seed sector are considerable, but an adequate review of national seed policy requires an examination of the rationale for farmers' utilization of purchased seed. Rather than assume that formal sector seed is necessarily preferable to farm-saved seed, it is helpful to look more closely at the specific characteristics of each type of seed in order to understand when farmers are most likely to benefit from the establishment of formal seed supply and, hence, where the most likely priorities and incentives for public or private initiative are to be found.

A reasonable starting-point is to remind ourselves that the vast majority of seed used in the developing world is farm-saved. For instance, only about 7 per cent of wheat seed and 13 per cent of rice seed planted in India is from the formal sector (Turner, 1994). The situation is not confined to developing countries; approximately 50 per cent of the cotton and barley, 60 per cent of the oats and 70 per cent of the wheat planted in the US is farm-saved seed (Pray and Ramaswami, 1991). On the other hand, virtually all of the sorghum, maize and vegetables in the US are planted using commercial seed. Vast differences between crops and between countries indicate that some disaggregation of the formal seed sector will be useful to help identify its potential and its limitations.

The most important distinction is based on the fact that seed is both germplasm (a collection of genetic information) and a physical input. Demand for seed may therefore represent the farmer's desire to acquire new germplasm (a variety), and/or a search for a renewable physical input (seed) that the farmer is unable to maintain for some reason. The distinction is clear, but it is remarkable how many proposals for promoting formal seed programmes are based on an inadequate understanding of the relative and absolute importance of these two factors in specific situations.

When formal plant breeding produces a new variety that farmers wish to use, they may gain access to it through seed purchase. The model of a seed company, public or private, offering seed of a new variety for sale does not necessarily dominate variety acquisition, however. The most notable example of varietal change in developing countries has been the spread of modern, input-responsive rice and wheat varieties as part of what became known as the Green Revolution. But in many cases the seed of these varieties was initially introduced to farmers as part of government programmes that offered incentives, or at times coercion (such as 'no seed-no credit' policies in Indonesia and the Philippines), to acquire the seed. These types of varieties have since spread because of farmer demand, but formal sector seed sale remains a relatively small contributor to the diffusion. Because rice and wheat varieties can be maintained fairly easily by farmers, much of the spread of these varieties has taken place through farmer-to-farmer contact; a farmer sees the variety in a neighbour's field and asks to buy or borrow a small quantity of seed to test the next season. For example, about 50 per cent of the acquisition of seed of new wheat varieties in Pakistan takes place in this way (Tetlay et al., 1990). Even for open-pollinated varieties of maize, farmers may depend more on their neighbours; a survey in Ghana showed that 40 per cent of farmers using new maize varieties originally obtained the seed from other farmers (GGDP, 1991). This capacity for farmer-to-farmer diffusion partly explains why non-hybrid seed production is slow to attract private sector activity.

The demand for seed as a vehicle for new germplasm is also affected by the capacity of modern plant breeding to develop new varieties. Wheat farmers in both industrialized and developing countries show a range of 5–10 years in the average turnover rate of varieties (Brennan and Byerlee, 1991), and in many cases farmer-saved seed is used until a new variety is sought. Modern plant breeding is still not able to address the conditions and

19

priorities of a wide range of farmers. The assumption that new varieties are always 'on the shelf', ready to be delivered to farmers, has been disproved by the disappointing experience of many extension programmes meant to deliver supposedly superior varieties that have not been sufficiently tested under farmer conditions. Ziegler (1986), for instance, describes the case of an improved maize variety in Burundi that outyielded the local variety, but whose late maturity made it unacceptable for the predominant crop rotations. This example is matched by many others where modern varieties have proved unsatisfactory because of their incompatibility with local cropping patterns, fodder needs, food preparation techniques or other conditions.

A common perception is that wealthier farmers are the ones who adopt modern varieties, but the situation is much more complex than this (Lipton and Longhurst, 1989). The success of modern varieties is not necessarily related to farm size. For instance, in Nepal, a new rice variety was originally taken up by larger farmers (who had better access to extension), but they later abandoned it, while smaller farmers in the same area placed increasing reliance on the variety because its cultivation requirements were compatible with their household labour supply (Ashby, 1982). Modern varieties are accepted or rejected on the basis of their compatibility with the complex characteristics of local farming systems.

Farmers may also adapt new varieties to their own conditions. Farmers in Malawi have been subject to a number of extension programmes promoting various improved varieties of maize. When a new maize variety is incorporated into local cropping patterns, its original name may soon be forgotten and it becomes known by the general term, 'maize of the ancestors' (Smale et al., 1991). Farmers in southern Mexico plant several local and improved maize varieties and there is opportunity for these to hybridize (Box 2.3). Many of these farmers plant an improved variety that is valued for its short stature, and tend to purchase fresh seed every third or fourth year, when they find that the variety is getting taller, probably because of outcrossing (Brush et al., 1988).

The demand for seed of new varieties, especially in the farming conditions that Chambers (1991) describes as 'complex, diverse, and risk-prone' will depend on the ability of modern plant breeding to adopt strategies that are better able to target these varied environments and to develop appropriate varieties. Much work is now being done on this issue (see Chapters 4 and 10 in this volume).

To summarize the situation with respect to variety-led demand for seed: although modern crop varieties are widely used in developing countries, there are still many conditions for which appropriate new varieties are not available, and hence do not provide a justification for seed programmes. Even when new varieties are appropriate, their diffusion is not necessarily matched by strong and consistent seed demand. Once farmers get a new variety, they are often able to maintain it themselves and may not return

20

Box 2.3   The use of traditional and modern maize varieties in Mexico

Farmers in a community in central Chiapas, Mexico, grow maize as their principal crop. Both local and modern varieties are grown, and each variety is recognized for its particular advantages and limitations. Sometimes a modern variety is introduced and becomes modified by farmer selection over many seasons, until it is classified as a 'creole' or a mixed variety. Farmers also recurrently buy seed of modern varieties to maintain their desirable characteristics. The following data compare Olotillo (a representative of the most important landrace found in this part of Mexico), Hibrido Amarillo (derived from a commercial variety sold in the area in the 1970s) and Tuxpeño (a marketed open-pollinated public sector maize variety).

	Variety		
	Olotillo	Hibrido Amarillo	Tuxpeño
Origin	Landrace	'Creole'	Modern variety
% of farmers growing	43	69	84
% of maize area	11	27	43
Storability	medium	good	poor
Performance on poor soils	good	medium	poor
Performance on good soils	poor	medium	good
Fertilizer response	poor	medium	good
Demand for weeding and fertilizer	low	medium	high
Wind resistance	poor	medium	good
Drought tolerance	good	medium	poor

Source: Bellon and Brush, 1994

for fresh seed from the formal sector for many years. In addition, when farmers wish to acquire seed of a new variety, they may go to an informal source, such as a neighbour or perhaps the market. Repeat seed purchases of the same variety are most likely when hybrids are involved, because hybrid vigour is diminished in the second and subsequent generations of seed. The most outstanding example is that of hybrid maize, and in a number of countries thriving hybrid maize seed companies serve the needs of small farmers (Lopez-Pereira and Filippello, 1995). The other factor that may affect a farmer's ability to save seed of the same variety is intellectual property protection of plant varieties, which in some cases may require a farmer to pay a royalty for the right to save seed. This is the issue of 'farmers' privilege', and is a concern for countries that are to join the World Trade Organization (WTO) (see Chapter 9).

However, farmers do not utilize the formal seed sector simply to acquire or maintain new varieties. As Fowler (1994:44) points out, many farmers in the United States were purchasing commercial seed well before formal plant breeding was developing new varieties. Farmers may find that the convenience and quality of formal sector seed outweighs the advantages of farm-stored seed. Certain crops such as soybean are difficult to store and maintain as seed in tropical conditions, and farmers often prefer to purchase seed. Farm-level seed maintenance may be difficult because of disease problems. Potato production in more tropical regions usually relies on seed supply from other areas, and even in regions of traditional potato production, disease build-up in local seed materials may be a problem. Scheidegger *et al.* (1989), for instance, showed that the use of clean seed potato could make an economically significant difference for highland Peru farmers. Farmers' capacity to control the presence of weed seed in their farm-stored seed may also be a problem; Fujisaka *et al.* (1993) show significant problems of weed contamination in farm-stored rice seed in the Philippines, a problem that will be exacerbated as farmers switch from transplanting to broadcasting rice.

For certain crops, such as many vegetables and fodder species, the crop is normally harvested before seed maturity and it may be difficult or inconvenient to reserve a portion for seed production. Even when farmers choose to produce their own seed, it may not always be of good quality. Louwaars (1994), for instance, discusses the problems that farmers have in selecting adequate seed for vegetable production.

An equally important factor affecting the potential contribution of farm-stored seed is the precarious economic status of many farm households. Inadequate harvests, household poverty or illness are all common threats to the capacity of households to store seed from one season to the next. Estimates made by members of peasant associations in Ethiopia indicated

Table 2.1 *Percentage of farmers using different sources for wheat seed in Bangladesh**

		Farm size **		
Source of seed	Marginal	Small	Medium	Large
Home storage	35.3	39.7	46.6	64.7
Public seed company	20.6	23.9	28.7	24.0
Market	34.9	29.6	19.1	10.1
Neighbours	4.5	2.7	4.8	0
Seed producers	4.7	2.0	0.9	0
No answer	0	2.2	0	1.2
Total	100%	100.1%	100.1%	100%

* Weighted average of responses in Dinajpur, Greater Jessore and Greater Faridpur Districts. Surveys of women in wheat-producing households.
** marginal = 0.5 acres or less
   small   = 0.51 – 2.5 acres
   medium = 2.51 – 5.0 acres
   large   = greater than 5 acres
Source: O'Donoghue, 1995

Table 2.2   *Farm and market as sources of bean seed for different classes of farmer in the Great Lakes region of Africa*

Source of seed	Social class of farmers	% of farmers using each source of seed in the long rainy season*		
		Zaire	Rwanda	Burundi
Farm saved	Poor	49	62	34
	Medium	64	85	73
	Rich	100	100	85
Market	Poor	60	26	80
	Medium	53	5	52
	Rich	17	0	32

* Sums for each class of farmer may be more than 100% because of multiple sources or less than 100% because of failure to plant that season.

Source: Sperling *et al.*, 1996

that between 25 and 50 per cent of farmers borrowed or bought seed of at least one crop in any given year (Henderson and Singh, 1990). These chronic seed shortages are rarely addressed by the formal seed sector, as most farmers turn to neighbours or to the market in search of seed, but local seed systems are not always able to cope with the requirements of the poorest households who search for seed at planting time. Table 2.1 shows the range of seed sources used by wheat farmers in Bangladesh, and Table 2.2 shows the importance of markets as a source of bean seed in Africa. Both of these examples illustrate the fact that poorer farmers are particularly likely to use the grain sold in local markets as a source of seed.

It is proper to conclude this brief examination of varieties and seed with the reminder that formal seed systems have already made significant contributions to developing country agriculture and that there is considerable potential for the future. But an examination of the role of formal seed systems must include a realistic assessment of demand and priorities. Improved varieties are not always available, and even when they are, farmers may not utilize formal seed channels to acquire them. If farmers are saving their own seed, there may still be justification for encouraging the development of the formal seed sector, or for strengthening local seed systems, but each case must be decided on its own merits.

We now turn to a description of the elements of formal seed systems and an examination of how public and private sector roles are changing. We look first at plant breeding and then at seed production.

Plant breeding

The majority of plant breeding for food crops in developing countries is in the hands of public sector agricultural research institutes. These institutions

Box 2.4   Sources of breeding materials for private maize seed companies in India

The majority of formal sector maize seed in India is produced by private seed companies, both national and multinational. Most of this seed is hybrid varieties that companies find more profitable to produce. Many of the larger companies have their own plant breeding capacity, while the small companies, which account for 10–35 per cent of private sector maize seed marketed in a given year, produce mostly public maize varieties.

An examination of the sources of germplasm used by private maize seed companies in India for the development of their varieties shows that both public and private sources are important.

Sources of germplasm used in private sector maize breeding programmes in India

	National companies	Multinational companies
Percentage of germplasm that is:		
Developed in India by company	23	28
Obtained from another company in India	2	2
Developed outside India by company	0	33
Obtained from another company outside India	13	1
(Total private sources)	(38)	(64)
Obtained from Indian Council of Agricultural Research or universities	34	23
Obtained from CIMMYT or public institutions outside India	24	10
Collected locally from farmers' fields	4	1
Other sources	–	2
TOTAL	100	100

Source: Singh *et al.*, 1995

face three serious challenges. First, their budgets have stagnated or declined in recent years (Pardey *et al.*, 1991); this situation is the result of both a general decline in public sector spending under structural adjustment and a declining trend·in donor support to public agricultural research. Second, public plant breeding has been more successful in producing varieties for relatively favoured environments, and there is increasing concern about its capacity to serve farmers in more marginal environments. Third, in many countries there is growing competition from private sector plant breeding. One of the outcomes is that public breeding programmes are seeing many of their staff leaving for higher paid jobs in the private sector.

These challenges are a cause of considerable concern about the future of public sector plant breeding. The general trend towards privatization in developing country agriculture must be compared, however, with an assessment of the role of public sector agricultural research in industrialized countries. Although virtually all seed production in the US is managed by private enterprises, public sector plant breeding remains quite important. Even in the case of hybrid maize, certainly the most remarkable example of the success of the private seed sector, 72 per cent of maize hybrids available in 1979 were based on at least one inbred line of public sector origin (Butler and Marion, 1985, cited in Jaffee and Srivastava, 1994). In 1980, public breeders in the US were responsible for developing more than 70 per cent of the soybean seed that was planted (McMullen, 1987:82). The establishment of plant variety protection legislation in the US in 1970 is one factor responsible for moving the balance towards private sector breeding, and recent changes in the structure of the seed industry, combined with considerable investment in biotechnology, can also explain the relative growth of private sector plant breeding. But even when seed production is an entirely private activity, public plant breeding continues to be important. The contribution of public germplasm to private maize breeding in India is shown in Box 2.4.

The precise role of the public sector in plant breeding also depends on particular characteristics of individual national seed systems. For example, Young (1990) contrasts potato breeding in Canada, where there are no private breeders and all varieties are developed through research funded by Agriculture Canada, with the situation in the Netherlands, where basic research is done by government institutes and universities but all variety development is in the hands of private individuals or companies. Both of these countries provide examples of dynamic and competitive seed systems, and the contrast discourages any easy answers to specifying a division between public and private plant breeding responsibility.

In most developing countries, private plant breeding is just beginning to emerge. Because of the commercial advantage of hybrid technology, the maize seed industry is probably the most 'privatized' of any food crop. A survey carried out in 1992 revealed that about one-third of maize breeders in developing countries (excluding China) were in the private sector. The equivalent proportion in industrialized countries was almost 80 per cent (CIMMYT, 1994). For many other crops, there is still little private breeding activity. More than 80 per cent of developing countries reported no private wheat breeding activity, for instance (CIMMYT, 1993).

Virtually all seed policy analysts agree that there is an important role for public plant breeding in developing countries for the foreseeable future, which makes it imperative that the challenges mentioned earlier (financial support, equity of impact and division of labour) be addressed. Jaffee and Srivastava (1994) point to several justifications for the continued importance of public sector plant breeding, including the high costs of investment in plant breeding, the concern that private breeding investment may not be socially optimal and the fact that farmer seed saving may make it difficult to recover a private breeding investment. Knudson (1990) discusses the

Box 2.5   Local-level variety selection and conservation in Ethiopia

The Plant Genetic Resources Centre/Ethiopia (PGRC/E) is involved in several activities that include farmer participation in conservation and variety improvement.

The Unitarian Service Committee of Canada helps support a PGRC/E project in north-eastern Shewa and south-eastern Walo which helps farmers protect and improve local varieties. Materials that have been collected from nearby areas are given to farmers to plant and to carry out simple mass selection to improve their characteristics. Farmers select plant types on the basis of qualities important to them, such as pest or disease resistance or the period of time taken to mature. Farmers receive assistance from plant breeders in this activity, and PGRC/E scientists establish standard descriptor lists for the materials. Farmers evaluate their selections in experimental plots and compare performance and yields with the original seed stock. The plots are also used for on-site maintenance of landraces.

In another project, the PGRC/E is collaborating with Debre Zeit Research Centre to maintain indigenous material of tetraploid wheat. Wheat germplasm collected by PGRC/E is tested and multi-plied by breeders and then provided to farmers for further multiplica-tion and selection. This allows farmers to experiment with landrace lines while the indigenous populations are maintained in the gene bank.

Source: Worede and Mekbib, 1993

example of the privatization of the former government Plant Breeding Institute in the UK and points out that the private sector is not necessarily equipped to take responsibility for basic research that may have low mar-ket, but high social, value.

Complementing the output of public or private varietal development is the continuing ingenuity of farmer varietal development. Dissatisfaction with the capacity of public or private sector breeding to serve the needs of resource-poor farmers has led several NGOs to organize activities to establish local-level breeding or improvement systems run by farmers and based on local varieties. Salazar (1992), for instance, describes the activities of the MASIPAG programme in the Philippines, where farmer groups participate in the breeding and selection of rice varieties appropriate for their conditions, in collaboration with university scien-tists. Recent interest in the subject of *in-situ* germplasm conservation (Brush, 1991) also addresses the necessity of ensuring support to local varietal development capacity. In Ethiopia, the Plant Genetic Resource Centre has a project in which farmers help select and improve local landraces (Box 2.5).

Seed production

An estimate of the annual value of agricultural seed used worldwide in the mid-1980s was US$50 billion, roughly evenly divided among public, private and farm-saved seed (Groosman *et al.*, 1991). The proportion of seed from public sector enterprises is likely to decline in the future, but the pressures and prospects vary by crop and by region. In Africa, many public seed companies have based their sales on maize seed, often benefiting from monopoly status. The partly government-owned Kenya Seed Company has enjoyed considerable success, while the parastatal Tanseed in Tanzania has been notably less able to develop a market (Friis-Hansen, 1989). The Ghana Seed Company, which sold seed of open-pollinated maize varieties, was forced to close in 1989. The National Seed Company of Malawi was sold to the grain trading company Cargill in 1988 (Cromwell, 1996).

In Asia, public seed companies tend to be based on rice and wheat, and although these self-pollinated crops lend themselves to on-farm seed saving, the large numbers of farmers served and the political importance of these crops have meant that public companies are still in operation. For

---

Box 2.6 The public and private seed sectors in India

India has a growing private seed sector that includes both plant breeding and seed production. It also has very strong public plant breeding institutions and large state seed companies. Private participation is largely for those crops whose seed is sold as hybrids, or whose open-pollinated varieties have a high replacement rate.

The following figures provide an estimate of the division between the public and private sectors in plant breeding and seed production.*

Crop	Total area (m of ha)	Average seed replace-ment rate (%)	Seed market volume (000 t)	% Market volume in hybrids	% public/ private varieties	% public/ private seed
Wheat	24.1	7.3	145 000	0	100/0	90/10
Rice	42.4	13.5	136 000	0	100/0	80/20
Maize	5.9	13.5	25 000	90	67/33	20/80
Sorghum	14.4	22.3	38 000	90	80/20	20/80
Pearl millet	10.5	44.0	18 000	90	85/15	20/80
Rape/mustard	5.8	33.7	6 600	0	95/5	70/30
Sunflower	1.4	59.2	10 000	35	65/35	10/90
Soybean	2.5	13.2	9 100	0	100/0	90/10
Castor	0.7	27.8	2 500	75	100/0	30/70
Cotton	7.5	15.11	21 000	35	90/10	40/60

* Figures based largely on data from 1990/91

Source: Turner, 1994 (Annex 6)

---

crops such as maize, sorghum or sunflower, where hybrid seed is available, private seed companies are coming to play a predominant role in several Asian countries. Box 2.6 illustrates the mix of public and private involvement in India's seed industry. Seed production in China is organized through a hierarchy of public seed enterprises, based on 500 prefecture and 2200 county seed companies (FAO, 1994a).

The challenges for public seed companies are common to many public sector enterprises. Incentives for efficient operation are often lacking. Abeygunawardena et al. (1990) demonstrate the superior efficiency of private outgrowers compared with government seed farm production in Sri Lanka. Public seed companies often benefit from government subsidies (Dalrymple and Srivastava, 1994) which discourage competition and make the companies complacent about their operations. A guaranteed market is often provided by large government purchases for various agricultural development programmes. Even with these advantages, public companies are often unable to deliver the seed they have been mandated to supply (Due, 1990). This is especially true for crops where seed demand is low. If the public company is the only conduit for new varieties, a serious bottleneck exists, and this has led Grisley (1993) to propose the possibility of publicly funded distribution of small quantities of new varieties as a cost-effective alternative to the pretence of a full-scale seed production operation.

The economics of seed production is well understood (Cromwell et al., 1992), but the nature of seed demand in many areas is still sufficiently uncertain to make it difficult to predict how public and private seed enterprises will evolve over the next decade. As national policies become more supportive of private sector activity, there will undoubtedly be an increase in the number of small, commercial seed enterprises. However, there are questions regarding the degree to which commercial enterprises will be attracted to seed production for crops where on-farm seed saving is feasible and widely practised, or where demand is low or uncertain because of the low purchasing power of farmers. One important factor is that economies of scale are not as evident in the seed industry as in many other endeavours, and there is certainly room for small companies to exploit local niches of demand. As McMullen (1987:83) points out, an important part of seed marketing is confidence and familiarity with the supplier, which explains why until recently most seed companies in industrialized countries were small, local operations; even today, many large seed companies in the US market their products through local farmer agents (Zulauf and King, 1985).

Recent changes in the seed industry have led to the formation of large multinational companies, and many of these are entering developing country markets. National regulations have kept such companies from competing in many countries (Pray, 1990), but that situation is slowly beginning to change. Large companies have the advantage of considerable production and marketing experience, strong reputations and the capacity to introduce varieties from other countries. But these companies are, of course, only interested in large and secure markets, so there is considerable doubt as to the proportion of developing country farmers they might be able to serve, even when trade and other regulatory barriers to their operation are removed. Perhaps more important is the fact that multinational (and indeed national) companies will not address the needs of those farmers who have little voice in the market. The responsiveness of the public sector in this regard has been far from satisfactory, however. An appropriate example of the dilemma occurs in Zimbabwe; it would appear that private seed companies based in South Africa are better able than the Zimbabwean public research system to meet the varietal needs of maize farmers in the more marginal farming areas of the country (Rusike, 1995:124). But this is mostly due to the fortuitous circumstance that these drought-prone conditions are similar to those of South African commercial farmers, who are the principal clients of the seed companies.

Co-operative seed production is also an option. For instance, much of the wheat seed for farmers in north-west Mexico is supplied by a well organized co-operative system. Janssen *et al.* (1992) describe how co-operatives in Colombia successfully began producing and marketing seed of a newly introduced bean variety. Agricultural co-operatives have long been important in France, providing many services, including seed production, for their members. In the 1960s some of these co-operatives began to establish successful joint ventures with public research and private seed companies to develop and market their own varieties (McMullen, 1987:148).

There are a growing number of local-level seed production activities as well. Cromwell *et al.* (1993) describe the various types of NGO seed activity that have been developed, and further detail is provided in Chapter 11. Some of these are related to the provision of seed as part of emergency relief operations during drought or civil conflict. But a number of NGOs have recognized a need to strengthen the sustainability of local seed systems. In some cases this has meant helping to organize local farmers to be outgrowers for state or commercial seed enterprises. In other cases, NGOs have embarked on the development of local seed enterprises whose goal is operational and economic self-sufficiency. Sometimes these moves toward developing a decentralized seed supply system have been purely an NGO initiative, while in other cases they have been supported by government policy. There are at least a dozen separate projects in the hill regions of Nepal aimed at reaching the farmers not served by the public seed sector (ibid.). Box 2.7 shows the impact of small-scale seed projects on vegetable seed production in Nepal.

Ashby *et al.* (1995) describe how some 'farmers' research committees' that were established in villages in southern Colombia to facilitate farmer participation in public sector adaptive agricultural research have expanded

Box 2.7   The impact of local-level seed production projects in Nepal

Small-scale seed production projects, many initiated by NGOs, have had a significant impact on the production and marketing of vegetable seed in Nepal in the past decade. At the present time, the output of contract seed producers accounts for about half of the vegetable seed used in Nepal.

Source of vegetable seed in Nepal (tons)

Year	Contract seed producer farmers	Government farms	Imports	Seed from on-farm or other sources
1984	21.4	11.8	1.74	762.4
1985	38.7	11.0	1.12	783.9
1986	58.5	11.0	0.54	785.7
1987	70.0	11.0	2.05	805.4
1988	120.0	11.0	0.60	759.3
1989	171.9	10.4	2.05	718.7
1990	215.6	17.1	9.20	535.0
1991	262.5	17.2	NA	509.9
1992	312.0	17.4	NA	491.0
1993	363.5	17.5	NA	453.4
1994	420.7	17.6	NA	416.1

Source: Munankami and Neupane, 1994

into seed production. In six cases, the committees' experience in testing new crop varieties led to the development of small-scale seed enterprises. The committees have received training in seed production, processing and quality control. In one season, these enterprises produced 147 tonnes of bean seed and eight tonnes of maize seed. CIAT (International Centre for Tropical Agriculture) has supported the development of 'artisanal seed production' for beans in Latin America, and Lepiz *et al.* (1994) outline how small enterprises have been developed in several countries to meet the demand for bean seed not covered by the conventional formal sector.

The only certainty is that the future will see an increasing diversity of seed enterprises being initiated in developing countries. Table 2.3 shows how the sale of seed of open-pollinated maize varieties is divided among public, commercial and non-conventional seed enterprises.

Another important source of seed, mentioned earlier, particularly for poorer farmers, is market grain trade, which usually escapes the official statistics. This type of local trade falls somewhere in between the formal and informal seed systems. It is usually condemned by public officials for distributing low quality seed, but in fact it is often responsible for a service that neither the state nor conventional commercial seed sources are likely

Table 2.3   *Sales of seed of commercial maize open-pollinated varieties (OPVs) in developing countries by type of company, 1992*

Region	Share of commercial OPV sales by company type				Total commercial OPV seed sales (000 t)
	Multi-national (%)	Private national (%)	Other non-public (%)	Public (%)	
Sub-Saharan Africa	0	18	17	65	24
West Asia and North Africa	0	0	0	100	2
Asia, less China	33	25	24	18	38
China	0	0	0	100	24
Latin America	0	53	26	21	25
All developing countries	11	24	17	48	113
Developing countries, less China	14	30	22	34	89
Industrialized countries	0	0	100	0	3
World	11	23	19	47	116

Source: Lopez-Pereira and Filippello, 1995

to provide. Van Santen and Heriyanto (1996) describe the operation of the *jabal* system in Indonesia, where market traders are able to move soybean from areas where harvest has just been completed to areas where planting is about to begin, and provide a more reliable service than the national seed company. In many countries, seed potato is produced in areas far removed from principal production zones because of disease problems, and the seed is carried long distances by indigenous traders (e.g., Scheidegger *et al.*, 1989; Rhoades, 1985).

Beyond 'public' and 'private'

The history of the development of most national seed sectors in industrialized countries is characterized by a progression towards increasing dependence on the private sector. Recent trends in developing countries indicate a similar shift. Even in 1980, when there was still strong donor support for public seed activities, Douglas (1980:23) emphasized the importance of strengthening commercial seed production activities. Pray and Ramaswami (1991) present a four-stage outline for the development of the seed industry in developing countries; the final stage ('mature seed industry') sees private firms responsible for the majority of varietal development, while the public sector concentrates on basic research and minor crops. Similarly, private companies (and farmer co-operatives) are seen as dominating seed marketing and distribution.

But another feature of many seed policy analyses is the demonstration of the need for effective collaboration between the public and private sectors. Douglas's (1980) comprehensive treatment of the organization of seed systems describes a range of types of public-private collaboration in the development of seed enterprises (ibid.: 83–92), and Kelly (1989) devotes a chapter of his book on seed policy to the possibilities of public-private collaboration.

The perception of a trend towards private sector ascendancy in national seed systems is certainly accurate, and the appeal for more attention to public-private linkages is sensible. But national seed sector development is more complex than this. In the first place, the distinction between private and public is not always clear. The private sector includes both commercial and voluntary activities, and even the definition of voluntary may be problematic. There are some large NGOs that behave more like parastatals, for instance, and some co-operatives have many of the characteristics of commercial firms (Brett, 1993).

Thirtle and Echeverria (1994) offer a useful analysis of the privatization of agricultural research, pointing out that few research activities can be seen as purely private or public. Their criteria for analysing research activities can be applied to seed systems in general:

○ *Source of funds:* Varietal development or seed production activities may be supported from public funds, from levies on selected groups (such as producers of a specific commodity), or from private commercial or voluntary sources.
○ *Execution of activities:* Independent of the source of funding, activities may be implemented by publicly owned, commercial or voluntary organizations.
○ *Profit motive:* The profit motive may or may not be dominant in stimulating the activity. The simple public/private dichotomy does not always give a clear indication of actual conduct. Public plant breeding programmes may reorient their work towards seeking royalties in order to counteract declining public budgets, for instance.
○ *Output utilization:* The output (a new variety or improved seed supply) may be in the public domain, directed or restricted to particular users or privately controlled.

National seed systems

The classification of formal seed systems as public or private is complicated by the fact that they involve several distinct levels of activity. Figure 2.1 is an attempt to represent the most important elements of national systems. It identifies four principal levels of activity (variety development, seed production, seed marketing and utilization), divided among government, commercial and voluntary endeavours. Compartmentalization such as this runs the risk of emphasizing distinctions that, as discussed above, are more

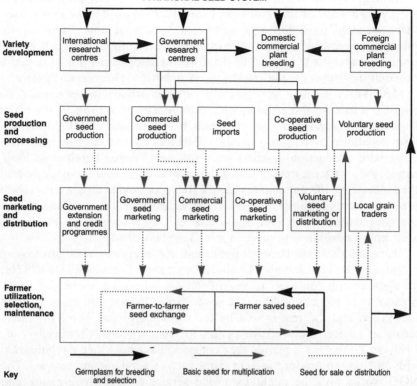

A NATIONAL SEED SYSTEM

Variety development
- International research centres
- Government research centres
- Domestic commercial plant breeding
- Foreign commercial plant breeding

Seed production and processing
- Government seed production
- Commercial seed production
- Seed imports
- Co-operative seed production
- Voluntary seed production

Seed marketing and distribution
- Government extension and credit programmes
- Government seed marketing
- Commercial seed marketing
- Co-operative seed marketing
- Voluntary seed marketing or distribution
- Local grain traders

Farmer utilization, selection, maintenance
- Farmer-to-farmer seed exchange
- Farmer saved seed

Key
- Germplasm for breeding and selection
- Basic seed for multiplication
- Seed for sale or distribution

Figure 2.1 *A national seed system*

apparent than real, but the complexity of formal seed systems is illustrated by the diverse flows from one level to another.

With respect to the flows of germplasm for breeding and variety selection, public plant breeding maintains links with international research centres supported by donor funding, utilizing germplasm from the centres and contributing materials to international trials. There is also a flow of germplasm from the public sector to private commercial companies. This has been a feature of plant breeding in industrialized countries for some time, and there are several examples from developing countries as well (see Box 2.4). Germplasm also flows from farmers' fields to plant breeding programmes. Until recently this has been a one-way flow representing the collection of germplasm for *ex-situ* conservation and breeding purposes. The development of *in-situ* conservation systems will allow more of that germplasm to be used directly on farmers' fields. In addition, and depending on the orientation of the particular *in-situ* programme, there is the possibility of partially reversing the flow, with public breeders providing materials that farmers may be able to use in their own varietal improvement activities (Chapter 10).

33

Although it has been most common for public breeding programmes to supply basic seed of their varieties to public seed production enterprises, there are many possibilities for more complex interactions. There are, for instance, a growing number of examples where public sector breeding provides materials for commercial seed production. Since 1987 the maize research institute of the Brazilian Agricultural Research Enterprise (EMBRAPA) has had an agreement with an association of small-scale regional commercial seed companies (UNIMILHO) to provide inbreds of its lines in return for royalty payments based on sal̓es. EMBRAPA was instrumental in helping to organize UNIMILHO and ensuring that adequate seed production practices were followed (Lopez-Pereira and Filippello, 1995). In some cases, the linkages may even be more complicated. In the Philippines, the national maize research programme is paid a royalty to provide inbreds to commercial seed companies, who in turn sell the seed to the government which then subsidizes the sale of the seed through its agricultural development programmes (Logroño,1996).

There are also links between public and voluntary organizations in seed production. In The Gambia, the government Seed Technology Unit (STU) provides foundation seed to several NGOs who take responsibility for organizing farmers to multiply the seed. Part of the seed is bought back by the NGOs and the rest is sold by the farmer growers. The STU offers technical advice and seed inspection for this scheme (Cromwell et al., 1993). In Zimbabwe, a private seed company has established a relationship with an NGO to produce seed of crops such as sorghum and cowpea. The NGO works with the public extension service to identify, organize and supervise the growers; the seed is mostly exported to neighbouring countries (Rusike and Musa, 1996).

Institutional collaboration also benefits the development of seed marketing. A project in Nepal supported 'private producer sellers', with the Department of Agriculture training participating farmers in seed multiplication and providing foundation seed and technical advice; the farmers were then responsible for marketing their own seed (Bal and Rajbhandary, 1987). There are a number of NGO seed projects in Nepal, including the Koshi Hills Seed and Vegetable Project (KOSEVEG) which organizes seed production groups. The seed producers obtain foundation seed from the local government research station, which also provides technical advice, as does the District Agricultural Development Office. Seed sale is arranged by the producers, and contracts for vegetable seed are established with members of the Seed Entrepreneurs Association of Nepal (SEAN) (Joshi, 1995).

These examples should be sufficient to illustrate that complex linkages are already being formed in national seed systems and that the potential exists for even broader collaboration. Figure 2.1 is dominated by the formal seed sector, but it is important to remember that the size of the bottom portion representing farmer seed selection, saving and exchange is not proportional to the overwhelming importance of the local seed system. Just as the private/public dichotomy has its limitations for understanding formal seed system development, the formal/local distinction is also insufficiently precise. The discussion above has provided examples of local seed selection interacting with formal plant breeding, local seed production being upgraded to provide wider coverage and local seed distribution networks being developed on a commercial basis. All of this supports the contention that the concept of 'integrated seed systems', combining elements of local and formal seed systems, is particularly useful for helping to stimulate innovative ideas for strengthening national seed systems (Louwaars, 1996). 'Such integrated approaches have to seek a balance between the vertically organized and thus vulnerable, but potentially dynamic formal seed system, and the diverse but insufficiently plastic local systems' (ibid.:9).

It should be clear that seed system development will depend critically upon the provision of adequate linkages: from one level of the formal seed system to the next; between public, commercial and voluntary entities; and supporting an integration of local and formal systems. It is the task of regulation to define, underwrite and maintain these linkages, hence the focus on regulation in this book. Regulation, as we shall discuss in Chapter 3, goes far beyond the usual concept of government intervention, and includes a wide array of methods by which participants in a transaction define, monitor and control their activities. Before examining the nature of regulation, however, it will be useful to review the potential challenges for national seed regulatory frameworks.

Seed regulation

Until recently, seed regulation in most developing countries was associated with a fairly straightforward set of objectives. Figure 2.2 presents, without too much simplification, the regulatory responsibilities that have been typical of seed systems dominated by the public sector. Plant breeding was usually the exclusive responsibility of public agricultural research institutions, which developed varieties that were then multiplied by public seed enterprises for distribution to farmers, either through commercial sale or as part of agricultural development projects. It is easy to be critical of this strategy, but it must be acknowledged that in many cases these public seed systems have played an important role in agricultural change, particularly in areas where relatively favoured growing conditions were addressed with programmes that supplied complementary inputs and extension advice.

Although not always considered part of formal seed regulation, the organization and strategies of plant breeding are also included in this book as an integral part of the regulatory process. The way in which priorities are set in plant breeding is influenced by, and interacts with, the regulation of variety approval and release. Plant breeding procedures adopted in public research institutes are a reflection of national seed policy and regulation. In

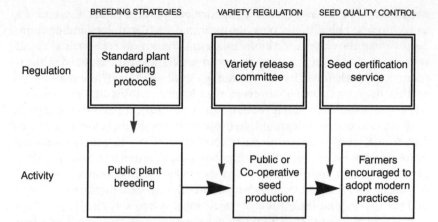

What rules and regulations should be applied to government plant breeding and government seed production to meet the needs of a homogeneous target of 'modernizing' farmers?

Figure 2.2   *The past scenario: the regulation of the public sector seed system*

addition, perceptions of the nature of the target farming populations who will use the products of the seed industry play a large role in determining how plant breeding is carried out. Thus it is appropriate to begin an examination of seed regulation with the conduct of plant breeding.

Public plant breeding has understandably devoted most of its efforts to major food crops, but although research has addressed differences among various agro-ecological environments, insufficient attention has often been paid to the specific socio-economic conditions of farmers. Most plant breeding has typically been carried out on experimental stations where crop management standards are superior to those that are feasible for many farmers. This strategy is often justified by the belief that farmers' management practices will improve, that input use will increase and that plant breeding should lead the way for agricultural 'modernization' rather than try to correct for the deficiencies of 'traditional' practices. One of the consequences of this strategy has been reliance on the goal of breeding varieties for wide adaptation rather than for specific niches. Breeding lines are moved through a well-ordered progression of trial types, selection is based primarily on yield performance under standard conditions and the end product is a variety that will be acceptable for the release criteria that have been established by the research institute itself.

A general description such as this runs the risk of underestimating the skill and dedication characteristic of the public plant breeding endeavour, but it must be acknowledged that much breeding carried out by public research institutes has been based on an assumption of broad, homogeneous targets. The efficiency justifications for such a strategy are obvious, and the diffusion and utilization of modern varieties of crops such as wheat and rice are testimony to the relevance of the strategy, but the vast numbers of resource-poor farmers who are as yet untouched by the public seed system calls attention to the urgency of examining alternative strategies.

When the public research institute has developed a new variety, it is usually presented to a variety release committee, typically composed of members of the research institute (plant breeders, pathologists, entomologists, etc.) plus other representatives from public agricultural institutions such as extension. Because both the research and the release are essentially in the hands of the same people, this is in a sense an internal review, designed to ensure that new varieties are appropriate and useful. The evidence required for release typically includes a description of the new variety and data on performance. The latter are usually provided through a series of standard field trials, carried out over several years, which in fact can be seen as the final stages of the research trials that progressively narrow the range of breeding lines to identify varieties that are candidates for release. If the variety is accepted by the release committee it is then eligible for seed production.

After release is approved, the research institution must produce sufficient foundation (basic) seed. Seed production, by public enterprises or others, has usually been regulated by a public agency responsible for seed quality control. The certification process ensures that the seed being produced is of acceptable genetic purity, and seed testing procedures monitor characteristics such as moisture content, germination capacity and physical purity of the seed. The responsibilities of the certification agency include field inspections of production plots, as well as laboratory tests after the seed is harvested. The same agency is usually responsible for licensing and inspecting seed merchants as well.

Thus the public seed system that has been predominant until recently has featured quite clear-cut regulatory procedures. Plant breeding is carried out under conventional protocols that emphasize wide adaptation and feature a uniform progression of field trials designed to select varieties that will excel under the requirements of the standardized tests required for release. Variety approval is managed by a committee dominated by the public sector and designed to ensure an orderly release and promotion of new varieties. The majority of seed production, whether carried out by public enterprises, co-operatives or private seed producers, is subject to control by a public certification agency that mandates uniform standards for seed purity and quality, and may also monitor seed sale.

Such a description is inevitably oversimplified, but is a useful profile of the seed regulatory structure in place in many developing countries until very recently. The changes and pressures evidenced in national seed

37

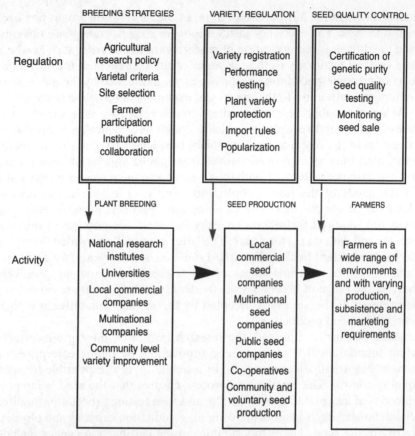

BREEDING STRATEGIES	VARIETY REGULATION	SEED QUALITY CONTROL

Regulation

Agricultural research policy	Variety registration	Certification of genetic purity
Varietal criteria	Performance testing	Seed quality testing
Site selection	Plant variety protection	Monitoring seed sale
Farmer participation	Import rules	
Institutional collaboration	Popularization	

PLANT BREEDING	SEED PRODUCTION	FARMERS

Activity

National research institutes	Local commercial seed companies	Farmers in a wide range of environments and with varying production, subsistence and marketing requirements
Universities	Multinational seed companies	
Local commercial companies	Public seed companies	
Multinational companies	Co-operatives	
Community level variety improvement	Community and voluntary seed production	

What rules and regulations are needed, and what types of institutions should administer them, to promote a dynamic seed sector that involves public, commercial and voluntary activity to meet the needs of a diverse farming population?

Figure 2.3 *The future scenario: the regulation of national seed systems*

systems that have been outlined earlier in this chapter give rise to a much more complex set of regulatory challenges, however. The major features of this new scenario are presented in Figure 2.3.

There are now many more institutions involved in the national seed system. Plant breeding is being done by commercial enterprises as well as public institutions, and there are also many community-level projects aimed at the preservation and enhancement of local varieties. The proliferation of seed production possibilities is even more extensive, and many different types of commercial seed enterprises are increasingly evident, replacing, or competing with, the public seed companies. Local-level seed projects are also becoming more important. Finally, although diversity has

38

always been a feature of the farming sector, the multiplicity of goals and procedures brought by these new actors to the seed system has served to emphasize the importance of targeting seed regulation to specific groups of farmers.

The organization of plant breeding is now a much more complex task. Public sector plant breeding is being forced to consider how it can address the needs of farmers who have so far not been able to take advantage of the products of public agricultural research. The degree to which breeding for wide adaptation can meet their needs is being called into question (Simmonds, 1991). This implies significant changes in the way that sites for variety trials are chosen and managed, as well as a re-examination of the characteristics that are used for variety selection. These considerations argue, in turn, for significant changes in the management of the breeding process, including the interactions between breeders and their clients, the possibilities for greater farmer participation and the increased use of local varieties and landraces in the development of varieties.

These potential changes in the organization of the breeding process are matched by pressures to review institutional mandates. Commercial plant breeding has a comparative advantage for certain crops (particularly those with high value seed, such as hybrids) and certain farming populations (particularly those that offer large, stable markets). The public sector is likely to have increasing responsibility for the crops and farmers that are not attractive to the commercial sector, but exactly how this division of labour is to be mandated and supported by national seed and research policies has yet to be articulated. Of equal importance to such an assignment of responsibilities is an agreement on interactions among plant breeding institutions. It is often said that the public sector will take responsibility for more basic plant breeding research, while the commercial sector concentrates on applied research and variety development, but again, the modalities have not been worked out. Similarly, there is an urgent need for public plant breeding institutes to develop better relations with community-level activities aimed at varietal improvement. The challenges facing public sector plant breeding are the subject of Chapter 4.

If the plant breeding process is to be reorganized and non-public institutions are to have an increasing presence, the procedures for variety release and approval must also be reformed. To begin with, there is the question of whether varieties from outside the public breeding system must pass through the same release process. Do new varieties simply have to be registered, or do they have to undergo performance testing as well? The criteria for registration usually include strict requirements on varietal uniformity but this may not always be appropriate, particularly for marginal farming conditions. The performance standards also need to be reviewed, especially in the light of evidence that they do not necessarily reflect farmers' priorities. If a mandatory variety release procedure is to be maintained, who should manage it? What was previously an internal procedure for public plant breeding is now potentially a method for controlling the commercial sector's access to the market, and changes in the membership and procedures of any release authority would have to be considered. The reform of variety regulation is the subject of Chapter 5. In addition to these challenges, seed regulatory systems must address the requirements of plant variety protection. Because this issue is a particularly prominent topic of debate, it is briefly addressed in the following section, and a more complete analysis is presented in Chapter 9.

Just as the growing range of plant breeding endeavours necessitates a change in the way variety approval is regulated, so too does the diversification of seed production require a re-examination of the regulations related to certification and seed testing. Among the issues that need to be addressed are whether seed certification is to be voluntary or mandatory, and whether only the government, or independent agencies as well, should be able to certify seed. No matter what regulatory mechanism is chosen, there are also questions about the appropriate standards to be applied, bearing in mind the tremendous diversity of seed producers and farmers. In addition, there are important challenges for encouraging wider access to seed, while at the same time ensuring that the expansion of seed distribution does not compromise seed quality. The themes are addressed in Chapter 6.

To recapitulate, we are interested in how plant breeding should be organized, how new crop varieties are to be approved for use and how the quality of seed is to be controlled. The answers to these questions constitute a definition of seed regulatory reform and are the motivation for the analysis presented in the rest of this book. There is no other set of issues that so strongly affects the future of national seed system development.

Plant variety protection

The recently concluded GATT negotiations require countries who join the World Trade Organization (WTO) to provide some type of intellectual property protection for crop varieties. Systems of plant variety protection (PVP) are in place in most industrialized countries, and the possibility of their application to developing countries has caused a considerable amount of debate. The basic concerns include the question of access to breeding materials, the possibility of commercial (and perhaps external) control of national seed supply and the impact on farmers' entitlement to save seed on-farm. These are all important issues and obviously part of any discussion on seed regulatory reform. They are examined in more detail in Chapter 9. The purpose of the present section is to explain why the concerns of conventional seed regulation, outlined above, deserve prior attention.

First, it must be borne in mind that the issue of PVP is still being debated, that its implementation is still several years away in many countries, and that its effects will not be felt until some time in the future. The issues of regulatory reform — the orientation of plant breeding and the organization of variety approval and seed certification — are, on the other hand, immediately accessible in most countries and are responsible for determining the efficiency of national seed systems *today*. In addition, PVP will have an immediate effect only on the relatively small proportion of a national seed system that is highly commercialized.

This is not to downplay the potential importance or consequence of PVP, however. Pressures for its adoption come particularly from the commercial seed sector, which wants to be assured of adequate incentives and protection before making substantial investments. This is understandable, but incentives for commercial seed production are affected much more strongly by the management of the current seed regulatory system, including requirements for variety release and certification. The seed regulatory environment defines the type of seed industry that emerges, and if current regulatory systems are perceived to be uneven, arbitrary or poorly managed, then consideration of the potential impact of PVP on commercial seed activity is purely academic.

There is also concern that PVP can limit the interchange of germplasm or redirect public plant breeding towards more commercially attractive targets. It is thus critically important that a debate be initiated *now*, with the object of better defining public sector plant breeding commitments and procedures for addressing the needs of farmers not likely to be served by the commercial seed industry.

In addition, some types of PVP may affect farmers' opportunity to save their own seed of protected varieties. One of the principal objectives of our analysis of seed regulatory reform is to support and strengthen the access of resource-poor farmers to appropriate varieties and seed. Stronger farmer participation in seed systems is one of the most important steps towards countering any excessive restrictions regarding seed use or seed saving that a PVP system may engender.

Finally, it is not always realized that if PVP is to be established in a country, this requires a variety registration and monitoring process that is more technically sophisticated and organizationally demanding than many currently in place. As Jaffe and van Wijk (1995: 77) observe, the implementation of PVP requires a national-level structure that is capable of controlling the seed market. Thus an examination of opportunities for the reform and refinement of conventional regulatory systems must precede any consideration of the establishment of PVP.

Summary

National seed systems have progressed from exclusive reliance on farmer variety selection and seed saving to a much more complex pattern in which public sector, commercial and voluntary activities all contribute to varietal improvement and seed provision. In developing countries, the formal seed sector has been dominated by public plant breeding and seed production, but that situation is changing rapidly, as commercial and voluntary endeavours play increasingly important roles.

There is still considerable uncertainty, however, regarding the future division of responsibility in national seed systems. The public/private dichotomy is less important for formulating national seed policy than a willingness to promote collaboration among farmers, public agencies, commercial enterprises and voluntary projects. The development of dynamic and responsive national seed systems will involve widespread participation. There are many reasons why the strong trend towards commercial domination and concentration witnessed in industrialized country seed systems need not be an inevitable blueprint for developing countries.

An increasing diversity in national seed systems, and increasing interactions among different sectors, imply a need to reconsider the management and purposes of seed regulations, which are currently based on the assumption of public sector dominance. As commercial seed interests assume a more important role in many countries, issues of intellectual property protection attract attention, but these must be seen within the context of broader seed regulatory frameworks.

Before considering specific regulatory alternatives in Part 2, we turn first to a brief review of the nature and purpose of regulation.

3 Regulation and regulatory reform

ROBERT TRIPP

The nature of regulation

THE FAMILIARITY WITH which the subject of regulation is often discussed conceals the complexity of its character. Although a common reaction to problems affecting public welfare is to call on the government to establish 'regulations', and an equally common response to perceptions of government bureaucracy and red tape is to demand 'deregulation', a precise definition of regulation is difficult to find. In his comprehensive review of the subject, Mitnick (1980) points out that the concept has no single accepted meaning, and that the distinction between regulatory and non-regulatory government activities is often problematic.

A sharper contrast would seem to be offered by the distinction between those activities conducted through open markets and those that are subject to government regulation, but on closer examination this too requires defining the nature of markets. Although individual market transactions may be seen to take place as discrete, isolated interchanges among independent decision-makers, Goldberg (1976:52) points out that these in fact 'are nested in a complex pattern of contractual jurisdictions which, taken together, establish the rights, obligations, and ultimately the transaction costs of the respective parties'. Thus, 'the line between private and public rules . . . is blurred, and . . . to achieve desirable results society will have to erect a set of barriers or restrictions . . . to channel behaviour; this set of barriers will establish a complex admixture of public and private jurisdictions' (ibid.:53).

Although the separation between 'public and private jurisdictions' is not perfectly distinct, and the boundary between regulatory and other government conduct is similarly imprecise, we should identify the limits of the subject of our discussion before proceeding. A reasonable place to start is one definition offered by Mitnick (1980:7) that sees regulation as 'the public administrative policing of a private activity with respect to a rule prescribed in the public interest'. Thus, with respect to the subject of seed regulation, we are concerned with government control of the production and distribution of plant varieties and seeds through rules enacted to protect public welfare.

A second feature that is important for our discussion is the identity of the actors responsible for the conduct of regulation. The activities usually associated with regulation involve the 'detailed, continuous monitoring of

43

economic processes [that is] beyond the capacity of legislatures [and implies] boards, agencies, and commissions'. (Friedman, 1985:111). Thus we will be interested in the actions and responsibilities of the special government entities (such as variety release committees, seed boards and certification agencies) that are charged with managing seed regulation. We are interested in examining the conduct and the effectiveness of these agencies, the degree to which their actions may diverge from the original intention of regulation and the possibility that their responsibilities may be redefined to lend greater support to the development of national seed systems.

An understanding of the appropriate scope and limits of government regulatory responsibility requires a recognition of alternative means for achieving regulatory goals. These are what Ayres and Braithwaite (1992:3) refer to as 'private regulation — by industry associations, by firms, by peers, and by individual consciences'. They point out that the challenge is more complex, and more subtle, than is implied by the simple dichotomy that pits the 'free' market against government regulation. We shall refer to this search for an appropriate combination or 'interplay' (ibid.) of private and public regulation as 'regulatory reform'. This is preferred to the term 'deregulation', which has performed too much service as a political slogan to be useful for policy analysis. It is also important to distinguish regulatory reform from another slogan, privatization, which as Ayres and Braithwaite (1992:11) point out, may in fact be associated with increased regulation.

The rhetoric of privatization and deregulation serves as a reminder, however, that any debate about regulatory conduct or reform will inevitably be embedded in a broader political context. Wilson (1980) provides an analysis of the political motivations behind the establishment of regulatory policy. He argues that the outcome of regulatory debates is often determined by how the costs and benefits of regulation are distributed. If the benefits of a particular regulatory policy are concentrated (say, in providing significant advantages to firms in an industry) while the costs are diffused, the industry will lobby vigorously for the policy. If, on the other hand, the benefits of a proposed policy are diffused among consumers, but the costs are borne by the industry, legislators and public advocacy groups will face stiff opposition from the industry.

Ideology as well as economic interest shapes the formulation of regulatory policy. Eisner (1993) identifies four separate 'regulatory regimes' that have characterized government action in the United States over the past century. Regulatory regimes 'are political-institutional arrangements that define the relationship between social interests, the state, and economic actors such as corporations, labour unions, and agricultural associations' (ibid.:2). These regulatory regimes are the product of new regulatory policies that emerge in the presence of significant institutional and economic change. 'Each generation interprets regulatory policies and state-economy relations from its own historical position as part of a specific political-economic milieu' (ibid.:1).

44

Many developing countries are in the midst of profound debates regarding the proper role of the state and its relation to an emerging private sector, and their regulatory regimes are thus subject to redefinition.

Although the theme of regulation is potentially quite broad, the goals of this book focus our attention on the specialized government agencies that control and police both public and private activities related to crop variety development and seed production and distribution. We wish to examine these agencies' roles, and the possibility that they can share some responsibilities with other regulatory bodies. Our interest is regulatory reform, which can best be described not in terms of an absolute choice between idealized models of 'state' or 'market' performance, but rather as a complex process of policy formation that seeks to encourage an effective conjunction of public and private responsibility in the development of a dynamic and equitable seed sector.

The next section of this chapter examines the motivations for government regulation, and relates these to national seed systems. The remainder of the chapter attempts to set the scene for the discussion of seed regulatory conduct and options in subsequent chapters. This is done by examining some general characteristics of regulation that can then be applied to the challenge of seed regulatory reform. The discussion outlines problems with government regulation, examines possible regulatory alternatives and points out that because regulation is composed of three elements (setting standards, monitoring and enforcement) there are many opportunities for sharing regulatory responsibility. The final section of the chapter returns briefly to the specific theme of seed regulation by suggesting three basic principles for analysing seed regulatory alternatives: participation, differentiation and evolution.

Why does the government regulate?

There are a number of legitimate reasons for a government to establish a regulatory system for a particular area of economic activity. These are usually related to various types of market failure, instances where competitive markets are unable to be established or are not capable of providing goods at the desired level. The causes of market failure most relevant to seed regulation are information asymmetry, externalities and the 'public good' character of some seed production.

In order for market transactions to be efficient, buyers and sellers must have access to adequate information about the product and the conditions of sale. If one party has a significant advantage in the control of information, this asymmetry will affect the nature of the transaction. If, for instance, the buyer cannot easily acquire sufficient information about the nature of the products, sale may not be possible. In some cases this will lead to the establishment of regulation, where a government agency takes responsibility for obtaining information about the products offered for sale and approving those that meet safety, performance or other standards. Even when the necessary information is potentially available to consumers, it may be more efficient for a government agency to analyse and process it than to expect individual consumers to do this. Farmers who buy seed may not be familiar with the characteristics of a particular variety, or even if they are, will have difficulty judging if the seed that is being sold is indeed of that variety, or if its physical quality is adequate. This 'information' may be available only at harvest, and the cost of obtaining it may represent a significant loss of income for the farmer.

A second argument for the establishment of government regulation is related to externalities, where individual economic activity has consequences for the wider public. If one person's economic activity imposes costs on the rest of society without affecting his/her own welfare, some external control may be necessary. Probably the most common example is that of industrial pollution, which is often met by government regulations aimed at protecting public health or welfare. Government responsibility for safeguarding national agricultural production and food supply motivates those seed regulations which are aimed at controlling the availability of varieties or seed that may contribute to the spread of pests, plant disease or weeds. A related argument, concerned with national food security, is sometimes used to justify government regulation of the source of seed as well. In particular, government regulations sometimes limit the degree to which foreign (or at times even domestic commercial) sources of seed, particularly of basic food crops, are marketed.

A third factor that may justify seed regulation is the 'public good' character of some seed production. In some cases, governments assume responsibility for variety development and seed production because it is felt that the products in question are unlikely to be supplied by conventional markets. A characteristic of public goods is their non-excludability; once they are provided to one consumer it is difficult to limit further access. Private firms cannot be expected to provide such goods, and hence the government must supply them; common examples are national defence or street lighting. Because seed can often be easily reproduced once an initial quantity is obtained, it has some public good characteristics, which help explain the existence of public agricultural research services and parastatal seed production enterprises.

Seed only very partially qualifies as having public good characteristics, however (indeed, there are relatively few examples of indisputably public goods). Hybrid seed is certainly not a public good, for instance, and the advent of intellectual property protection for plant varieties has made it possible to limit the degree to which purchased seed is reproduced for further use. In addition, as was discussed in Chapter 2, farmers are often willing to pay seed enterprises for the convenience and physical quality of their product, rather than simply for the genetic content of the variety itself. Nevertheless, many national seed regulatory systems are still based on the rules and operating procedures established for public sector variety development and seed production.

The weaknesses of government regulation

Despite clear justifications for the establishment of government regulation, there are a number of problems with the conduct of public regulatory agencies. These include bureaucratic misconduct and inefficiency, and the possibility that regulatory agencies are not politically independent.

Bernstein (1955) analyses the histories of several US regulatory commissions and describes a common life cycle that involves four stages. In the 'gestation' stage, the regulatory agency is established, often in response to a crisis and with strong public support. In the 'youth' stage of the agency, it adopts a crusading attitude, although it may begin to suffer from a lack of public support or comprehension. In the third, 'maturity' stage, agency procedures become routinized and the regulated industry begins to establish influence over the regulators. In the final stage, 'old age', the agency suffers from excessive bureaucracy, fails to adapt to changing conditions, and often serves the needs of the regulated industry rather than those of the public.

Bernstein's analysis has been criticized for being oversimplified and insufficiently analytical (Mitnick, 1980:48), but it does serve to focus attention on the fact that regulatory efficiency cannot be understood in isolation from the composition, motivations and resources of the implementing agency. Mitnick (1980:94) discusses three reasons why regulation may not serve the public interest in the way that it is intended. The first is venality or corruption; regulatory agencies may provide opportunities for staff to line their own pockets through the acceptance of bribes or the diversion of public funds. The second possible failing of regulatory agencies is incompetence. The agencies may be subject to inadequate management, and government salaries may be insufficient to attract adequately trained or motivated staff, or to provide sufficient resources for the performance of the agencies' mandated duties.

The third possible failing discussed by Mitnick, regulatory capture, deserves separate attention. Regulators are in a difficult position in that they must often depend on the regulated industry itself to provide the information that they need. In addition, as time passes, it is not uncommon for a symbiotic relationship to develop between the regulator and the regulated. Indeed, there is often a confusion about which part of the public interest a regulator is supposed to protect. A good example is provided by the case of BSE ('mad cow disease') in the UK, where public perceptions have been divided between the view that regulation should have done more to protect the meat-consuming public and the view that regulation was harmful to the interests of the national beef industry.

There are undoubtedly situations in which the regulated industry exerts undue influence over the actions of the regulatory agency. Bernstein's (1955) description of the history of US regulatory commissions contends that, despite their initial dedication to the public interest, their common fate was capture by the industries they were supposed to regulate. One influential analysis (Stigler, 1971) goes as far as proposing that regulation often has its very origin in the political pressure exerted on government by the firms in an industry to provide subsidies, limit access to the market by rival firms, control competition or fix prices. This may be an extreme interpretation, but regulation often evolves to serve purposes other than those identified with the public interest.

There are thus a number of problems that can occur when too much dependence is placed on government regulation. Chapters 4–6 look at these problems in more detail with respect to the conduct of plant breeding, variety regulation and seed quality control. In those chapters, regulatory performance is analysed in terms of efficiency, standards, participation and transparency.

Alternative regulatory frameworks

The previous sections have shown that although government regulation is often established because of market failure, problems arising from government regulation may themselves be responsible for serious inefficiencies. This is an example of what is, in North's (1990:58) judgement, 'the fundamental dilemma of economic development. If we cannot do without the state, we cannot do with it either. How does one get the state to behave like an impartial third party?' In seeking a way out of this conundrum, it will be best to look in more detail at the strengths and weaknesses of various regulatory options, and to understand how regulatory responsibilities may be shared among institutions. The resulting compromises will surely be more complex than is implied by 'state versus market' arguments, but they should also be politically realistic and able to adjust to evolving economic and political conditions. In short, we are seeking more responsive regulation; 'for the responsive regulator, there are no optimal or best regulatory solutions, just solutions that respond better than others to the plural configurations of support and opposition that exist at a particular moment in history' (Ayres and Braithwaite, 1992:5).

The following discussion is concerned with examining some of the most common alternatives to government regulation. These include various types of market mechanisms, the use of industry associations and the establishment of independent certifying agencies.

First, we should review the ways in which markets can deal with some of the problems of information asymmetry that are often used to justify government regulation. Akerlof (1970) argues that the variation of quality in products offered for sale in developing countries is a serious impediment to progress; excessive effort by both consumers and entrepreneurs is devoted to assessing the quality of inputs and outputs rather than being invested in more productive activities. He points out that several market mechanisms may counteract this problem of quality uncertainty, including guarantees offered by the seller and the establishment of brand names. Guarantees are useful where there is an effective system of commercial law in operation so that consumers are assured that any complaints will receive a fair hearing.

Brand names are an example of the use of reputation to regulate the quality of products offered for sale. Klein and Leffler (1981) discuss the conditions under which reputations are a useful means of enforcing contracts. Reputation is most effective when the firm has the possibility of attracting frequent repeat purchases of its products and if it depends upon a continual stream of income. In addition, investments by the firm in advertisement and in facilities provide further signals to consumers of its stability. These conditions may or may not be met by various types of enterprises in developing countries. Advertisement is most useful in promoting quality through reputation when consumers have several alternative sources of information through which they can verify the claims being made.

The possibility of rogue companies taking advantage of market imperfections is a concern not only for consumers, but for legitimate firms as well. The actions of a minority of unscrupulous firms can seriously damage the reputation and viability of the industry as a whole. One response in such cases is the use of industry associations to regulate quality and to enhance the reputations of their members. An industry association may set quality standards and enforce compliance among its members.

Another alternative to government regulation is the establishment of independent certifying agencies. In such cases consumers have a choice of whether or not to purchase products that have been certified. The advantage of such a system is that it allows market forces to dictate quality standards, while leaving quality control to an independent and specialized third party. The disadvantages of independent certification are characteristic of the weaknesses of market mechanisms generally, in particular the responsibility placed on the consumer for obtaining and managing sufficient information. Consumers may be tempted to buy non-certified products against their better judgement, and the costs to the consumer of gathering and assessing information about certified products may be excessive (Kelman, 1983).

The possible application of some of these alternative regulatory mechanisms to national seed systems is discussed in Part 2 of the book.

Standards, monitoring and enforcement

The challenge for regulatory reform in the seed sector is to balance the advantages and disadvantages of various modes of regulation in order to provide an effective framework for promoting seed system diversification. One helpful approach is to break regulation into its components. Regulatory duties can be seen as comprising: setting standards, monitoring performance and enforcing compliance. This division is certainly not perfect, but it is useful for helping consider how the regulatory process can be shared among different institutions. The following discussion examines each of these elements and provides examples of how regulatory options may be applied to each component of the regulatory process.

Standards

The first step in regulating for quality or safety is to determine the standards against which products are to be assessed. This usually implies the technical definition of feasible and acceptable performance or safety levels. Standards are often imposed by a regulatory agency drawing upon its own, or outside, technical expertise. But there is a danger of ignoring the range of conditions under which purchasers may use the product, and their particular requirements and priorities.

There are possibilities for standards to be tailored to the needs of individual firms. Ayres and Braithwaite (1992:116) describe the US Mine Safety and Health Act as an example of 'enforced self-regulation', where a government regulatory agency establishes standards, but responds to petitions from individual firms (mines in this case) for modifications that will still meet the agency's guidelines. This opens the possibility of developing more responsibility for individual firms in the regulatory process, and for tailoring standards to the conditions of the firm and its clients.

There are also possibilities for including several sets of standards under one regulatory umbrella. The organic farming movement grew rapidly in the UK in the 1980s and led to several sets of standards, representing different philosophies and definitions, although the predominant one was provided by the Soil Association. When the Ministry of Agriculture, Fisheries and Food (MAFF) moved towards the establishment of organic standards in response to European Union proposals, it received a mixed reaction from organic farmers. On the one hand, they tended to favour the involvement of the government as a way of promoting their industry abroad, but they also pushed for the Soil Association to maintain control of administration and monitoring (Clunies-Ross and Cox, 1994). Under current arrangements, the Soil Association and several other independent bodies offer organic certification alternatives that are in line with MAFF standards (BOF/OGA, 1994).

As competition grows within an industry, firms may feel that they need to seek advice on standards that will help them maintain their share of the market. One example is the movement towards 'Total Quality Management' (Dale, 1994), and the emergence of independent certifying agencies that establish standards not for products themselves, but rather for the production process.

Finally, the 'market' option for setting standards is to leave the decision to the individual firm. This is the usual practice in the production and sale of many products. As discussed above, the provision of brand names, mechanisms for establishing a firm's reputation and the existence of a responsive system of commercial law all add to the argument for choosing this type of performance standard.

Monitoring

Once standards have been defined, someone must monitor and measure a firm's production or activities to make sure that the standards are being followed. Again, the conventional solution is for the regulatory agency that sets the standards to carry out the monitoring as well.

In some cases the regulatory agency may assign considerable responsibility to firms themselves for monitoring adherence to standards. A system of Good Laboratory Practices (GLP) was established by the US Food and Drug Administration to control fraud during drug-testing experiments (Ayres and Braithwaite, 1992). The GLP requires that each firm establish its own quality assurance unit that keeps records and is responsible for enforcement.

Independent certification agencies may be able to offer better monitoring services than a public agency tied to government budgets. In addition, possible competition among independent certifying agencies provides an incentive to provide the most up-to-date technology for monitoring. Industry association monitoring may also be quite efficient, although there is a greater possibility that such monitoring may be tempted to overlook transgressions of member firms that are likely to escape public notice or that imply significant financial sacrifice for the firm to correct. In cases where independent or industry monitoring is established, there is still the possibility of government regulatory oversight to ensure that the monitoring meets established standards.

In cases where no formal regulation exists, and firms set their own standards, monitoring will correspond to a firm's internal quality control procedures. In a well-functioning market, a decline in the firm's quality control will be noted by consumers who will change allegiance or take the deficient firm to court. This type of monitoring requires alert consumers and competitive markets. The California Safe Drinking Water and Toxic Enforcement Act (Helfand and Archibald, 1990) provides an innovative example of incentives for public monitoring of water quality. A 'bounty hunter'

51

provision allows private citizens to monitor water quality; if they uncover a violation they are allowed to initiate legal action and are entitled to 25 per cent of the fine levied on the violating firm.

Enforcement

One of the greatest difficulties with regulatory mechanisms is faulty enforcement. Harriss-White (1995:593) comments on the large amount of regulatory law governing markets in India that 'in lying unimplemented or useless, threatens state legitimacy'. If regulations are perceived as unenforceable, they are worse than useless and they jeopardize the more feasible duties of a regulatory agency. Enforcement, of course, depends on effective monitoring, but implies an additional step, which is the subject of this section.

If regulations are in place, the regulatory agency must have the capacity to impose sanctions, or to instruct the legal system to do so. Choosing the correct level of enforcement may be difficult; some regulatory agencies are seen as toothless collaborators of the regulated industry, while at the other extreme the agency may adopt such an adversarial role that any cooperation from the industry is impossible.

Ayres and Braithwaite (1992:35) discuss the useful concept of 'the enforcement pyramid' which offers a range of sanctions of increasing severity

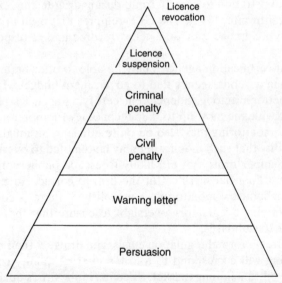

The proportion of space at each layer represents the proportion of enforcement activity at that level.

Source: Ayres and Braithwaite, 1992

Figure 3.1 *Example of an enforcement pyramid*

(from simple persuasion to licence revocation) that can be applied according to the circumstances (Figure 3.1). The bottom of the pyramid includes sanctions that imply a more co-operative relationship between the regulator and the firm. Their suggestion that successful regulators behave like 'benign big guns' (ibid.: 40) is based on the idea that 'the greater the heights of punitiveness to which an agency can escalate, the greater its capacity to push regulation down to the co-operative base of the pyramid'. Or, in more practical terms, 'punishment is expensive; persuasion is cheap' (ibid.: 19). At a minimum, regulatory agencies must have access to a range of enforcement capabilities if their standards and monitoring are to have any effect.

If independent agencies or industry associations have responsibility for monitoring, they may handle enforcement as well. If a firm's product fails to meet the standards of the certifying agency, it cannot be sold with the agency's or association's mark of approval. In extreme or repeated cases, the agency may refuse to monitor or collaborate further with the firm. Industry associations may warn or fine their members for breaches of regulations or, at the extreme, bar them from membership.

When no formal regulation is applied, enforcement is effected in one of two ways. Dissatisfied customers may punish the firm by taking their business elsewhere, or, if the firm has sold its product under some sort of guarantee or subject to other aspects of commercial law, consumers may take it to court.

The examples discussed above for assigning responsibility in the management of standards, monitoring and enforcement in regulation are far from exhaustive. They are presented as reminders of the wide range of possibilities, and in particular the opportunities for collaboration among organizations, that may characterize regulatory reform.

Principles for regulatory reform

The preceding discussion on the options for managing the setting of standards, monitoring and enforcement of regulations leads to the identification of three important principles for the development of seed regulatory reform. These are discussed below under the headings: participation, differentiation and evolution.

Participation

We have seen that many other organizations besides regulatory agencies can play important roles in the regulatory process. When it is deemed necessary to depend upon a state regulatory agency, Paul (1992) urges that citizens' lack of the 'exit' option (i.e. no alternative regulatory options are allowed) must be offset by attention to 'voice'; he points out that in developed countries many regulatory processes include strong public participation.

Ayres and Braithwaite (1992) discuss participation under the term 'tripartism', which emphasizes the key role of public interest groups, in addition to regulatory agencies and firms, in the conduct and direction of regulation. Their analysis assumes that firms already have a voice in the regulatory process but, in the case of seed regulation in developing countries, participation in regulatory management is often not available to private entities, including local groups and commercial firms involved in variety development or seed production. Much of the discussion in the following chapters will be concerned with how to achieve the widest and most effective participation in the definition and conduct of seed regulation.

Differentiation

One of the most serious problems with conventional government regulation is its monolithic character. When it comes to setting performance standards, the fact that 'a government agency must make a single choice, despite existence of diverse preferences among citizens' (Kelman, 1983:233) is a serious drawback. The discussion in the previous section showed that it is possible to allow more flexibility in regulation, however, and to encourage the tailoring of standards to the conditions of different producers and to the priorities of a range of consumers. This is particularly important for promoting dynamic seed systems in developing countries. Chapter 2 emphasized the great diversity within national seed sectors. The resources and skills available to different types of seed enterprise vary enormously; both voluntary farmer group seed production and large-scale commercial seed production may occupy important niches in developing countries, for instance, and it is most unlikely that they will be adequately served by a single, inflexible regulatory system. Public regulation of agriculture tends to be highly centralized (Smith and Thomson,1991), and there is a need for a more targeted approach.

Differentiation among consumers is also of importance for analysing seed regulatory reform. The needs of different types of farmers must be taken into consideration if adequate seed systems are to be developed. Of particular importance for national seed policy is the state's obligation to promote equitable development. As Carney (1995) points out, much of the current discussion about the role of the state in addressing market failures tends to ignore the fact that this debate is merely academic for the large numbers of poor people who are excluded from meaningful participation in the market. The seed and varietal needs of resource-poor farmers must be a touchstone for judging the adequacy of seed regulatory reform.

Evolution

A legal and regulatory system must be responsive to changes in economy and society. 'Law is to be viewed *instrumentally*, not as a doctrine deriving worth from its integrity or normative unity as a system of abstract ideas but as a means to practical ends . . . ' (Cotterrell, 1989:185). We need to be more pragmatic about seed regulation and to acknowledge that it should respond to changing economic and technical conditions. The history of seed regulation in industrialized countries, which will be touched upon in Chapters 5 and 6, provides ample evidence of this. One of the problems with seed regulations in developing countries is that they have often been transferred from developed countries with vastly different conditions. Regulatory reform must be seen as a continuous process, and regulatory structures must be sufficiently flexible to respond to and promote the evolution and diversification of the national seed sector.

Summary

Besides responding to technical and economic conditions, regulatory reform will also be the product of political debate. We have seen this in our discussion of the origins of regulation, and acknowledge it in the emphasis placed here on participation and differentiation. We should not pretend that regulatory reform is a technocratic process of simply identifying 'optimum' arrangements and then applying them. To say that regulation is a political process is not to be pessimistic. An acknowledgement of its political character allows regulatory agencies to define their role as not merely (or even primarily) to police and control, but rather also to encourage and enable the development and diversification of seed sector institutions, paying particular attention to equity and participation in the political process. More specific treatment of the political character of regulation is provided in Chapter 7.

Regulatory reform will reflect a compromise among competing interest groups (Needham, 1983:15), and such a compromise will not necessarily be easy to achieve. A realistic analysis of commitments and sympathies is necessary. 'Reform means indicating just where the interests are grounded, where the lines of opposition are drawn, the pain and guilt felt and hidden' (Schaffer, 1984, cited in Harriss-White, 1995: 595). But the effort is undoubtedly worthwhile. More-responsive seed regulation can make a significant difference to the development of seed systems that contribute to improving farmer welfare.

PART 2

THE ORGANIZATION OF SEED REGULATION

4 New directions for public sector variety testing

J.R. WITCOMBE AND D.S. VIRK

Introduction

THIS CHAPTER DESCRIBES the most important characteristics of the variety testing procedures that form an important part of the plant breeding programmes of public agricultural research systems. It points out where management reform is desirable and suggests measures that can make public sector plant breeding more supportive of national seed systems and more responsive to the needs of low-resource farmers.

Public sector plant breeding in developing countries

Farmers in developing countries have, with few exceptions, been dependent on public plant breeding programmes for modern varieties of staple crops. In many countries, a national agricultural research institute has responsibility for plant breeding. In others, plant breeding is carried out by several different entities, including national and regional research institutes and agricultural universities.

Many national plant breeding programmes collaborate in the international exchange and testing of germplasm co-ordinated by the International Agricultural Research Centres funded by the Consultative Group on International Agricultural Research (CGIAR). A few national plant breeding programmes also participate in bilateral or multilateral exchanges and testing programmes with neighbouring countries, although this type of activity is relatively uncommon.

In order to co-ordinate the range of plant breeding activities and to control the release of new varieties, nearly all developing countries have established a variety testing system that is used to identify promising materials and to decide which ones will be submitted to the official release authority. When there are several public plant breeding entities in a country, they are usually governed by a single national variety testing system, or by a well-defined hierarchy of regional and national testing procedures. Where varieties from the private sector must be officially released, commercial plant breeders have to enter them in the public testing system.

Box 4.1 Examples of variety testing authorities

National testing network and regional testing authorities
India
Plant breeding is carried out by a network of research institutes under the Indian Council of Agricultural Research (ICAR) and by state agricultural universities. Variety testing for major crops is conducted by ICAR through a series of All India Co-ordinated Crop Improvement Programmes (AICCIPs) that manage a nationwide testing scheme. State-level variety testing is under the authority of the state agricultural universities.

National testing network
Philippines
For rice, a National Co-operative Testing (NCT) project is run by the Rice Varietal Improvement Group (RVIG), whose participating agencies include the Philippine Rice Research Institute (PhilRice), the Bureau of Plant Industry (BPI), the University of the Philippines at Los Baños (UPLB), state colleges and universities and the International Rice Research Institute (IRRI). Entries for the testing system come from PhilRice, UPLB, IRRI and other state institutions and private companies. A similar testing system for maize and sorghum is run by the Corn and Sorghum Varietal Improvement Group (CSVIG).

Single research institute managing testing
Kenya
Most plant breeding is done by the Kenya Agricultural Research Institute (KARI); the partly government-owned Kenya Seed Company also has a breeding programme, and there is a small amount of private plant breeding for certain crops. KARI is in charge of managing National Performance Trials (NPTs) for all varieties, with monitoring by the National Seed Quality Control Service (NSQCS).

Single research institute responsible for all testing
Nepal
The Nepalese Agricultural Research Council (NARC) includes 10 national commodity programmes that are responsible for research and variety development for major food crops. Each commodity programme conducts trials through a network of regional research stations and other testing sites.

Testing by individual institutes
Bolivia
Variety testing is organized by individual commodity breeding programmes under the Bolivian Institute of Agricultural Technology (IBTA) or other public, private or international research institutes. Where more than one entity does plant breeding for a particular crop there is not necessarily a co-ordinated testing system. Application for the release of a variety is made by the individual breeding programme to a regional seed council, which may accept the results of the validation trials already conducted by the breeding programme, or commission further independent trials.

Source: Project case studies

An overview of multilocational trials systems

Systems of multi-locational variety trials are established for two reasons: to identify varieties that are superior to those currently available, and to determine the area of adaptation of the selected varieties. Assessing the performance of varieties across time and space helps to identify varieties proposed for release not only in regions where they have been bred, but also for other regions as well.

In those countries where a single national agricultural research institute is responsible for plant breeding, it is usually charged with co-ordinating variety testing. In many cases, however, there are several plant breeding institutes or regional plant breeding organizations, and the co-ordination of a testing system becomes more complex (Box 4.1).

It should be emphasized that the subject of this chapter is the variety testing systems that plant breeders use to select varieties that are *proposed* for official release. Although the decision of the variety release authority may be at least partially based on data from these variety testing systems, regulation of actual variety release is, in theory, a process separate from, and additional to, the testing that is part of public plant breeding programmes. The variety testing that is commissioned by variety release authorities is discussed in Chapter 5.

The variety testing systems are the products of scientific principles of experimental design, the organizational rules of the national research institutes and protocols borrowed from other established trial systems. The organization of the trials system responds to national agricultural policy and to the structure of national seed regulatory frameworks, including the control of variety release and seed quality control. Despite an image of scientific rigour, national variety testing systems are also influenced by assumptions about the directions of agricultural development, the demands of the public sector seed system and the constrained resources that limit the number of test sites and the number of varieties and traits that can be evaluated. As the policy and institutional environment changes, the variety testing system must be capable of evolution and adjustment.

The changing environment of variety testing

Until recently, public sector plant breeding enjoyed a privileged position in most developing countries. The impact (or promise) of the Green Revolution was sufficient to attract both public funds and foreign donor support for breeding programmes. Public seed companies were established to market the output of these programmes, and extension programmes encouraged the use of new varieties and the adoption of crop management practices that would enhance their performance. Competition from private plant breeding was either limited by law or discouraged by a perceived lack of opportunity. National variety testing systems evolved and became established in this environment, but these conditions are now changing rapidly.

Table 4.1   *Adoption of modern varieties of rice in India*

District class	Number of districts	Production statistics of districts with different classes of adoption rates of HYVs		
		Area (000 ha)	*Production (000 t)*	*Average yield (t/ha^{-1})*
0–50%	62	5003	4896	0.98
50–75%	34	3254	5577	1.71
75–100%	53	6277	12782	2.04
All districts	149	14534	23255	1.60

Source: Virk *et al.*, 1996

The general budgetary crisis affecting all public sector activities has been felt in a general decline in support for agricultural research, and foreign donors are also becoming less willing to contribute to agricultural research budgets. Part of this decline in support can be attributed to increasing scrutiny of the impact of public plant breeding. Most public sector crop varieties are being grown in areas of relatively superior agricultural resources, while more marginal farming environments and resource-poor farmers are still not well served (Table 4.1). There is also growing concern about the effectiveness of the public extension and seed production systems that are meant to popularize and deliver the new varieties.

Variety testing systems were established at a time when agricultural development strategy was based on the success of the Green Revolution. The strategy comprised two elements: the concentration of plant breeding resources on the breeding of varieties that were widely adapted to a range of environments; and the belief that farmers' crop management practices would follow a 'modernization' path towards the increased use of external inputs. There is now ample evidence that these assumptions about the effectiveness of breeding for wide adaptability and the feasibility of achieving uniformly high crop management standards are not applicable to many farming situations.

In addition, countries are beginning to change their policies and attitudes toward private sector plant breeding, and both domestic and multinational seed companies are gaining ground in a number of countries. At the same time, a growing number of community-based varietal selection and *in-situ* conservation projects are promoting the preservation and enhancement of local crop varieties. These developments place public plant breeding systems under increasing pressure to demonstrate impact.

Variety testing systems will have to respond to these changing conditions. The plant breeding strategies on which the testing systems are based have not been successful in delivering improved crop varieties to all farmers. The public agricultural research and input delivery systems that implemented these strategies are losing support while community and commercial alternatives are gaining increasing ground. Farmers' requirements are much more diverse than previously envisaged, and a much wider use of participatory approaches in plant breeding is essential if the needs of low-resource farmers are to be met.

Problems for the management of variety testing

A review of the management of variety testing systems in developing countries reveals a number of serious problems that need to be addressed. Some of the most important of these are discussed below. They can be divided into issues of: *efficiency* (low adoption of new varieties, uneven resource allocation, delays and inappropriate site selection), *standards* (unrepresentative trial management and analysis procedures), *participation* of farmers and organizations that represent farmers and *transparency* (lack of co-ordination and accountability) (Box 4.2).

The frequency of variety replacement

The frequency with which farmers replace older public varieties with newer ones is one measure of the success of both a plant breeding programme and a varietal testing system. Evidence shows that farmers quickly replace older varieties when public plant breeding produces new superior alternatives (Cuevas-Perez *et al.*, 1995). When farmers continue to use older varieties, there are three possible explanations: public plant breeding and variety testing are not producing superior new varieties; the variety release system does not allow farmers access to new varieties; or popularization mechanisms do not provide farmers with sufficient information about new varieties. Estimates of the speed and frequency of variety replacement do not distinguish among these three factors, but they do offer one means of assessing the overall efficiency with which new varieties are bred and selected for release.

There are several different measures that can be used to estimate the rate of varietal replacement. One method is to calculate the average age of the varieties available for a particular crop, weighted by the area currently sown to each variety (Brennan and Byerlee, 1991). Calculating the average age of varieties requires data on current variety use. The most useful source of information is agricultural census data on the varieties grown by farmers, but such data are often unavailable or out of date. Alternative sources of data include statistics on certified seed production of individual varieties, or seed producer demand for breeder seed by variety.

A study in India (Virk *et al.*, 1996) utilized both of these latter sources to estimate average age of varieties for wheat, pearl millet, groundnut, sorghum, rice, chickpea and maize. National estimates were based on breeder seed indents (the quantities of breeder seed of each variety requested by all seed producers). Breeder seed is the first stage in commercial seed production, and the pattern of current breeder seed indents is an

Box 4.2   Problems with the management of variety testing

Efficiency

Low frequency of variety replacement. Analysis of variety use in many countries shows that the turnover rate of modern varieties is quite low, indicating problems with the variety testing system, variety release or popularization.

Uneven resource allocation to different trial stages. A large proportion of the varieties submitted for testing do not survive the early stages, but there is rarely an increase in plot size or number of testing sites to balance the decreased number of varieties in later stages.

Prolonged variety testing. Varieties can be kept in the various stages of the testing process for six years or longer.

Inappropriate site selection. Sites for variety testing are often chosen for convenience of access rather than as true representatives of the major growing environments of the crop.

Inappropriate zoning. There is insufficient attention given to grouping and targeting variety testing for different environments.

Standards

Unrepresentative trial management. The levels of trial management (such as fertilizer application) are often much higher than average farmer levels; unwarranted assumptions are made about the capacity of farmers to use higher levels of external inputs.

Trial analysis biased against poor environments. Trial sites with low or variable yields are likely to be eliminated from the overall analysis.

Lack of attention to farmer-relevant variety traits. Many varietal characteristics that are important to farmers, such as fodder yield, earliness and marketability, are often overlooked in variety testing systems.

Participation

Lack of participation from related organizations. There is little opportunity for a wider range of agricultural research and extension organizations to participate in the design or interpretation of the trial system. Private commercial breeders usually have little voice, even when their varieties must be tested before official release.

Lack of farmer participation. There are few mechanisms through which farmers can participate in establishing priorities or expressing preferences in the standard variety testing system.

Transparency

Lack of co-ordination between national and regional testing systems. In countries with both national and regional testing systems there is often poor co-ordination between the two levels and inadequate exchange of information between regional authorities.

Lack of accountability and linkages. Variety testing tends to be tightly controlled by commodity programmes and there is not sufficient accountability to other parts of the research and extension system.

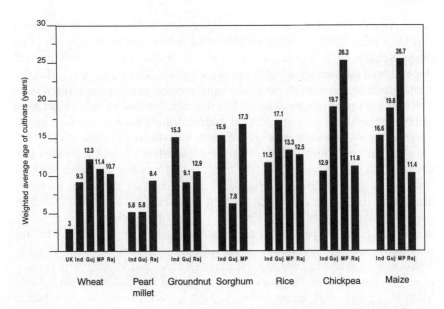

Weighted average age of cultivars of important crops estimated from breeder seed indents in India (1984–93), and certified seed production statistics for Gujarat (1992–93), Madhya Pradesh (1993–94) and Rajasthan (1992–93). (The age of certified seed of wheat in the UK is also indicated for 1987 to 1993.)

Source: Virk *et al.*, 1996
Figure 4.1 *Weighted average age of varieties of important crops in India*

indication of the relative importance of different varieties that will be offered for sale three or four years in the future. The weighted average of breeder seed indents over the past five to 10 years (depending on the availability of data) was calculated. For three states, data on certified seed production from state seed companies were used, based on studies carried out by Jaisani (1995) for Gujarat, Upadhyaya (1995) for Madhya Pradesh and Vyas (1995) for Rajasthan.

The estimates from certified seed production in the individual states were generally higher than those expected by adding 3–4 years to the ages calculated from breeder seed indents, but the general conclusions are quite consistent (Figure 4.1). The majority of the average ages were above 10 years, and in some cases (maize and chickpea in Madhya Pradesh) well above 20 years. This is higher than would be expected if variety testing, release and popularization functioned efficiently. Brennan and Byerlee (1991) calculated weighted averages of wheat varieties for a series of developed and developing countries with strong wheat breeding programmes. They found a range of 5–10 years, with an average of about

65

seven years. Wheat varieties may experience a somewhat more rapid turnover than varieties of some other crops because of rapidly evolving disease pressure, however, and the rate of replacement of varieties will depend on a number of other factors (Heisey and Brennan, 1991). But the Indian figures are considerably above the seven-year average for wheat. For many crops it can be argued that the calculations using breeder seed indents or certified seed production underestimate the real average age of varieties in use because they ignore farmer-saved seed of older varieties.

In the case of hybrids, farmers have less incentive tó sow their own seed, because advanced generations of a hybrid yield less and are more variable than the original hybrid generation. Hence, statistics on seed sales more accurately reflect the age of cultivars in hybrids than in self-pollinated or open-pollinated varieties. In Kenya in 1994, the average age of public sector maize hybrids and varieties, weighted by the quantity of each hybrid or variety sold by the Kenya Seed Company (Kimenye and Nyangito, 1996), was 13 years. In 1993 in Zimbabwe (Rusike and Musa, 1996), the age of maize hybrids was 20 years, when weighted by the sale of individual hybrids. In the Philippines there is high private sector activity which

Table 4.2 *Examples of variety testing systems*

Country	Crop	Stages in variety testing system	Years in each stage	Number of entries per trial
India (national release)	rice, wheat, sorghum, pearl millet	Initial Evaluation Trials (IET)	1	45–51[a]
		Advanced Variety Trials (AVT)	2	14–31[a]
Kenya	maize	Preliminary Yield Trials (PYT)	1	64
		Advanced Yield Trials (AYT)	2	25
		National Performance Trials (NPT)	3	20
Philippines	rice (irrigated)	Preliminary Yield Trials (PYT)	1[b]	10–20
		Advanced Yield Trials – 1 (AYT-1)	2[c]	20
		Advanced Yield Trials – 2 (AYT-2)	1[d]	10
Bolivia	potato	Comparative Yield Trial (CYT)	2–3	25–30
		Regional Trials (RT)	2–3	10–15
		Validation Trials (VT)	2	1–5

a Averaged across years and trials. Individual trials will have more extreme values
b 1 wet season and 1 dry season
c 2 wet seasons and 1 dry season
d 1 wet season and 1 dry season

Sources: authors' research; Njoroge, 1996; Hernandez and Borromeo, 1996; Romero, 1995.

appears to have resulted in more rapid replacement of hybrid maize cultivars (Logroño, 1996). In 1995, the average age of hybrids, weighted by area of cultivation, was eight years for public sector hybrids and four years for private sector hybrids. In general, even in maize hybrids the average age of cultivars is again considerably higher than the ages of wheat varieties found by Brennan and Byerlee (1991), and reflects more closely the situation described for India.

Uneven resource allocation across trial stages

Most variety testing systems test entries over a number of years in a progression from initial to advanced trials. The number of entries tested in the first year is far greater than those tested for a second or third year. The number and nomenclature of the stages varies across countries and crops. Table 4.2 presents some typical examples.

In multi-stage variety trials, the most efficient results can be obtained by devoting equal resources to each stage of testing (Finney, 1958; Curnow, 1961). This strategy requires that a constant proportion of entries are promoted at each trial stage and that the declining number of survivors is balanced by increasing the intensity of assessment. For example, breeders can halve the number of entries at each testing stage, whilst doubling the land devoted to each entry (through any combination of larger plot size, more replicates or more sites). But such a strategy is rarely practised in national breeding programmes.

The survivorship in most testing systems is very low, resulting in a rapid elimination of the majority of the varieties under examination. Despite the low survivorship in the variety testing programmes, there is usually not a concomitant increase in plot size or number of replications in succeeding stages of variety trials (Table 4.3).

Prolonged variety testing

Another indication of inefficiencies in the variety testing system is the length of the testing process. Although variety testing should avoid the hasty release of inappropriate varieties, more attention should be focused on addressing avoidable delays in the testing system. Given the number of generations and years required to breed a variety before testing is initiated, any time that can be saved in the testing process would make a significant contribution to efficiency. The time taken to breed varieties depends on the type of product (hybrid or variety), on the breeding system (open or self-pollinated) and the number of generations that can be grown per year (from one to three). Consequently, the time required varies from three to 10 years with five to eight being the most typical. Once a variety is in the testing system it can take six years or more before it is proposed for release (Table 4.2).

Table 4.3   *Characteristics of different stages in the variety testing system*

Country and crop	Stage	Year of testing	% survival to next stage	Plot size (m²)	Number of replications	Number of sites per trial
India,	IET	1	25	8.3	3	5–31
wheat	AVT-I	2	32	16.6	3	2–39
	AVT-II	3	28	16.6	3	2–39
India, rice	IET	1	43	10	3	2–7/zone
	AVT	2	45	12	3	2–8/zone
	AVT	3	53	12	3	2–8/zone
Nepal,	IET	1	–	4–18	1–3	3
wheat	CVT	2	–	4–16	4	4
	CVT	3	–	4–16	4	4
	FFT	4	–	20–100	1	8
Nepal, rice	IET	1	–	4–6	1–3	2
	CVT	2	–	9–15	4	4
	CVT	3	–	9–15	4	4
	FFT	4	–	20–100	1	8
Pakistan,	A	1	33	2.8	3–4	1
wheat	B	2	–	6.9	3–4	2
	Micro	3	20	6.9	3	18–20
	NUYT	4	10	6.9	4	18–20
Pakistan,	PYT	1	60	4.5	1	1
rice	OYT	2	–	50	1	1
	RYT	3	25–30	12	3–4	7
	NUYT	4	–	12	3–4	8
Philippines,	PYT	1	10–20	9.6	3	–
rice	AYT-I	2	10–15	24	3	10 (irrig), 4–7 (up) †
	AYT-II	3	30–50	24	3	15 (irrig), 4–7 (up)
Philippines,	PYT	1	20–30	3.75	2	2–3
maize	AYT-1	2	25–30	15	3	5
	AYT-2	3	25–30	15	3	5
	OFT	4	10–20	75	3	20

† irrig = irrigated, up = upland

IET   = Initial Evaluation Trial
AVT   = Advanced Variety Trial
CVT   = Co-ordinated Variety Trial
FFT   = Farmers' Field Trial
'A'   = Initial Trial
'B'   = Second Stage Trial
'micro' = Third Stage Trial

NUYT = National Uniform Yield Trial
PYT   = Preliminary Yield Trial
OYT   = Observation Yield Trial
RYT   = Replicated Yield Trial
AYT   = Advanced Yield Trial
OFT   = On-Farm Trial

Sources: authors' research; Sthapit, 1995; Rao, 1996; Hernandez and Borromeo, 1996; Logroño, 1996

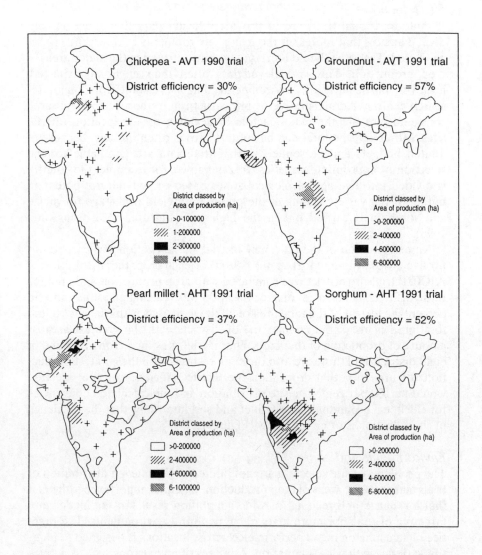

Location sites of AICCIP trials for chickpea (1990), groundnut (1991), pearl millet (1991) and sorghum (1991) in relation to area of production by district. Areas within the thicker black lines have no recorded cultivation of the crop.

Figure 4.2   *The efficiency of trial site locations in India*

Source: Virk *et al.*, 1996

Site selection

If multi-locational trials are to provide relevant data they must be conducted at sites that represent the major environments in which the crop is cultivated. Test sites should therefore be concentrated in the major areas of crop production. This is achieved less often than might be expected, however, particularly for environments that are distant from major research centres. Administrative or infrastructural, rather than agricultural, considerations are the major factors in deciding on the location of trial sites. Moreover, the total number of test sites is often too low, because of limited budgets and personnel, so that trial data are unreliable for the selection of appropriate varieties. In Zimbabwe, for example, the country is divided into five agro-ecological zones based on agricultural potential, but all of the variety testing at the preliminary yield trial stage for maize and sorghum is carried out in the high potential area (Mashiringwani, 1996).

An examination of the efficiency of trial site allocation was carried out for five crops in India (Virk *et al.*, 1996). For each crop, the distribution of AICCIP trials by district was compared with crop production and area for those districts. Efficiencies of site allocation were calculated as the ratio (in percentage terms) of the total area of all the n districts with trial sites to the total area of the same number (n) of districts with the greatest area or amount of production of that crop. Thus if trial sites for a crop are found in eight districts and those are also the eight districts with the greatest production (or area) for that crop, then the district efficiency of site selection would be 100 per cent. The site distribution and the calculated efficiencies for chickpea, groundnut, pearl millet and sorghum show that the efficiency of site selection is often quite low (Figure 4.2).

Environments and zones

The problems of site selection are not limited to the uneven distribution of trials across major areas of crop production. Of equal importance is the fact that a reliance on breeding for wide adaptation results in the inadequate targeting of trials for more marginal agricultural environments. The practice of selecting on mean performance across locations is designed to identify varieties with wide adaptation. Analyses of many crops such as cereals (rice, wheat, pearl millet and sorghum) and legumes (groundnut and chickpea) tested in multi-locational trials in India (Virk *et al.*, 1996) showed that this strategy selects for entries that yield more than the average in low-yielding environments, but it does not always identify the best cultivar for these environments. This was also shown to be the case in pearl millet multi-locational trials, analysed by Witcombe (1989).

Many national commodity breeding programmes are divided into zones based on agro-ecological or production systems. In Kenya, for instance, maize trials are designed specifically for five agro-climatic regions, and

70

each region has its own breeding sub-programme and set of trials (Njoroge, 1996). Wheat variety testing in the Punjab of Pakistan is divided into three zones, based on the cropping system. In the vast country of India, the greatest number of zones is seven in the case of wheat, and several crops have only three, or fewer, zones. These types of trial zoning improve the precision of the variety testing system, but are usually insufficient to address the challenges of breeding for specific adaptation to marginal environments.

Centralized breeding employing multi-site trials is not the most efficient way of producing varieties adapted to marginal environments (Simmonds, 1984). There is growing evidence that selection is more effective if it is carried out in target environments (Smith *et al.*, 1990; Simmonds, 1991; Ceccarelli *et al.*, 1994). Selection under low-input management is essential if significant yield gains for such conditions are to be achieved, as this will reduce the magnitude of genotype x environment interactions. The bias towards high-input farming systems in the trials system, on the other hand, is responsible for large differences between the performance of varieties in research station trials and their performance in farmers' fields. The disparity is so large that there is a risk of selecting varieties specifically adapted to favourable environments that will perform poorly in farmers' fields. For the evaluation in multi-locational trials to be relevant to the target environments, the trials must be conducted, as far as possible, in environmental conditions that represent farmers' fields. Imperfect site selection leads to a sub-optimal identification of cultivars, and the recommendation domains of identified cultivars are imperfectly defined. Greater participation of farmers, in a more decentralized system, can make the system much more relevant to farmers' needs.

Trial management
In addition to the problems associated with unrepresentative trial site selection, trial management can impose further biases on the interpretation of variety test data. Variety trials are typically planted on experimental stations, where the management is often very different from that of the typical farmer's field. In Zimbabwe, for instance, maize variety trials receive a 400kg/ha basal dose of compound fertilizer and 400kg/ha of ammonium nitrate as top dressing, while maize farmers, particularly in lower potential areas, apply little or no fertilizer to their maize. Similarly, the majority of millet and sorghum farmers use no chemical fertilizer, but it is regularly applied to all trials at research stations (Mashiringwani, 1996).

Exact comparisons between research station and farmer management may be hampered by a lack of statistics on typical farmer practices, but an indication of the bias is provided by examining differences between trial mean yields and average yields in farmers' fields. An analysis was done for India in which the mean yields from AICCIP trials were compared with

71

agricultural census data on crop yields in the districts where the trials were located (Virk *et al.*, 1996). For some crops, the differences were startling. The minimum difference found in 1989 and 1990 between the mean yields of pearl millet trials and those of the districts in which they were located was 260 per cent (a difference of over 1 t/ha); for sorghum, the difference was 270 per cent (over 2 t/ha). Some of this difference can, of course, be explained by the fact that the trials include genetic material that is superior to that grown by farmers, but the differences are much too large to be completely explained in this manner. The most reasonable interpretation is the high level of inputs applied to the trial plots, particularly chemical fertilizer. Indeed, the exceptions in the study serve to confirm this hypothesis. Groundnut and chickpea variety trial yields tend not to differ as greatly from their respective district yields as in the case of pearl millet and sorghum. The minimum difference found in 1989 and 1990 in chickpea was 140 per cent (a difference of 0.4 t/ha), and in groundnut, which was only studied in 1988, the difference was 150 per cent (0.5 t/ha). This may be because differences between nitrogen levels in research trials and farmers' fields are less extreme for legumes, which naturally fix nitrogen, than for cereals.

The differences between yield levels in trial plots and farmers' fields in India is more remarkable, because the districts where the research sites are located have higher yields than those of the country as a whole. This is an indication of the fact that the research sites are in more favoured environments; the yields from the sites are not representative of the districts, and the trial districts are not representative of the country.

Trial analysis
The techniques used for analysing trial results tend to exacerbate the effects of unrepresentative management practices. In many cases, trial sites with low or variable yield results are eliminated from further analysis, even though such sites may provide exceptionally relevant information for addressing the needs of farmers in marginal environments. In India's AICCIP system, most crops trials having a mean yield lower than the state average are not even considered in the data analysis for determining promotion and release of entries. If we assume that yield on farmers' fields is normally distributed, then half of the fields would be expected to yield less than the state mean. Consequently, trials that are rejected because they are below the state mean are representative of 50 per cent of farmers' fields!

In many countries a further problem with the analysis of variety trials is an excessive reliance on the use of the coefficient of error variation (CV) as a measure of trial efficiency. CV is the error standard deviation (SD) expressed as a percentage of the mean yield in the experiment. Trials that exceed a pre-set level are rejected as unsatisfactory without any regard to the significance of differences among entries. Rainfed sites, or those in harsh environments, tend to produce a high CV, but often this is because the trial mean is low rather than because the standard deviation is particularly high. Following a pre-set limit of CV, data from low-yielding sites tend to be excluded from the across-site analyses.

The maximum acceptable CV for the inclusion of trial data varies across crops and countries. In India, this limit is as low as 20 per cent in chickpea irrigated trials while it is 30 per cent in pearl millet and rainfed chickpea trials. In the Philippines, a maximum CV of 20 per cent for irrigated lowland rice trials and 30 per cent for rice trials in other ecosystems has been set (Hernandez and Borromeo, 1996).

In fact, the CV is a statistic that is really intended to provide a measure of variability that is independent of large differences in overall mean because different traits are measured, or to compare trials that, because of very different treatments, have large differences in overall mean. In typical multi-site variety trials, on the other hand, the same trait is measured on the same set of entries, and other statistical measures are more appropriate. Under these circumstances, adherence to the dogma that rejects results from trials above a pre-set CV simply acts as one more impediment to the examination of variety performance in marginal environments.

Assessing farmer-relevant traits

The major criterion for the promotion of a variety from one trial stage to another is that it yields more than the trial mean or more than check varieties, and the major criterion for release is that the variety has survived for three years in the trials and yields more than previously released varieties. The overwhelming attention given to yield means that other traits of economic importance often take second place. In practice, varieties with significantly superior disease or pest resistance, early maturity or improved fodder yield or grain quality are not promoted or released unless they also have a higher yield. In many cases these traits are not even measured during the trials, and the assessment of many traits, such as cooking quality, taste, market acceptability and storability, is often delayed until the variety has been released.

For example, although high fodder yield is an important trait in cereal crops for resource-poor farmers in India (Jansen et al., 1989), varieties will be promoted only if they satisfy the criterion for grain yield. If promotion criteria are to give due consideration to farmer-relevant traits, selection must be made using multiple-trait selection indexes. For many crops, high fodder yield needs to be part of such a selection index, or specific trials need to be created for dual-purpose varieties that are grown for both fodder and grain. In many countries, fodder yield is not even measured in variety trials.

Grain quality is also crucially important. In a study in India, farmers preferred a variety of rice, Kalinga III, for characteristics never assessed in

73

formal trials—thin husk, non-breaking grains at dehulling and high market value of grain (Joshi and Witcombe, 1996b). Market value is important for resource-poor farmers, and selling staple crops is a common transaction. When choosing which varieties to grow, farmers pay more attention to the total value, rather than the absolute quantity of the yield.

One of the most important traits for farmers that is often overlooked in conventional variety trial systems is maturity. Although some trial programmes specifically recognize the importance of early maturity for the needs of farming systems and divide their trials by maturity class, many breeding programmes still pay insufficient attention to this trait. Early-maturing varieties are likely to yield somewhat less than other varieties, and this puts them at a disadvantage in trial systems that base promotion and release on yield criteria. An excellent example is the early-maturing Indian pearl millet variety 'MP 124' (ICTP 8203). Its yield advantage in the trials was below the requirement of yielding more than the trial mean and it failed to meet a criterion, currently applied in other crops, of yielding 10 per cent more than the best check variety. Nevertheless, in a rare example of promotion on the basis of multiple traits, it was promoted for its earliness and large grain size and was officially released after three years of testing. Its supposed yield disadvantage has proved to be no barrier to its adoption, as its extreme earliness is much appreciated by farmers, and it is now widely grown in Andhra Pradesh, Karnataka and Maharashtra (Bantilan et al., 1996).

Participation from related organizations

Most national variety testing systems are controlled by public plant breeding institutes. Commodity co-ordinators are usually in charge of managing the national trials, and there are frequent meetings involving scientists to plan the trials and assess the results. But the breadth of participation from other organizations involved in agricultural research or extension is often disappointing.

In India, Singh (1992) observed that the participation of high-level scientists from national and state agencies had declined in AICCIP workshops. He also observed that, although workers from extension and rural development agencies are often invited to these meetings, their participation is almost always poor. He suggested the desirability of better interaction between the research and development staff at the time when national trials were being planned.

In some countries, private sector plant breeding is still discouraged, but in countries with commercial breeding, private sector varieties may or may not be required to be officially released (see Chapter 5). In those cases where official release is mandatory, the commercial variety must usually be included in the variety testing system. Where official release is voluntary (as is the case in India if only truthfully labelled seeds are sold) private breeders may still submit some of their varieties to the public testing system in order to enable them to sell certified seed. In either case, it is unusual for private commercial breeders to have much say in the organization of the testing system or the interpretation of the results.

Farmer participation
There is a complete absence of farmer participation in the planning of variety trials in most developing countries. In some cases, national workshops may consider feedback from farmers expressed through the participation of extension workers invited to the meetings. Farmers are conspicuously absent from the initial stages. In some countries, such as Nepal and Bolivia, farmer field trials are part of the later stages of the testing process, but the extent of farmer involvement in these researcher-managed trials is not well defined. In most countries, farmers are included in on-farm trials only at the pre-release or release stage when it is considered desirable to expose them to the new varieties in order to promote adoption. Farmers are not consulted in the development stage, and varieties are often released without consideration for the requirements of client farmers.

Regional versus national testing systems
In some larger countries, such as Pakistan and India, there are parallel systems of variety testing at state and national levels. These allow for national and state releases and theoretically help to cater for both the concerns of wide adaptation and the requirements of regional specificity. But conflicts in management are often responsible for inefficiencies. In India, state-released varieties have to be notified by the central (national) variety release committee, in order to qualify for certification. This is interpreted locally as an unnecessary interference from the centre. In the state system, nearly all released varieties are bred by the state agricultural universities, with national and out-of-state releases rarely, if ever, being recommended (Jaisani, 1995; Upadhyaya, 1995; Vyas, 1995). These conflicts lead to incorrect definition of the cultivation domain of a variety, and the recommended areas are often too small because widely adapted cultivars continue to be recommended only in the individual states where they were bred.

Joshi and Witcombe (1996b) describe one example where the upland rice variety Kalinga III was never promoted beyond the preliminary trial stage in the national testing system. It was, however, tested and released in the state of Orissa. Despite its popularity there, no other state officially released it, although it is recommended for cultivation in Bihar and eastern Madhya Pradesh. Later, farmer participatory varietal selection studies in districts of Madhya Pradesh, Rajasthan and Gujarat showed that the variety was highly accepted by low-resource farmers in those states, and breeder seed indents show that it is widely grown in many northern states.

Accountability and linkages

Accountability is not an inherent feature of public sector varietal testing systems. Trial systems are established and maintained with little consideration for improving their efficiency. For instance, even if trials conducted at a research site have been consistently unsatisfactory over a number of years, the site will often continue to be included in the trial system. Other disciplines that could improve the farmer relevance and efficiency of the trials, such as socio-economics and biometrics, are rarely included in the varietal testing system. Their inclusion could act as a catalyst for profound changes.

Trial systems are often very rigid and do not allow the integration of data from other sources, such as private companies, other national research institutes, or extension trials in farmers' fields. The issue of linkages between research and extension is particularly crucial. The sharp distinction that is maintained in most countries is artificial and counterproductive. Farmer participatory research lies on the boundary between research and extension and requires more flexible and accountable management of the variety testing system.

Alternatives for managing variety testing

In order to compete effectively with private plant breeding, and to guarantee continued access to public funds, the variety testing systems managed by public agricultural research institutes must become more efficient. This section examines strategies for improving the efficiency of public sector plant breeding. First it reviews the procedural changes that will have to be made in the variety testing process to address the deficiencies outlined in the previous section. It then examines the organizational implications of these changes, including the possibilities for decentralization, the requirement for greater farmer participation and the need for wider links between public plant breeding institutes and other organizations. It concludes by reviewing the risks and incentives for changes in the conduct of variety testing.

Reforming variety testing procedures

An inevitable conclusion of the discussion of deficiencies presented in the previous section is the need to increase the quantity and diversity of variety testing. Plant breeders should invest in a wider range of trials and a greater number of test sites. They should collect more information from the trials on traits important to farmers, and should be prepared to release a greater number of varieties to meet diverse needs. At first sight, such conclusions may seem impractical when confronted by the realities of decreased public funding for agricultural research. However, certain types of activity can be balanced by decreased investment in other areas (for example, more

76

farmer-managed trials can lead to a reduction in scientist-managed test sites); a reorientation of variety testing is needed to improve efficiency (for example, by increasing the proportion of released varieties that are actually used by farmers); and an increase in variety testing activities will have to seek broader participation from farmers and from extension services and NGOs.

It is clear that the absolute level of variety testing managed by most public agricultural research institutes is inadequate to address farmers' needs. In particular, the later stages of the testing do not include enough locations to provide sufficient information about the performance of varieties in diverse environments. Instead of relying on a few test sites with complex, replicated trials, plant breeders should place more emphasis at the initial stages of testing on using a greater number of sites, often with single replications. An indiscriminate increase in the number of trial sites will not be helpful, however, and increased attention should be placed on choosing sites that are more representative of well-defined environments.

An important tool for increasing the efficiency of multi-locational trials is better zoning. Zoning helps to identify varieties adapted to specific agro-ecological regions. The use of geographic information system (GIS) technology, meteorological records and crop models makes it possible to consider much more sophisticated zoning techniques to enhance the efficiency of variety testing (Muchow and Bidinger, 1996). Unfortunately, many of these techniques go beyond the scope of the limited meteorological data that are available in many developing countries, and beyond the scope of the analytical resources of many national research programmes.

The greater number of test sites provided by farmer participation and the more detailed zoning made possible by the increased number of test sites will allow more efficient breeding for specific adaptation and contribute to an understanding of the limits to breeding for wide adaptation. Under current variety testing protocols, breeders have little incentive to test genotypes that have highly specific environmental adaptation (such as extremely early- or late-maturing varieties) because they will rarely perform well across the majority of test sites in a single, broadly defined zone. Because these types of material are eliminated on the basis of their *average* performance, their *specific* contributions to more precisely delimited environments remain untested. A greater (and more targeted) dispersion of trial sites will encourage the use of more specifically adapted material for the marginal environments currently neglected by conventional variety testing.

Not only do plant breeders need to invest in a wider range of trials, they also need to reconsider the way their trials are managed. A corollary of the strategy that increases the diversity of trial sites is an acceptance of greater diversity in trial management. The ability to detect differences in varietal performance across environments is greatly diminished by the practice of applying high and uniform levels of external inputs to trial sites. Varietal performance needs to be evaluated under the actual management conditions of target farmers. Rather than following textbook recommendations for crop management, varieties should be tested with the inputs, planting dates and other management practices actually used by farmers.

A greater diversity in trial management also implies a broader evaluation of variety performance. Breeders need to extend the scope of the data they use for assessing varieties beyond simple yield and disease-resistance parameters. In addition, greater familiarity with farmer priorities will suggest further traits (such as fodder yield, cooking quality or market acceptability) that need to be assessed. These increasing demands for data collection can be met in two ways. First, breeders can invest more time in identifying and recording new measures of variety performance; in some cases they will be able to substitute these for some of the less relevant parameters that are currently recorded but rarely analysed. Second, when farmers play a greater role in variety testing their observations throughout the growing season and post-harvest, this will provide much additional information. As breeders become more familiar with the relevant parameters for variety evaluation, they can determine the appropriate division of responsibility for observation and data collection with farmers. It is very likely that it will always be more cost-effective for farmers to assess post-harvest traits, particularly those like taste, cooking quality and market value.

In addition to broadening the coverage of trial sites, breeders need to make better use of the data generated at each site. For instance, a selection for variety performance under difficult growing conditions requires changing the practice of automatically discarding data from low-yielding sites or where the CV is above a certain limit. In addition, breeders need to ensure that varieties do not spend more than three years in the trials system before a decision is taken on their eligibility for release. Finally, and perhaps most fundamentally, the diversification of the variety testing process should lead to a greater number of varieties being released. Indeed, the justification for the investment necessary to reform variety testing procedures is the promise of a wider range of useful varieties being made available to farmers.

Decentralization and information exchange
It is obvious that the diversification of variety testing requires decentralization. Managing plant breeding from a central institute that relies on relatively few experimental stations as testing sites does not adequately test varieties, as variety testing is not sufficiently dispersed to representative farming areas. Plant breeding institutes need to examine the correspondence between the current distribution of trial sites and the location of target farming populations, and then make appropriate adjustments.

One solution is to assign more plant breeders to regional research sites and to provide facilities to support agricultural research away from the

78

central research station. The administrative challenges involved in such a strategy are similar to those faced by adaptive on-farm research programmes, and experience has shown that greater decentralization of agricultural research is both managerially and financially feasible (Merrill-Sands et al., 1991). Another solution is to provide more support for the variety testing programmes of regional organizations, such as local agricultural universities. The regionalization of plant breeding is not a new idea; Pain (1986) describes how Sri Lanka successfully regionalized its rice breeding programme in the 1970s in order to provide greater environmental specificity.

But there are limits to the capacity of a small research institute to disperse its staff. Any decentralization strategy for variety testing must also include increased collaboration with other organizations, such as NGOs and extension services. It must also involve a significant increase in farmer participation in the testing process. (These options are discussed in the following two sub-sections.)

There are also dangers of isolation and loss of critical mass that can affect decentralization efforts. The potential gains of focusing on local conditions and concerns will be sacrificed if the result of decentralization is a set of inward-looking plant breeding programmes. One of the great advantages of conventional plant breeding is the capacity to test a wide range of materials in diverse environments. Decentralization must enhance and refine that capacity to move and exchange varieties, rather than encouraging the formation of small, isolated efforts. The problem is well illustrated by the experience of the Indian plant breeding system. A high proportion of the approval and recommendation of new varieties is handled at the state level (although the size of India's states hardly qualifies as a typical example of decentralization). The individual state programmes are often exceptionally productive, but because of a lack of mechanisms (and incentives) to exchange materials and information among individual state breeding programmes, many varieties developed and used in one state never reach farmers in similar environments in other states (see Box 4.3).

Arguments have recently been made for improving agricultural research efficiency by reducing the size of plant breeding programmes in many developing countries and relying instead on materials developed by a small number of national and international breeding efforts (e.g., Maredia and Eicher, 1995). These arguments do not necessarily contradict our strategy for decentralization. Indeed, they emphasize the need to identify situations where the testing of varieties bred elsewhere is sufficient, and to identify conditions which require a separate breeding programme. Concentration on testing varieties bred elsewhere saves resources that can then be used for more extensive decentralized testing. Individual programmes that largely depend on introduced material can still carry out decentralized breeding that relies on exploiting local germplasm.

Box 4.3   Financial losses to farmers caused by inefficient regulation

The Case of Kalinga III Rice

Kalinga III is a rice variety developed for rainfed, drought-prone upland environments in India. The variety was entered into the All India Co-ordinated Crop Improvement Programme trials in the early 1980s, but was rejected after two years of testing, at least in part because the high input conditions of most trial sites were inappropriate for showing the advantages of a variety bred for drought-prone areas.

Kalinga III was then entered in state-level performance trials in Orissa, where it was released in 1983. The variety became very popular in Orissa and spread by farmer-to-farmer exchange to areas in neighbouring states. It has recently been included in farmer participatory variety selection tests run by the Krishak Bharati Co-operative Indo-British Rainfed Farming Project (KRIBP) and farmers have been impressed by its performance and have sought seed. The variety is now being promoted by KRIBP in upland rice areas in six states. The variety has been officially released and recommended for eastern Madhya Pradesh and it has entered official state variety testing programmes in Rajasthan and Gujarat.

The experience with Kalinga III points to failures in the national testing system to identify varieties suitable for marginal conditions, and subsequent failures of state testing systems to take full advantage of materials bred in other states.

It is possible to estimate the magnitude of loss to farmers caused by this type of inefficiency. It is conservatively estimated that Kalinga III has an adoption potential in 10 per cent of the 8.7m ha of upland rice land in these six states of India. KRIBP data show that Kalinga III gives about a 30 per cent yield advantage (1.3 t/ha vs. 1.0 t/ha) over farmers' current varieties. Using data from other adoption studies, it is also assumed that once released, Kalinga III will take nine years to achieve its maximum diffusion (i.e. 10 per cent of the target area).

These figures can be used to compare two scenarios: first, an assumption of efficient national-level variety testing that would have led to the release of Kalinga III in all states in 1983; and second, an assumption that the recent interest in the variety will lead to state-level release in the year 1998 (and maximum diffusion in 2006). Calculations for both scenarios can estimate the total (discounted) benefits to farmers over the course of adoption and diffusion of the new variety. The difference between the two scenarios amounts to Rs 10,702m. or £198m. at 1996 prices. This estimate of total benefits forgone is equivalent to 40 per cent of the value of annual upland rice production in the target area.

Such calculations are of course subject to various assumptions, but any reasonable alternative estimate would still indicate losses of this magnitude. This particular case points to inefficiencies in the exchange of information among state variety testing systems in one country, but a parallel argument can be made for a more open exchange of information and breeding material among countries.

Source: Balogun, 1996

The arguments for improving plant breeding efficiency are also based on an acknowledgement of the value of widespread exchange of materials among breeding programmes. At a time when greater interchange and communication among public plant breeders is called for, it is particularly unfortunate that the advent of PVP has made many national programmes increasingly reluctant about exchanging materials. In some cases this is based on hopes of deriving commercial gain from public varieties in the domestic market, while in other cases it is based on a fear that other public or private breeders will derive commercial advantage from a programme's own materials. This problem underlines the importance of ensuring that public (and farmer) varieties remain in the public domain.

Links with other organizations

The diversification and decentralization of variety testing not only requires more effective exchange between plant breeding programmes, but also depends on collaboration between public plant breeding institutes and other public and voluntary organizations. Such collaboration is necessary to provide a broader contribution to variety testing and to improve the dissemination of new varieties.

The extension service is often in a position to collaborate in decentralized variety testing, especially because extension agents are generally much more widely dispersed than the members of research institutes. Public agricultural extension is currently under considerable financial pressure, but contributions to an expanded variety testing programme may be one way to justify the continued presence of extension agents in the field.

In many cases NGOs and farmer organizations can also be effective collaborators in the management of a variety testing programme, identifying farmers to host trials, helping to collect data and observations on variety performance and organizing farmer participation in the definition of plant breeding priorities.

Public plant breeders also need to establish much better links with the parastatal, commercial and community-level seed production enterprises that will be responsible for diffusing new varieties. There is no sense in promoting more targeted plant breeding and variety testing if the products are not utilized. Public sector plant breeders need to do a better job of promoting their varieties, as well as understanding the variations and limitations in demand that affect seed producers' choice of the varieties to multiply.

A final example of the links that public plant breeding must develop to support a decentralized variety testing strategy is the definition of the relation between public and private plant breeding. Our emphasis has been on the responsibilities of public plant breeding, particularly their attention to resource-poor farmers, but a more efficient division of labour with the private sector can make an important contribution to effective resource use. The private sector will increasingly take the lead in certain markets, as they

81

already have done in hybrid breeding of maize, sorghum and pearl millet, for example, in several developing countries. Increased private sector involvement should free public resources that can be invested in breeding efforts for the environments and farmers that are not likely to attract commercial interest.

Farmer participation

An effective variety testing strategy will not only depend on decentralization and the development of more effective organizational links. It will also require much more farmer participation. Some recent experiences with farmer participation in variety improvement are discussed in Chapter 10, but it will be useful to outline the range of possibilities for collaboration between farmers and formal plant breeders.

It is possible to distinguish between farmer participation in varietal selection when the objective is to choose among the finished products from breeding programmes (e.g., Joshi and Witcombe, 1996a), and farmer participation in plant breeding when farmers contribute to the selection or the crossing of material that is still segregating (e.g., Sthapit et al., 1996).

The degree of involvement of farmers in the selection of varieties can differ greatly (see Table 4.4). On-farm variety trials are common at the final stage of the variety testing process, and when they are controlled by researchers, often involve unrepresentative management practices. Formal replicated variety trials that feature more typical farmer management are

Table 4.4 *Methods of participatory varietal selection with varying degrees of farmer participation*

Methods in increasing order of farmer participation	Evaluation	Typical institution involved
1. On-farm trials, researcher managed. Replicated design.	Yield data	Research
2. On-farm trials, farmer-managed with scientists' supervision. Several entries per farmer. Replicated design.	Yield data	Research
3. Farmer-managed trials. Replication across farmers. One or a few cultivars per farmer.	Yield data Farmers' perceptions	Research Extension NGO
4. Farmer-managed trials. Replication across farmers. One or a few cultivars per farmer.	Farmers' perceptions	NGO Extension Research
5. Farmer-managed trials. No formal design.	Informal observations	NGO with limited resources. Extension

also possible, and are a step in the right direction. In both cases the emphasis is on quantitative yield data only. An alternative is to plant unreplicated trials, with one or a few varieties, under farmer management. Yield data may still be collected, but farmers' observations on variety performance assume increasing importance. Finally, varieties to be tested may simply be distributed to farmers, who plant them as they wish and report qualitative observations.

Farmer participation can be extended to plant breeding procedures involving segregating material (see Table 4.5). There are relatively few examples of this type of activity to date. It generally represents a greater investment than more straightforward varietal selection. For these reasons, Witcombe *et al.* (1996) suggest that participatory plant breeding should be undertaken only after participatory varietal selection (PVS) has been tried.

Table 4.5   *Some examples of plant breeding methods in predominantly self-pollinating crops with varying degrees of farmer participation*

Methods in increasing order of farmer participation	Site specificity	Example
1. All generations on station and grown by plant breeders. Farmers involved at pre-release stage or even after release.	Wide adaptation targeted. Early generations may all be in single location followed by multi-locational testing.	National breeding programmes
2. Early generation (F_2) in farmers' fields. All other generations and procedures with plant breeder.	Single location testing site for F_2.	Thakur (1995)
3. Best advanced lines at F_7 or F_8 given to farmers for testing. Closest method to participatory varietal selection since farmers given nearly finished product.	Easy to test best advanced lines across locations.	Recommended by Galt (1989)
4. From F_3 or F_4 onwards farmer and plant breeders collaborate to select and identify the best material. Farmers select. Plant breeders facilitate the process. Release proposal prepared by plant breeder.	Possible to run selection procedures on early generations in more than one location.	Sthapit *et al.* (1996)
5. Breeder gives F_3 or F_4 material to farmers. All selection left to farmers. At F_7 to F_8 or later, breeders monitor diversity in farmers' fields and identify best material to enter in conventional trials.	Easy to run selection schemes in many locations.	Salazar (1992)
6. Trained expert farmers make crosses and do all selection with or without assistance from breeders. Breeders can place best material in conventional trials.	Specific to farmers' requirements.	None yet

Moreover, the participatory plant breeding programme can then use cultivars, identified by PVS, as parents of crosses. Compared with conventional plant breeding, participatory methods are more likely to produce farmer-acceptable products, particularly for marginal environments. At least one parent of any cross is well adapted to the local environment and genotype-by-location interactions are greatly reduced because selection is always in the target environment. Usually few crosses are made, so, in an inbreeding crop, large populations of early generations can be grown to increase the possibility of identifying desirable progeny.

These advantages also apply to decentralized breeding, regardless of whether increased farmer participation in the form of on-farm collaborative research is employed. Farmer participation where selection is in farmers' fields can reduce demands on research station land, and reduce or eliminate the need for breeders to do single-plant selection in many of the generations. Most importantly, it ensures that all farmer-relevant traits are evaluated. It is particularly efficient when important post-harvest quality traits that are difficult to assess in the laboratory can be selected by farmers. Farmers' selection for such traits is most appropriate because farmers and their families are the ultimate judges of quality in any cultivar.

Even though participatory plant breeding does not target broad adaptation, there is no reason to suppose that the products will be narrowly adapted. A farmer's field will always lie within a wider agro-ecological zone. Conventional breeding often produces widely adapted cultivars even when selection in the early generations is at only one location. In contrast, when farmer participation is employed, early-generation testing using more than one environment ensures that cultivar domains are not too narrow.

The risks of decentralized variety testing

Proposals for decentralized and farmer participatory plant breeding are often met with scepticism and concerns that such strategies may entail unacceptable risks. The arguments are often similar to those offered for the strict regulation of official variety release. A closer examination of such concerns shows that they are largely unfounded.

One of the most frequent apprehensions is that working with unreleased or segregating material on farmers' fields may cause the spread of inferior varieties. Indeed, there are some national agricultural research programmes that forbid experimentation with any unreleased variety on farmers' fields for this reason. But farmers are perfectly capable of recognizing varieties that are inferior, and their increased access to potentially superior materials can only stimulate their interest and participation in decentralized variety testing.

The greatest concern is that participatory approaches may lead to the spread of varieties that are susceptible to important plant diseases.

84

However, plant breeders will continue to screen materials for the major diseases affecting the crop, whatever the participatory approach employed. Moreover, decentralized plant breeding exposes varieties to the most relevant pathogen populations, those that occur in the fields in which the crop will be grown. In contrast, centralized disease nurseries can over- or underestimate the susceptibility of a variety in a specific geographical area or ecosystem.

Increasing concern is also being expressed about the impact of formal plant breeding on crop genetic diversity. The case for decentralized breeding and variety testing seems clear-cut here, as the likelihood of developing a greater range of varieties is increased (Witcombe *et al.*, 1996).

Incentives for decentralized variety testing

In order for decentralized plant breeding to function, public plant breeders will need adequate incentives to change from their current models. To some extent the increasing pressure on public sector agricultural research to demonstrate results will contribute to changing procedures, but policy changes are also required. In particular, a clear definition of the priorities and clientele for public sector research is necessary. Decentralized plant breeding responds particularly to the needs of resource-poor farmers, and only if they receive priority in agricultural development policy will there be a significant change in plant breeding strategies.

Under the current system, public plant breeders receive recognition for the number of officially released varieties they produce; professional promotion is, unfortunately, less often based on the extent of actual varietal adoption. Under a more decentralized breeding scheme, where more varieties are made available, often without official release, the reward system, although potentially less clear-cut, will be related more to actual impact. Leaders of breeding programmes should make it clear that the primary measure of success is farmers' utilization of the programme's materials, whether acquired through farmer-to-farmer seed exchange, local seed production schemes or certified seed production.

Other incentives can also be provided for public plant breeders in developing countries, many of whom will compare their positions to those of higher-paid counterparts in the private sector. Research administrators need to provide working conditions that are conducive to job satisfaction by offering opportunities for research, publication and professional advancement, and by fostering ever closer links between farmers and plant breeders.

A summary of the alternatives and goals for the reform of variety testing is presented in Table 4.6.

The role of public sector agricultural research is changing, and regulatory reform of national seed systems puts increasing pressure on public plant breeding to develop new models and procedures. Public breeders will

85

Table 4.6   *The evolution of variety testing in public plant breeding systems*

Current status	Alternatives	Goals
Variety testing procedures		
o Few zones; reliance on breeding for wide adaptation o Sites chosen on administrative criteria o Uniform level of trial management o Yield is major criterion for selection o Analysis of trials eliminates results of low yielding or variable sites o Few varieties proposed for release	o Invest more in adequate zoning and site selection o Change trial management to represent better actual farmer conditions o Use a wider range of criteria for promoting varieties o Devote more emphasis to low yielding test sites o Propose more varieties for release, targeted to a wider range of conditions	o An understanding of when breeding for specific niches is more effective than breeding for wide adaptation o A more complex set of criteria for variety testing is established o A shift from breeding for uniform management and market conditions to tailoring varieties for specific requirements o A much wider range of varieties, offering more choices to farmers, is available
Organization of variety testing		
o Variety testing centrally administered o Low utilization of materials and data from other breeding programmes	o Decentralize research; develop better collaboration with extension, NGOs, farmer groups o Develop more interchange with other breeding programmes o Develop relations with seed production to help popularize varieties and understand client needs	o Effective zoning and decentralization places plant breeders in contact with target farmers o Public and private plant breeding programmes collaborate effectively, within and between countries o A wide range of seed production enterprises have access to public varieties
Farmers' role		
o Farmers are rarely consulted about breeding priorities o Farmers do not have a chance to test new varieties until the final stages of development	o Place more emphasis on farmer-managed variety trials o Develop programmes with farmer input in early stages of variety selection o Enhance farmer selection and breeding skills	o Farmers are seen as clients *and* collaborators for public breeding programmes o Farmer skills and local materials are fully utilized in plant breeding
Incentives		
o Breeders are not directed towards addressing needs of resource-poor farmers o Breeders are rewarded for variety release rather than variety utilization	o Change research policy to emphasize needs of resource-poor farmers o Devote more resources to monitoring and analysing variety use	o Resource-poor farmers are recognized as targets and partners for plant breeding programmes, and success is measured by the degree to which their problems are solved

be asked to define their contributions *vis-à-vis* the expanding commercial seed sector and to devote more attention to those farmers who have not yet benefited from the products of formal plant breeding.

A significant reorientation is required to the centralized plant breeding and variety testing system that has evolved in conjunction with Green Revolution models of agricultural development. The diverse and complex requirements of resource-poor farmers will require a more location-specific approach to plant breeding and a considerable change in the numbers, types, distribution and interpretation of variety testing experiments.

The change in research methods brings with it a concomitant change in organization, and public plant breeders will have to build better links with extension services, seed producers, NGOs and farmer organizations. Of equal importance, plant breeding protocols will have to include more farmer participation.

Seed regulatory reform identifies clear responsibilities for public plant breeding: the development of an expanding range of varieties useful for all the nation's farmers; the preservation and enhancement of plant genetic diversity; the protection of public and farmer varieties that contribute to strengthening local crop improvement capacities; and the exchange of those materials among an increasingly complex network of farmer and formal breeders.

5 The conduct and reform of crop variety regulation

ROBERT TRIPP AND NIELS LOUWAARS

Introduction

Registration, performance testing and release

AGRICULTURAL POLICYMAKERS FACE important decisions when they consider how to regulate crop varieties. The procedures that are chosen play an important role in determining the incentives for both public and private plant breeders and hence affect the range and type of varieties that farmers may use. Three procedures need to be distinguished when examining variety regulation: registration, performance testing and release.

Variety registration involves recording sufficient morphological and agronomic data about a variety so that it can be identified and distinguished from others. Variety registration helps control the nomenclature of varieties offered for sale so that farmers are not confused by synonyms and name changes. The data for variety registration can also be used if seed is to be certified. In addition, applications for plant variety protection require extensive information about a new variety. Variety registration includes technical observations from field plots of the new variety and the maintenance of an official register. Field tests may not be necessary for imported varieties if foreign registration is accepted.

Performance testing of new varieties is an attempt to ensure that they meet certain standards (such as yield) and that they compare favourably with varieties already available. Performance testing is usually carried out by assessing trial data from a specified number of sites and seasons. The testing may also include assessment of the consumption or industrial qualities of the variety. In many developing countries performance testing is part of the management of public sector plant breeding, and is the final stage of the variety testing sequence described in Chapter 4. The results of performance testing may simply be used to provide recommendations to farmers and seed producers, or they may form part of the variety release decision.

Most countries have some type of *variety release* process, which is based on the results of registration and/or performance testing. Variety release is an official authorization that allows seed of the variety to be sold or otherwise made available. Variety release may serve several purposes. It provides an official sanction for a variety, and hence offers protection to farmers. In public plant breeding systems, variety release is also a way of offering recognition to plant breeders and of increasing the efficiency of public seed provision by officially notifying the availability of new varieties. By including data on a variety's response to plant diseases or pests, the release process also attempts to guard against externalities such as epidemics and national crop loss that could be caused by the widespread use of a susceptible variety. In addition, some countries require that new varieties of important export crops conform to standards that maintain the country's advantage in export markets.

The origins of variety regulation

In many industrialized countries variety regulation was initiated in response to concerns about the type of seed available in rapidly developing commercial markets and to address the growing confusion about the proliferation of varietal names. One of the first examples of seed regulation was the effort of the German Agricultural Society (DLG) at the end of the nineteenth century to establish rules for seed sale. As the seed industry developed, there was great confusion regarding varietal names, and companies tried to introduce varieties with names similar to those that had experienced earlier success. By 1905, the DLG had established a register of qualified varieties which included morphological characterization and performance testing results (Rutz, 1990). In the UK, the National Institute of Agricultural Botany formed committees in the 1920s to help eliminate synonyms from the growing number of names of marketed varieties. It was not until 1964, however, that a National Seeds Act was passed in the UK which established a voluntary index of approved varieties (Kelly and Bowring, 1990). In the US, many states passed seed laws in the early twentieth century to help regulate the emerging seed industry, and a Federal Seeds Act of 1939 prohibited the use of synonyms for a single variety (Kloppenburg, 1988:133).

The evolution of variety regulation took quite different directions in Europe and the US, however. Performance testing has long been a part of variety release in several European countries, for instance, and European Union regulations specify that all field crop varieties offered for sale must pass national performance tests and be included in a national list. They can then be included in the EU Common Catalogue, which makes them eligible for sale in any Member State. In the US, on the other hand, compulsory registration has been vigorously opposed by the seed industry. In 1962 the US Department of Agriculture (USDA) proposed a law that would entail compulsory review and registration of all new varieties, but seed companies were successful in opposing this move (Kloppenburg, 1988:137). Although variety registration is voluntary, varieties of many important crops are submitted to National Variety Review Boards, managed by the independent Association of Official Seed Certifying Agencies (AOSCA), which have representation from the seed trade, research services and USDA (Lowry, 1995).

More recently, the increasing use of biotechnology in plant breeding has led to the development of special regulations for the testing and release of

89

transgenic crop varieties (Krattiger and Rosemarin, 1994). Because most of this testing is done in industrialized countries, and because the regulation often involves environmental and public health authorities separate from the seed regulatory establishment, the subject is not covered in this book.

The management of variety regulation

Table 5.1 presents a summary of variety registration and performance testing for a number of countries. The US is one of the few countries where variety registration is not required. New Zealand does not require varietal

Table 5.1 *Variety registration and performance testing requirements*[a]

Country	Variety registration	Performance testing
EU	Mandatory. Common catalogue.	Mandatory
USA	Voluntary.	Voluntary
New Zealand	Voluntary, but required for certification.	Voluntary
India	Mandatory for public sector; voluntary for private sector. No formal variety register.	Mandatory for public varieties; voluntary for private varieties
Pakistan	Mandatory for public varieties. A list of registered varieties is published.	Mandatory for public varieties and for imported rice and wheat varieties
Nepal	Mandatory for all varieties, which are placed on a notification list.	Mandatory for all varieties
Philippines	Mandatory for public varieties; voluntary for private maize and sorghum varieties. List of released varieties is published.	Mandatory for all public varieties
Kenya	Mandatory for all varieties. Catalogue of all released varieties.	Mandatory for all varieties
Zimbabwe	Mandatory for all varieties. National list introduced in 1994.	Mandatory for all varieties
Bolivia	Mandatory for all varieties. National variety register.	Mandatory for all varieties, but only to show adaptation
Argentina	Mandatory for all varieties.	Mandatory for all varieties
Mexico	Voluntary for private sector varieties. (Previously mandatory.)	Voluntary for private sector varieties

a The requirements generally apply to major food crops, but there is considerable variation in the breadth of regulatory coverage across countries.

Sources: Country case studies; author's research; Hampton and Scott (1990); Jaffe and van Wijk (1995).

Box 5.1   Variety release procedures in three countries

India
Procedures for the national release of public sector varieties:

o Varieties are tested for three years in nationwide trials run by All India Co-ordinated Crop Improvement Projects (AICCIP).
o AICCIP Variety Identification Committee considers data and makes recommendations based on yield superiority and other characteristics.
o Central Sub-committee on Crop Standards, Notification and Release of Varieties of Department of Agriculture and Co-operation, Ministry of Agriculture, considers recommendations.
o Central Seed Committee of Ministry of Agriculture notifies variety (places it under the seed law).

Bolivia
Procedures for all varieties (public or private):

o Organization developing (or importing) a variety presents data on varietal description to Regional Seed Board (in the *departamento* where release is sought).
o Data and samples are passed to National Seed Board. Up to two years of tests may be required before it is registered.
o Once registered, National Seed Board authorizes Regional Seed Board to conduct agronomic tests to establish if variety is adapted (but not necessarily superior). Data from the breeder may be accepted, but up to two years of tests, usually conducted by a local research institute, may be necessary.
o Regional Seed Board authorizes variety for release.

Kenya
Procedures for all varieties (public or private):

o National performance trials are conducted. Three seasons of data required for consideration.
o DUS testing carried out by National Seed Quality Control Services (NSQCS).
o A Specialist Variety Release Committee (SVRC) meets once a year to consider results of national performance trials.
o SVRC recommends varieties for provisional release, meaning that some seed production by Kenya Seed Company may begin and on-farm trials are organized.
o Several years after provisional release, SVRC considers performance and, if warranted, recommends release to National Variety Release Committee, which meets at the request of SVRC.

Sources: Turner (1994); Rosales (1995a); Kimenye and Nyangito (1996).

registration, but unregistered varieties cannot be sold as certified seed (Hampton and Scott, 1990). In other cases registration involves field tests to determine that the variety is distinct, uniform and stable (DUS) and these may involve a considerable investment of time and resources. (DUS testing is also a component of all plant variety protection (PVP) systems.) In addition, some countries require registration for all varieties, while others make this optional for privately developed varieties.

Table 5.1 also shows that performance testing is quite common, but in some cases privately developed varieties may be exempt. Countries usually make variety registration and performance testing mandatory for a specified number of crops. In the EU, performance testing is mandatory for field crops but not horticultural crops, and is described by the term 'value for cultivation and use' (VCU). In Nepal, the rules hold for food grains but not vegetables, while in the Philippines the rules are more strictly observed for rice than for maize or sorghum.

There is a range of institutional mechanisms to address variety registration and performance testing. In some cases, different institutions have responsibility for the two functions, while in other cases a single entity manages both tasks. Most countries carry out these tasks at a national level, but in a few cases there is some decentralization. In Pakistan, for instance, varieties may be released based on performance testing at the national or provincial level, although registration is done at the national level. India also releases varieties at both the national and state levels. In Bolivia, authority for performance testing is devolved to regional seed boards operating in each *departamento* (Rosales, 1995a). Box 5.1 presents a few examples of the variety release process to give an indication of the variation that exists among countries.

Problems for the management of variety regulation

There are many problems regarding the management of variety release. There is ample evidence that many farmers are still not well served by the formal plant breeding system, for instance. Many commercial seed companies are lobbying for a reduction in release requirements. Local-level breeding efforts would benefit from a more flexible variety release system as well. On the other hand, the move towards PVP presages more complex registration procedures. An analysis of the current situation in developing countries identifies the following challenges (Box 5.2): *efficiency* (the delays of the release procedures, their costs and the ineffective transfer of information); *standards* (for registration and for performance, and lack of communication between countries); *participation* of all relevant parties in variety release procedures; and *transparency* (including unclear national policy towards seed enterprise development and lack of clarity in the scope of variety release authority).

Box 5.2   Problems with the management of variety regulation

Efficiency

Delays. The testing process for variety approval is often excessively long. In addition, meetings of release committees may not be organized in a timely manner. Addressing these delays could place new varieties in farmers' hands several years earlier.

Costs. An extensive performance testing system is expensive to maintain. Plant breeding organizations (public or private) will have to bear the cost of the testing. Registration requirements are becoming more sophisticated, especially those related to the establishment of PVP, and these involve considerable costs.

Popularization. Public sector variety release systems are not efficiently linked to extension and seed production. Extension agents and seed producers may have inadequate information about new varieties, and farmers often have little opportunity to learn about the varieties that have been released.

Standards

Standards for variety registration. The move towards more precise characterization of varieties means that an increasing proportion of time will be spent on establishing varietal distinctness, rather than on properties useful for production. In addition, demands for greater varietal uniformity may threaten attempts to enhance the useful heterogeneity of varieties, especially for farmers in more marginal environments.

Standards for performance testing. The performance standards for variety release are biased towards broad adaptation and rarely acknowledge the characteristics and growing conditions important to resource-poor farmers. Rigidities in official performance testing also limit the release of relevant varieties by private breeders.

Sharing data. There is insufficient attention given to using data from other countries or regions to speed the release of imported varieties.

Participation

Variety release authorities are subject to professional and political bias. In addition, they rarely provide any type of meaningful representation to private sector plant breeders, NGOs or farmers.

Transparency

National policy on seed companies and imports. Protectionist policies often limit the participation of foreign institutions, and sometimes of domestic private plant breeders, in variety development.

Uneven application of regulations. Variety release procedures are often poorly defined for minor crops, and the resulting uncertainty is a disincentive to variety development. The mandate and legal status of variety release authorities are sometimes in doubt.

Delays

Unnecessary delays in the variety registration and testing process are a cause for serious concern. Given the time required for plant breeders to develop new varieties, and the considerable gap between the release of a variety and its first appearance as commercial seed (in India the estimates are four to six years from notification to commercial production), any time that can be saved in the formal approval process would make a significant contribution to the efficiency of national seed systems.

Delays can be the result of both lengthy field-testing requirements and infrequent meetings of release authorities. Problems with the length of field testing are discussed in Chapter 4. In Bolivia, variety registration and performance testing are handled sequentially; in some cases the registration authority may require two years of field tests to establish the DUS characteristics of a new variety, after which it is turned over to the regional seed board for up to two additional years of performance testing (Rosales, 1995a). Regional release of maize varieties is possible in the Philippines, but because there are only a few accredited testing stations for each region, and there is a fixed number of test results required by the release committee, a regional release actually requires more time (Logroño, 1996). Joshi (1995) describes delays in the testing of a promising rice variety in Nepal because it had to wait its turn to begin a testing sequence that was constrained by a predetermined maximum of entries.

Committees may meet infrequently, further delaying release. Variety release is often a two-stage process, with a technical panel making recommendations to a second group for final approval. In Tanzania, bean variety release is initiated by the Grain Legume Co-ordinating Committee, which sends its recommendations to the Variety Release Committee, which in turn forwards instructions to the Seed Production Committee. Because funding for such committees is usually insufficient, and they often comprise representatives from geographically separate institutions, meetings are frequently cancelled or postponed (Due, 1990).

Every year lost because of unreasonable trial requirements or postponed meetings contributes to lower incomes and missed opportunities for farmers, and these costs may overwhelm any contributions that the variety release process makes to safeguard farmers from inappropriate varieties.

Costs

If a variety registration and testing system is to be maintained or established, secure financial support is required. The variety release systems currently in place in many developing countries are an integral part of, and supported by, the public agricultural research system (Chapter 4). The All India Co-ordinated Crop Improvement Programmes, for instance, include a comprehensive network of trials for variety release. As public agricultural research budgets come under increasing pressure, alternative sources of funding will have to be identified. The challenge is especially urgent where mandatory testing and registration of the growing number of privately developed varieties are contemplated.

In Kenya, variety release has been confined to materials developed by the Kenya Agricultural Research Institute (KARI) and the partially government-owned Kenya Seed Company (KSC) (Kimenye and Nyangito, 1996). The performance tests are managed by KARI with some land and other facilities provided by KSC. As other seed companies begin to operate in Kenya, it is not clear who will pay the cost of testing. In Bolivia, local research institutions are commissioned by regional seed boards to carry out tests. Fees are charged for the testing of private varieties, but the system is partially supported by government and external aid funds (Rosales, 1995a). The variety registration and release system in Zimbabwe is currently undergoing reorganization. One suggestion was to establish an independent (government) variety release authority, but on closer examination this was judged to be financially unworkable (Rusike and Musa, 1996).

Inadequate funding arrangements combined with comprehensive mandatory testing are serious disincentives to the development of independent plant breeding capacity. If the testing system relies on government funds, it may be unable to cope with an increasing number of varieties offered for testing. If, on the other hand, large fees are charged for an elaborate testing procedure, private plant breeding will be discouraged; this would have a major impact on smaller commercial or community-level efforts.

Popularization

Another cause of inefficiency in public variety release systems is their inadequate concern with popularization. In industrialized countries, information about commercial varieties is made available through advertising and a range of other media available to farmers. In developing countries, advice about a new variety is largely spread through the actions of public seed companies and the extension service, neither of which may have adequate incentives to provide information to farmers.

Release authorities usually consider their task completed when a variety has been approved. The information is made available, and interested seed companies, public or private, can then obtain foundation seed and initiate the production process. It is often the responsibility of the seed company to seek out this information, and private companies, especially smaller and more poorly connected ones, may have trouble keeping abreast of the latest developments. If, on the other hand, a public seed company is the principal producer of public varieties, it may have little incentive to switch production from a variety with an established market towards one that has been shown to be only marginally superior and which will require some time to establish a reputation among farmers.

Public extension services are potentially important sources of information about new varieties, but are often poorly connected to variety development, testing and release procedures. Virk *et al.* (1996) describe the inefficient communication between the Indian release authorities and state departments of agriculture and farm science centres. Extension personnel should be closely associated with the on-farm testing of new varieties and should then be in a position to provide useful information to farmers, but this connection is rarely effective. In countries like Nepal and India, varieties being tested are included in 'mini-kits' (seed packets of one or two promising varieties) that are distributed to farmers by the extension service. The results of farmers' tests are theoretically considered by the release authority, but they rarely carry any weight in the release decision (Singh, 1992).

In addition, the extension service in most countries is usually only able to recommend varieties that have been officially released, so private varieties that have not been through the official testing process cannot be included in extension messages. In many countries, only seed that is certified (and hence only varieties that have been officially released) can be included in extension or credit programmes.

There is a chicken-and-egg character to this dilemma as well. Seed companies will be cautious about moving production toward new varieties until they are certain that there is adequate demand. Extension agents, on the other hand, will be cautious about investing in demonstrations and other activities for varieties whose seed cannot be supplied. An argument for better co-ordination between the seed companies and the extension service is evident.

Many of these inefficiencies will be ameliorated as competitors to public seed companies emerge and as public extension is restructured and made to operate under more client-driven incentives. But public seed companies and extension services will certainly play an important role in a number of countries for the foreseeable future, and hence the connection between variety release, on the one hand, and public seed production and extension, on the other, must be strengthened.

Standards for variety identification

If varieties are to be registered before their seed can be sold, some set of standards must be agreed. Current national registration systems exhibit a wide range of standards. Some countries such as India simply ask breeders to provide a relatively few distinguishing characteristics for new varieties as part of the release process, while others attempt to employ the UPOV descriptors (designed for PVP), which provide an extensive morphological characterization.

The pressures towards increasing precision and sophistication in variety registration raise concerns that such systems further jeopardize crop genetic diversity and discourage attempts to utilize varietal diversity to address farmers' problems. If varieties must be registered before their seed is sold, and if registration requires evidence of high uniformity, this will deter many imaginative plant breeding initiatives. As evidence of the shift that commercial pressures and technological capacities have caused in the standardization of plant varieties, it is interesting to note that when certification procedures were being debated in the UK in the late 1940s, many plant breeders believed their responsibility was to continue to improve their varieties (under the same names) rather than maintain them as originally released (Kelly and Bowring, 1990).

Inter- and intra-varietal diversity are both important strategies for the selection and development of local varieties. The stability and adaptability of local landraces are due in part to their intrinsic variability. Bean farmers in Rwanda generally prefer to grow varietal mixtures; one analysis showed an average of 19.8 varieties in each mixture, with three varieties usually accounting for 50 to 90 per cent of the mixture (Voss, 1992). This may be an extreme example, but the strategy is a common one for providing a resilient combination of genotypes in the face of unpredictable and continually shifting plant disease and climatic conditions. In such circumstances, it is easy to imagine Rwandan farmers insisting on the certification of diversity rather than uniformity in any seed that they purchased.

The exploitation of diversity can be a useful strategy for formal plant breeding as well. Marshall (1977) discusses a number of possibilities for using intra-varietal diversity (such as multi-lines or mixtures) and inter-varietal diversity (such as employing different resistance genes for one variety destined to be grown in different areas of the country). Berg et al. (1991:123) point out that many US public wheat breeding programmes produce line mixtures to provide adaptation and resilience for variable growing conditions, but that such 'varieties' would not meet UPOV characterization requirements. Community-level programmes can err on the side of excess uniformity as well. A programme working with Bolivian farmers to develop a seed production system for diffusing local varieties of quinoa (an Andean small grain) uses mass selection to increase the yield and varietal purity of the materials. But genetic mixtures, as traditionally employed by the farmers, may provide more security in the harsh growing conditions that the crop must face (Pavez and Bojanic, 1995).

The challenges of designing an appropriate set of standards for variety identification are intensified with the advent of PVP, which demands exceptionally precise characterization (see Chapter 9). In the US, for instance, a maize variety submitted for PVP must be accompanied by a description of 47 morphological characters and data on reactions to 17 diseases and two insect pests (Smith, 1992). This type of data is quite expensive to collect, and requires sophisticated experimental design and data analysis (ibid.). In addition, despite the increasing cost of morphological characterization, it is sometimes unable to provide sufficient information for distinguishing among new varieties. Hence laboratory techniques (electrophoresis) are increasingly being employed to distinguish and register varieties.

PVP not only presents technical challenges for a variety regulation system, it may also distort the priorities of public plant breeding. There is the danger that public sector breeding institutions will be drawn to the possibility of earning royalties from protected varieties. This will divert attention from the needs of less commercially oriented farmers, and away from producing materials that are more diverse and adaptable to marginal environments.

The establishment of standards for varietal registration must be able to distinguish between the strict requirements of PVP systems for commercial purposes, and the value of a more agile approval system that stimulates variety development and promotes genetic diversity. It would be a tragedy if PVP were allowed to dominate national seed systems and threaten the basis of collaboration between public sector plant breeding and local-level variety development.

Standards for performance testing

In almost all countries, public varieties must pass through a performance testing system before being considered for release, and as private breeding enterprises begin to appear in developing countries their varieties must often be submitted to the same testing process. There are serious concerns regarding the adequacy and relevance of these testing procedures, however. The degree to which site selection for variety development and testing actually provides conditions representative of those of target farmers, and the relevance of the criteria that are used for promoting materials and making release decisions, have been discussed in Chapter 4.

Adoption rates for modern varieties in less favoured environments are generally much lower than in better environments. Several factors contribute to this situation, including the fact that the less developed infrastructure in these areas and lack of access to extension and credit programmes limit the development of effective seed provision. But one important factor is the lack of attention given to specifically addressing the conditions of resource-poor farmers in plant breeding programmes. National research policies are a product of political priorities. In Zimbabwe, plant breeding priorities became better focused on smallholder concerns after independence, but the fact that the Seed Co-op (dominated by commercial farmers) is a crucial source of support for plant breeding programmes partially explains a continuing concentration on varieties for commercial farming and on selection for wide adaptation (Friis-Hansen, 1992). Only rarely is the output of public sector plant breeders measured and assessed in relation to its relevance to resource-poor farmers.

It is thus not surprising that variety performance testing assesses yields under growing conditions different from those of many farmers. If there is

Box 5.3   Farmer variety development: escapes and selections

Pakistan
An advanced line in a national wheat evaluation trial was attractive to farmers who saw it growing in the plots. Farmers multiplied the seed and distributed it among themselves. The resulting selection soon became quite popular, and it was later officially released by provincial seed councils in Northwest Frontier Province and Baluchistan.

(Alam and Saleemi, 1996)

Nepal
The rice variety Pokhreli Masino spread widely through Terhathum District, Nepal, without being formally released. Seed of the variety was included in mini-kits distributed to farmers by the extension service. Farmers valued the variety for its good yield and high demand in the market. The variety spread by farmer-to-farmer exchange; 94 per cent of farmers using the variety obtained the seed from another farmer.

(Green, 1987)

India
The rice variety Mahsuri was introduced from Malaysia in 1967–8 and tested, but was rejected by rice breeders because of lodging. But a farm labourer carried some seed to a village in Andhra Pradesh. Farmers liked its performance, and it soon began to spread through farmer-to-farmer exchange. It is the third most popular rice variety in India, and has since been officially notified.

An American cotton variety did not perform well because of its late maturity, but a farmer in Rajasthan selected an earlier plant, multiplied it and began to grow it as a distinct variety. The variety became popular under the name Bikaneri Lerma and is now widely grown and officially recognized.

(Maurya, 1989)

Philippines
A farmer in Mindanao found an unusual rice plant growing in his field of IR-36. After several generations of selection the farmer was able to stabilize the population, producing a variety which has excellent palatability and that yields well without high applications of fertilizer. The variety spread rapidly to neighbouring provinces. In 1995 it was officially released as 'Bordagol'.

(Salazar, 1992; Hernandez and Borromeo, 1996)

insistence, on maintaining performance testing as part of variety release, the relevant question is, 'Whose standards are to be used?' In many countries cases can be found where breeding materials that have been officially tested and rejected have subsequently been used by farmers to develop popular varieties, or where farmers have developed varieties whose popularity later qualifies them for official recognition. A few examples of such escapes and selections are shown in Box 5.3, and these illustrate the lack of congruence between official testing criteria and farmers' priorities.

National-level performance tests and insistence on wide adaptability make it difficult for location-specific varieties to be approved. In Kenya, a private plant breeder developed an open-pollinated maize variety that performed well under the conditions of small farmers in western Kenya, but because it lacked wide geographical adaptability it was rejected by the release authority. Despite the fact that it has not been officially released, it enjoys considerable popularity among many farmers (Kimenye and Nyangito, 1996). Similarly, Joshi (1995) describes an early maturing rice variety in Nepal which proved popular among farmers who used it as a rotation crop with vegetables, but whose low yield made it ineligible for official release.

The problem of inappropriate standards for performance testing is not confined to developing countries. Canadian variety release standards originally dictated that commercial hybrid maize varieties had to be tested under management conditions appropriate for older, public sector maize varieties rather than the higher planting densities for which the hybrids were developed. Several years of negotiations between the seed companies and the government authorities were required to arrive at a protocol for collaborative testing managed by the companies and the government that facilitated the release of the new hybrids (Duvick, personal communication).

In considering the rationale for establishing registration and performance testing, it is worth listening to the views of an eminent plant breeder who is concerned about two issues:

. . . first, the possible stultifying effect of too rigid an application of DUS criteria (which are legal rather than agricultural in intent); and, second, the application of VCU principles (which are certainly unnecessary and expensive and can be regarded as potentially dangerous to farming) . . . The VCU criterion seems to have come to stay, however; if interpreted broadly it may work quite well but the risks and disadvantages of narrow interpretation are real; unrestricted lists, even if they were longer, would probably have served farming better (Simmonds, 1979:225).

This advice on adopting a broad interpretation of performance criteria is well taken. The evolving and heterogeneous nature of farming conditions argues against rigid interpretation of performance tests and suggests the necessity of a more open and participatory system for variety approval.

Sharing data for variety release

Industrialized countries that have established mandatory variety registration and release systems have found it increasingly effective to share responsibilities for carrying out tests. The prime example of sharing information across countries is the Common Catalogue of the European Union, where varieties that have been approved in one country can be sold in other member countries without further testing. In addition, data required for release may be provided by the plant breeders themselves or by independent agencies, rather than by the government.

This broader interpretation of responsibility for data provision is not much in evidence in developing countries. In India, varieties may be released at the state rather than the national level. But even if a neighbouring state shares an environment similar to the one for which the variety has been released, the variety must go through several years of testing in the second state before it is eligible for recommendation by the state extension service. The same lack of communication characterizes provincial variety releases in Pakistan.

The public plant breeding system in India often produces varieties that are appropriate for conditions across the border in Nepal. A number of Indian varieties are officially released in Nepal; these may skip the initial stage of the official release system but must still pass through several years of testing before release (Joshi, 1995). A more adequate sharing of testing data among the two countries should be able to speed up the release process.

Composition of the variety release authority

As was pointed out earlier, the composition of the variety release authority varies greatly among countries. In some cases there is a two-stage process, in which a technical panel of plant breeders reviews the information and makes recommendations to a second body, which ratifies final release. In

Table 5.2 *National variety release authorities*

Country	Body with final authority over variety release	Total members on body	Public sector members
India	Central Sub-committee on Crop Standards, Notification and Release of Varieties	45 (approx.)	40 (approx.)
Nepal	Central Variety Releasing Committee	15	14
Philippines	National Seed Industry Council	9	6
Pakistan	National Seed Council	26	14
Kenya	National Variety Release Committee	7	6–7
Zimbabwe[a]	Variety Release Committee (membership varies by crop)	Variable	Variable
Bolivia	Regional Seed Councils	8–22	50%

a Until 1991; currently undergoing reorganization.
Source: Country case studies

101

other cases the release process is handled by a single body. Table 5.2 shows how variety release is managed for a series of countries.

Release authorities are subject to professional biases and jealousies, interpersonal rivalries and ideological stances. Several commentators on seed systems are aware of the problems. Ferguson (1994) argues for more transparency in release authorities and warns that personal and prestige factors often play a role in decisions. Douglas (1980:57) cautions against appointing members on a political basis, but this may be difficult to avoid. Indeed, much of the membership on such committees is on an *ex-officio* basis. The senior plant breeders on a committee may have considerable power in determining which of their junior staff are rewarded by facilitating the release of their varieties.

The diversity of national seed systems is rarely evident in variety release committees, most of whose members are drawn from the public sector. Of the cases shown in Table 5.2, only Bolivia's release system involves significant participation from the private sector, which includes farmer organizations, NGOs and seed companies. Table 5.3 examines the composition of the release authorities of these same countries in more detail. When there is a two-stage release process, public sector breeders usually dominate the first stage but may not be represented at the second stage, which is often only a formality, serving to ratify the recommendations taken at the first stage.

Some of the countries in the table do not have private plant breeding capacity, so there is no private participation in the release process. India, however, has a strong private plant breeding industry which sometimes submits varieties to the national trials, but there is little provision for private sector participation in release decisions. Both Kenya and the Philippines provide one position for a private breeder on the release authority.

The concerns about private participation in release authorities are not limited to commercial enterprises. In Bangladesh, the Mennonite Central Committee (MCC) has had difficulty in securing the official release of soybean varieties that it identified for its development projects, and rice varieties that proved to be well suited to the conditions of its client farmers encountered problems with the rigid format of the official trial system (Lewis, 1992).

Farmer representation on release authorities is even more problematic. It can be argued that farmer participation is much more important in the earlier stages of variety development, but variety release authorities often have the power not only to accept or reject particular varieties but also to define priorities for national seed policy. Strong farmer representation should therefore be an important element here. Of the countries shown in Table 5.3, some give positions to individual (so-called 'progressive') farmers, as in India and Pakistan. It would seem more appropriate to

102

Table 5.3 *Representation on variety release authorities*

Country	Public plant breeders	Private plant breeders	Public seed company	Private seed companies	Farmers
India	Breeders constitute most of first stage. Crop project co-ordinator participates at second stage	No	Yes	Representatives of seed industry	Individual farmer(s)
Nepal	Chief of Disciplinary Divisions from National Agricultural Research Institute (NARI), but not crop co-ordinators	None	Yes	Representative of Seed Entrepreneurs Association	No farmers. (Chief, Agricultural Extension Division)
Philippines	At first stage. Directors of research institute at second stage	Yes (at first stage)	Yes	One representative	Representatives of farmer organizations
Pakistan	At first stage	No	Yes	Representatives of seed growers and seed traders	Individual 'progressive farmers'
Kenya	At first stage	Provision for one representative	Not necessarily	None	No farmers (Extension agents, to represent farmers)
Zimbabwe[a]	Yes	Yes (when relevant)	NA	Yes	Representatives of two farmer unions
Bolivia	Yes (when relevant)	Yes (when relevant)	NA	Yes	Representatives of farmers' organizations and/or NGOs

a Until 1991.

Source: Country case studies

include officials of farmer organizations, as is done in the Philippines and Bolivia. In Kenya and Nepal, no provision is made for farmer representation in the release authority, and extension officials are assumed to represent farmers' interests.

The composition of the national variety release authority is an important consideration in seed regulatory reform. These authorities should be broadened to become more representative of the diverse demands of the farming population and the interests of seed enterprises and independent plant breeders.

National policy on seed companies, imports and exports

Variety release and registration are often related to national policies on the development of seed enterprises. Policies may favour public sector plant breeding or seed production organizations and may limit or restrict the development of local private plant breeding capacity. They may also restrict access to foreign varieties or seed. The rationale often given is protection from dependence on private or foreign sources of seed, although such restrictions may only serve to protect public seed enterprises. Even where official policies promote the involvement of private enterprise, the existing regulations can seriously delay the implementation of this policy.

Private sector plant breeding is not yet active in many countries. Plant breeding requires more skills and longer-term investment than seed production, hence the usual sequence is for small- and medium-sized commercial seed production enterprises to become established before the initiation of private plant breeding endeavours. When companies begin their own plant breeding operations, the breeders are often those who have begun their careers in the public sector. Companies are not likely to invest in plant breeding capacity until they are certain that their products can be sold without undue restriction.

India has a dynamic private seed sector, but it has had to struggle against policies and attitudes that limited its development. An official from a government seed project described how he planned to drive several private companies out of business. 'We will take away their contract growers by paying them 20 per cent more for seed produced than they do, and their markets by selling seed for 20 per cent less than the price they set.' The justification was that the companies were 'too materialistic' (Delouche, 1969 cited in Pray, 1990:193). Since that time, however, many of the restrictions on private seed enterprises have been removed.

Privatization itself is not a guarantee of a competitive seed market. In Zimbabwe, the Seed Co-op is a private entity which was given exclusive rights to produce all public sector maize varieties, in return for guarantees to maintain a buffer seed stock; this agreement was revised in 1995 to allow other companies access to public varieties (Rusike and Musa, 1996). In Kenya, the Kenya Seed Company is partly government owned and has had the exclusive right to produce all maize seed for the country; this was modified in early 1996 to allow other companies to compete (Kimenye and Nyangito, 1996).

These two examples of maize in Africa illustrate the fact that government policy on private seed operations is often selectively applied to crops that are more important for national food security. This is particularly true of regulations governing the import of foreign varieties or seed. Liberalization of seed policy in India in the 1980s did not include imports of rice or wheat seed, although this has since been changed. In Pakistan, restrictions are also placed on foreign rice and wheat varieties, which must be submitted for national performance trials where they need to show yield advantages of 20 and 12 per cent respectively over the best public sector varieties, before they can be released (Alam and Saleemi, 1996).

It is understandable that policymakers are concerned about the food security implications of foreign seed or varieties, and not surprising that they are worried about the possibilities of domestic private sector influence over issues that have long been seen as the domain of the public agricultural establishment. Foreign seed companies can become potent symbols in political debates. Protests over the operation of Cargill Seeds in India are a good example; the company's offices were ransacked twice by members of a farmers' movement protesting about the implications of the GATT Uruguay Round negotiations for national sovereignty (Sharma, 1995). Disentangling political issues from effective seed policy is not always easy, but as a first step policymakers must ensure that regulations do not provide undue protection to public institutions that have ceased to serve the needs of the nation's farmers effectively.

Finally, policies that restrict variety availability in order to maintain the quality of national exports should be reviewed to ensure that the advantages of establishing a premium for national sales in export markets are not offset by losses to farmer welfare. If an export crop is difficult to grade and if there are significant differences in price based on quality, it may make sense for the government to restrict variety release. But this assumes that the government marketing authority is able to out-perform private efforts, and that farmers are not unreasonably denied access to varieties that can increase their welfare. Ulrich *et al.* (1987) analyse how Canadian farmers have been affected by restrictions on the release of productive new wheat varieties that did not conform to Canada's wheat export requirements.

Uneven application of regulations

A regulatory system should provide clear and unambiguous information to the industry so that it understands what is permitted and what standards are to be applied. Unfortunately, variety registration and release regulations are not always transparent.

Although variety release procedures may be defined for major crops, they may not be established for other crops, such as forage species. The uncertainty associated with this lack of definition may be a disincentive to breeders to develop new varieties. In Kenya, there is no established release procedure for sorghum and millet varieties, for instance. The Katumani Dry Land Research Centre has the mandate for these crops and has developed several varieties acceptable to farmers. These are made available through community-level seed production activities sponsored by NGOs, but are officially considered as being only 'pre-released' (Kimenye and Nyangito, 1996). There is certainly some advantage in the research centre being able to work independently of the national bureaucracy, but this must be balanced against the uncertainties of the present system, and the centre's breeders have asked that a formal release procedure be established for sorghum and millet.

The legal status of variety release authorities is also poorly established. A recent study showed that five out of seven southern African countries had release authorities with no legal backing (Commonwealth Secretariat, 1994). This lack of definition is one of the causes of the current uncertain status of variety release in Zimbabwe. The Seed Co-op, which has its own breeding programme, released seven maize hybrids in 1991 without going through the variety release committee. This was done in protest against what it saw as an unfair rejection of a Seed Co-op wheat variety, which the committee claimed was insufficiently distinct from a public wheat variety (Rusike and Musa, 1996).

Alternatives for managing variety registration and performance testing

The concerns outlined in the preceding section suggest that most national frameworks for variety release deserve re-examination. Changes can be made to improve the efficiency, participation and transparency of variety registration and performance testing. National seed systems differ to such a degree, however, that no single formula can be adequate for all situations. In addition, an adequate regulatory framework for today may prove deficient tomorrow because of changes in the seed system; hence accommodation must be made for adjustment.

Debates about seed regulatory reform often centre on the question of whether a variety release system should be mandatory or voluntary. The following discussion takes a different approach, choosing instead to examine a series of issues that should be considered in the design of useful regulatory frameworks. The choice between mandatory and voluntary systems is one, but probably not the most important, of these issues, and it is deliberately left until the end of the discussion. In many cases, consideration of the other issues, in the context of a particular national seed system, will play a major role in the voluntary/mandatory choice.

The following discussion of options for variety release treats variety registration and performance testing separately. It emphasizes that the management of standards, monitoring and enforcement for both can be undertaken by a range of organizations.

Variety registration

The management of registration standards
All participants in a variety registration system should contribute to defining the standards that are to be used. If commercial varieties are included in the registration system, then private sector plant breeders should have a voice in determining the parameters to be used, and the requirements should be reviewed periodically by a panel of public and private breeders.

The characteristics used for registering varieties should be few in number and as simple as possible to record, and should be in accordance with the purposes of the registration system. If registration is established to allow farmers, extension workers and seed merchants to distinguish among varieties, the registration system can be relatively simple. Even seed certification can be managed without relying on an exceptionally large number of registration characteristics. In India, which has one of the most advanced and productive public crop variety development and seed certification systems in the world, current variety registration procedures are quite basic. There is no independent registration authority, and breeders are asked only to provide a short list of distinguishing features of the new variety to accompany the release application (Turner, 1994:11).

There is considerable pressure for changing the Indian system, however, with the advent of plant variety protection (Arora, 1995). It is important that countries should not confuse the requirements for managing PVP with the much less rigorous demands of a system of registering non-protected varieties for the purposes of variety identification and control. As PVP becomes established in developing countries, many breeders both in the private and public sectors will choose to register their varieties, especially those that are not hybrids. But conventional and PVP registration may be handled with quite different standards (and indeed by separate organizations).

Coverage and clarity of registration standards
A particularly important concern for any mandatory variety registration system is the assurance that local varieties and landraces will not be adversely affected. A rigid and comprehensive registration system could restrict the use of local varieties. Although this may sound far-fetched, it is exactly what happens in the European Union with traditional crop varieties. There are many vegetable varieties, for instance, that are not commercially attractive and hence no company is willing to pay the maintainer's fee to keep them in the Common Catalogue. Because they are not officially registered,

no one may produce and offer their seed for sale, even for the limited use of home gardeners. A recent attempt to persuade the European Parliament to amend this rule was unsuccessful (Cherfas, personal communication). A similar situation has arisen in Argentina, where companies previously sold seed of local alfalfa varieties (under the name *alfalfa*) but are now prohibited from doing so by stricter registration requirements (van Wijk, personal communication).

Such examples are extremely important as lessons for designing variety registration that does not interfere with the use of local varieties or landraces for cultivation or hamper efforts to decentralize variety development. If variety registration is mandatory, clear exceptions must be made for all local materials that farmers use and exchange among themselves. This implies either exempting local varieties from registration or making the registration standards broad enough to include less uniform local varieties.

Many countries face the task of devising some type of PVP system in the next few years in order to conform to the requirements of the World Trade Organization. It is not clear that the UPOV conventions are going to be appropriate for many of them (Louwaars and Ghijsen, 1996), and the possible effects of adopting PVP in developing countries are still being analysed (see Chapter 9). There are also considerable uncertainties about the way in which the spread of PVP may affect plant genetic diversity, and the problem should not be compounded by establishing an over-zealous system of conventional variety registration that in any way limits the use of local crop varieties. A national PVP system should provide sufficient protection to stimulate competition among commercial seed companies, but should not interfere with the protection and enhancement of local crop genetic diversity.

Harmonization of registration

Any progress in the harmonization of national seed regulatory systems will help to promote the broader interchange of crop varieties among countries. Complete harmonization will not always be easy, but agreement on simplified procedures that can utilize varietal registration data from other countries will be an important step forward. If registration does not have to be repeated in the second country, this could reduce the time for the release of an imported variety by as much as two years. Clear policies for harmonized variety registration will encourage both public and private plant breeders to explore wider markets for their products and can stimulate plant breeding in countries whose national markets alone do not offer sufficient demand. Sharing registration data, most of which are not affected by environmental differences, is much easier than trying to standardize performance testing across countries.

Harmonization may be initiated between neighbouring countries that exchange many varieties (such as Nepal and India), or through regional groupings or organizations. The SADC countries of southern Africa are exploring possibilities for the harmonization of seed laws (Commonwealth Secretariat, 1994) and similar efforts are under way in east Africa and Central America. Malawi has recently revised its registration system so that varieties registered in neighbouring countries do not have to be tested again in Malawi (Luhanga, personal communication).

Linking registration with popularization

One of the principal uses of a registration system should be the provision of information about new varieties to farmers and extension agents. Extension bulletins and similar methods are often used to promote public sector varieties, but if private seed enterprises are to be included in a registration system, their varieties should also receive publicity. The registration of varieties of minor crops is voluntary in Bangladesh, but lists of private varieties that have been registered are passed to extension agents, and this is an incentive for private participation in the scheme (Milki, personal communication).

Funding variety registration

Any varietal registration system must be funded in a sustainable fashion. The charges for registration must be sufficient to cover the costs of the tests carried out, but should not be used as a means of limiting registration or raising revenue at the expense of plant breeders. There are cases, for instance, where registration fees in a mandatory system have been set deliberately high in order to discourage private sector entry. If a simple registration system is shown to be efficient and an effective means of informing farmers of new varieties, private variety developers will be encouraged to participate.

The costs of supporting a PVP system are greater than those of conventional registration, but the experience of the UK as it moved towards PVP is indicative of what national registration systems will face. In the 1970s, government funding supported an extensive system of performance trials as well as DUS testing carried out at two or three sites. As more varieties entered the testing system, the government began to charge a fee partially to cover the costs, but this was not sufficient. DUS testing was reduced to one site, bilateral agreements with other countries were established for the characterization of certain crops, and breeders began to pay the entire cost of the tests (Bould, 1992).

Voluntary or mandatory registration?

There are several arguments on either side of the debate about mandatory variety registration. On the positive side, a well-managed mandatory system helps prevent confusion in the seed market. It should be recalled that the inexperience (and at times dishonesty) that characterized the early development of commercial seed operations in industrialized countries led to the establishment of seed regulations, especially those that tried to control and rationalize the nomenclature of varieties being offered for sale.

An additional argument for mandatory registration is that it may be easier to control the diffusion of inappropriate varieties by removing them from the register. It is also argued that registration is required for seed certification, but if seed certification is not a requirement for sale, then registration need not be mandatory.

The danger of any mandatory system that controls all varieties entering the market (rather than simply having the power to ban specific varieties when there is clear justification) is that it can potentially be used to restrict the activities of certain types of enterprise. The usual example is the public regulatory system favouring public varieties, but if the registration authority were assigned to a private seed producers association, for instance, this too could limit further competition. An additional concern about mandatory registration is that, unless it is a very straightforward and inexpensive process, it will discourage new commercial enterprises and voluntary efforts.

On the other hand, it is important to realize that successful voluntary registration systems do not operate in an institutional vacuum. The role of national variety review boards in the US was mentioned earlier. New Zealand is another country with a voluntary registration system, but while 'there are no seeds acts or regulations as such, there are strict administrative rules, and seed certification is deemed to be an essential and integral part of the New Zealand seed industry' (Hampton and Scott, 1990:178).

Strategies for the evolution of variety registration

The preceding discussion has reviewed a series of factors that must be considered in the reform of variety registration. Particular regulatory systems will emphasize different priorities as they adjust to national seed system development. There are, however, several general principles which are useful for guiding the evolution of variety registration (see Table 5.4).

First, many national regulatory systems are under increasing pressure to record a large number of crop characteristics for variety registration, in preparation for (or in imitation of) PVP. It will be preferable instead to think of two separate approaches. National policy decisions will establish the type of PVP legislation acceptable for each country, and a PVP authority and registration system can then be defined. Independently, decisions need to be taken regarding the minimum amount of registration data that is useful and necessary for public and other varieties that will not be under PVP. It is particularly important to ensure that registration requirements do not interfere with the use or enhancement of diverse and 'non-uniform' local varieties and landraces.

In addition, variety registration is now usually the exclusive responsibility of a public agency. Moves could be made towards assigning more

Table 5.4   *The evolution of variety registration*

Current status	Alternatives	Goals
Registration standards		
○ Many characteristics used for registration, sometimes in preparation for PVP ○ Standards for registration not widely understood by industry or farmers	○ Identify a minimum set of characteristics for efficient (voluntary or mandatory) registration of non-PVP varieties ○ Guarantee protection for use and exchange of local varieties and landraces ○ Establish policy for a PVP system for commercial varieties	○ Incentives established for development of non-PVP varieties ○ Increasing attention to maintaining and enhancing plant genetic diversity through local crop improvement ○ Promotion of commercial seed sector through an acceptable PVP scheme ○ Farmers have confidence that varieties are clearly identified
Data sources		
○ All field tests and data for registration managed by public agency	○ Give plant breeders increasing responsibility for providing registration data ○ Use data from other countries (increasing harmonization) ○ A PVP agency (public or private) establishes clear procedures for private companies participating in system	○ Efficient registration policy that relies on plant breeders to provide and manage data, with supervision from public agency

responsibility to plant breeders themselves for providing these data, and for promoting various types of harmonization that allow the efficient use of registration data that have been developed elsewhere.

Performance testing

The management of performance standards

The choice of standards for performance testing is much more complex than for variety registration. There are many possible interpretations of the term 'value' (for cultivation and use) and many decisions about the environments and farming conditions under which the tests should be performed. These potential difficulties in setting standards indicate that strong representation from all concerned breeders, seed producers and farmers should be included in the management of variety performance testing.

As we saw earlier, one of the principal concerns with performance testing, especially for resource-poor farmers, is that test conditions often do not reflect the crop management practices or circumstances of most farmers. Testing is often carried out under experimental station conditions and management. If on-farm trials are included in the evaluation, the conditions usually still do not match those of the average farmer, and in any case these results are rarely used in the final decision. The establishment of meaningful performance testing in most countries implies a significant revision of the testing conditions.

Of equal importance are the standards used in performance testing. As we have seen, yield ranking is overwhelmingly the major criterion, whereas farmers make judgements about varieties based on a much broader set of characteristics. Furthermore, release decisions are usually made on the basis of best average performance over a range of sites, and such varieties may not be superior for particular environments. Performance testing that is little more than a mechanical set of multi-locational yield trials should be replaced by a more open-ended evaluation in which the suitability of the variety for a particular set of conditions is the basis for approval rather than absolute superiority on narrowly defined criteria.

Responsibilities for monitoring performance testing

Much data for performance testing can be provided by variety developers themselves. Even a mandatory testing system can utilize test data provided by plant breeders, with occasional spot checks and supervision from a regulatory agency. This is in a sense what already happens in many public breeding systems, where the data from the research institution's own variety testing programme are considered by a variety release committee. Such systems need to be transparent, however, and to include publication of trial locations and identification of the check varieties.

Commercial seed companies could be encouraged (or required) to manage their own testing system in a similar fashion. A seed producers' or breeders' association could establish a performance testing scheme for its members. If the scheme were voluntary, private breeders would have an incentive to participate in order to assess their materials against other potential entrants to the market, and to be able to provide farmers with a recognized standard for performance. If such a scheme were mandatory, however, care would have to be taken to ensure that the association and its testing programme were accessible to all variety developers.

Besides placing more responsibility for variety assessment with the plant breeders and seed companies, it is equally important that farmers have a

Box 5.4   Variety pre-release in Zambia

Most plant breeding in Zambia is done by researchers belonging to the Department of Agriculture (DOA). In the past, their varieties have had to go through a testing and approval process managed by the DOA. Seed of public varieties is produced by the parastatal seed company, ZAMSEED. Recently, however, there has been increasing activity from private seed companies in providing varieties and seeds of commercial crops such as maize, sunflower and soybean. This broader participation has required a readjustment of variety release and approval procedures.

In the current system, both private companies and government plant breeders who wish to propose a new variety for release and seed production must submit the variety to a registration and testing scheme managed by the Seed Control and Certification Institute (SCCI). The testing process lasts two years and the charge is approximately US$700 per year for each variety submitted. In the early years of the scheme government varieties were not charged, but now they must pay the same fee as the private companies.

The testing involves two issues. The new variety is grown and morphological characteristics are recorded. This DUS testing is done at two sites over two years. The varieties are also included in performance trials that are planted at a minimum of 12 sites in the country. Seed company and public breeders are encouraged to visit these trial sites.

The results of the performance trials are passed to a variety release committee, composed of three representatives from the public sector (extension, adaptive research, plant pathology), a representative from the Zambia Seed Producers' Association, two representatives from the Zambia National Farmers' Union and a representative from the University of Zambia.

The release committee is more concerned with the adaptation of the varieties rather than with strict yield criteria. If the committee feels that the variety is suitable, it is released for seed production. If companies observe that a variety does not perform well after the first year of testing, they can withdraw it from further tests.

When a variety is accepted for initial testing, the private company (or ZAMSEED) is allowed to market small quantities under a pre-release arrangement. For maize, the company can sell up to 100 tons of seed of the new variety during each of the two years of the testing process. This allows the company (or the public breeders) to assess the performance of the proposed variety in farmers' fields and to gauge potential demand. If the first year's experience is positive, the company can prepare to multiply more seed of the variety, in anticipation of its official release. Thus, when the variety is released, the company will be prepared to bring a sufficient quantity of the seed to market.

Source: Muliokela (personal communication)

113

central role in the monitoring of performance testing. Farmer groups or associations can take the lead in establishing and organizing local, voluntary testing procedures in which public and private varieties are entered. The endorsement provided by such tests would be a strong incentive for participation. If performance testing is mandatory, on the other hand, a considerable investment in understanding farming conditions and much better collaboration with farmers in the testing process are prerequisites for any meaningful reform of the testing system.

One way to take advantage of farmer observations regarding new varieties is to include some type of 'pre-release' arrangement in the monitoring process, with a company being able to begin limited seed production and sale of a variety that is still under test. This is a system used in Kenya, where once a variety has passed the first stage of approval by the variety release committee, it is used in on-farm tests and the Kenya Seed Company is able to begin production and marketing. A final release decision is postponed until after several years of experience, and there have been cases where varieties under pre-release have ultimately been rejected (Kimenye and Nyangito, 1996). This allows the seed company a chance to judge the size of demand for a new variety. In Zambia, commercial seed companies are required to submit varieties for performance tests, but may market limited quantities of seed while the tests (which require two years) are carried out (see Box 5.4). Pre-release is not without problems, however, and it may cause considerable uncertainty for seed companies trying to decide when to increase stocks of seed of a variety under test.

If performance testing is mandatory for privately developed varieties, significant changes in the composition and conduct of variety release committees need to be made. Any comprehensive release system must be managed by a neutral body, and as competition between the public and private (commercial and voluntary) sectors increases, release authorities composed largely or exclusively of public sector officials and scientists will be unacceptable. The establishment of a truly representative and transparent release authority is a prerequisite for encouraging the diversification of national seed systems.

Linking performance testing with popularization
There are tremendous opportunities for reforming performance testing (voluntary or mandatory) so that it supports variety popularization. In many current systems, as noted already, variety testing is simply a set of multi-locational tests with no farmer input, at times complemented by a few token on-farm trials. It is only after a release committee has made its decision that extension agencies and seed enterprises become involved in attempting to popularize the newly released varieties and farmers become familiar with their characteristics. If the variety assessment process were carried out in a more public and participatory fashion, it would not only

provide more opportunity to incorporate farmers' observations in the evaluation, but would be an excellent way of introducing farmers to new materials and developing the demand necessary to encourage investment from seed producers.

In the US as early as 1920, many state crop improvement associations began voluntary testing programmes in which companies could enter their new materials. The University of Illinois began to sponsor a 'Corn Yield Contest' in 1930, in which private companies could enter their varieties. This provided valuable information about the characteristics of commercial varieties to farmers, and allowed the companies to promote and assess their new lines (Fitzgerald, 1990:127). Such testing programmes are only useful, however, if the participating companies agree to follow standard rules and are convinced that the tests are managed in an unbiased fashion (ibid.:204).

The problem of popularization is particularly important for public sector breeding and seed production. At the present time, most public sector breeders have little connection with seed production. Their task is completed with the release of a new variety, and they may be quite frustrated by the public seed company's delays in producing and distributing the variety. A more public testing system would help expose both public breeders and seed producers to the pressures and realities of farmer demand. It would also allow public breeders to promote their varieties more aggressively to the parastatal and to develop interest among various private (commercial or voluntary) seed producers in public varieties.

Funding performance testing

Financial support for performance testing is a crucial issue. As long as it is part of the public research service's variety development programme, the costs may be hidden. But as public budgets are squeezed and testing is expanded to include more environments and an increasing range of private varieties, attention to funding is essential. If performance testing is voluntary, a wide range of funding sources is possible. Farmer organizations may be willing to sponsor local tests, for instance, and individual seed enterprises or seed producer associations can provide substantial support for testing.

If the performance testing system is mandatory, on the other hand, it is obvious that plant breeders who submit materials will have to support the cost of the testing. In the UK, performance testing responsibilities are shared with organizations contracted to the British Society of Plant Breeders, who operate trials under licence at their own expense (Bould, 1992). This simplification of the testing process and the sharing of costs and responsibilities with variety developers will certainly be features of most variety registration and release systems in the future.

In a public testing system there are serious potential disincentives for the private sector, especially if the tests are seen to be poorly managed and biased against non-public materials. Any mandatory testing system will need to present an efficient set of procedures that all breeders are willing to support; if it cannot, it must be prepared to accept partial blame for the stagnation of the national seed system.

Enforcement of performance testing

In a mandatory performance testing system, major responsibility for enforcement rests with the public regulatory agency, which must have powers to discipline breeders or seed producers who try to avoid the testing process. Only if the mandatory system is able to secure the whole-hearted endorsement and participation of seed producers can they be expected to help in enforcement, by applying sanctions to seed association members who violate the system, for example. If a performance testing system is voluntary, on the other hand, this implies a willingness to co-operate on the part of participants, and more collaboration can be expected in legitimizing and promoting the voluntary system.

Voluntary or mandatory performance testing?

Defending a mandatory performance testing system is difficult. In many countries all variety development is still in the hands of the public sector, and the 'mandatory' release system is part of the public variety testing and approval process. But even here, the evidence presented in Chapter 4 indicates that a significant reorientation is required. Expanding such a testing system to include the potential range of domestic and imported commercial varieties, as well as those developed by community efforts, is even more problematic. A bureaucratic, costly and unrepresentative performance testing system will discourage much public and private breeding activity.

This is not to say that it is impossible to justify some type of performance testing, however. The intent is to protect farmers from unsuitable varieties and to provide advice regarding the most appropriate materials. The products of inexperienced or unscrupulous companies may cause considerable short-run losses for farmers. Farmers are, of course, continually trying new varieties that they exchange with neighbours or acquire from more distant sources. This would argue for relying on farmers' own experimental capacities to choose new varieties. There are differences between the indigenous testing and commercial seed systems, however; if farmers have to buy seed for an entire planting, or seed packaging precludes experimentation with small quantities, more risk is involved. The issue is further complicated by the potential effects of a few unrepresentative enterprises (public or private) on farmers' attitudes towards formal sector seed. If farmers' disappointment with a variety's performance is translated into avoidance of all formal sector seed, or all new varieties, then the industry as a whole may suffer from the incompetence or dishonesty of a small proportion of its (unregulated) members.

An example illustrates the dilemma. Vegetable seed may be imported to Nepal without testing, and in one recent case a company (apparently innocently) imported cauliflower seed from India that was not appropriate for Nepal's growing conditions. Many small farmers lost their harvest, and the income expected from it. They were eventually compensated, but only for the cost of the seed (Rajbhandary, 1995).

Many of the problems illustrated in this example could have been avoided with some type of simple screening system, one, for instance, that required seed companies to provide data supporting the adaptability of a new variety for the environment in which was to be grown. Such problems are also addressed by ensuring that seed companies are registered and clearly identifiable by farmers. Similarly, the development of official recommendations for farmers may be done through a voluntary testing system, as discussed above (pp. 114–15).

Farmers should be protected from the false or exaggerated claims of seed companies, but, equally important, they should be also protected from an ineffective or biased testing system that denies them access to superior varieties. Voluntary testing systems that attract the widespread participation of public and private breeders can be very effective, and as seed systems evolve, increasing reliance on business reputations and market discipline will identify and reward superior varieties. It must be remembered, however, that this will depend upon 'a discriminating population of farmer-customers and efficient and competitive breeders' (Simmonds, 1979:222).

Choices regarding the degree to which performance testing should be mandatory will also be influenced by the types of crop involved. National food security concerns imply that governments will be least likely to abandon mandatory testing systems for major food crops (even though some of these could benefit most from the stimulus of a more open approach). In these cases, it will be the responsibility of the plant breeders, seed producers and farmers involved with crops regulated by a voluntary system to demonstrate that this approach is in fact effective and then to lobby for gradual relaxation for the protected crops.

Strategies for the evolution of variety performance testing
Table 5.5 summarizes some of the paths that can be considered for moving variety performance testing regulations to be more supportive of diversifying national seed systems. Under most current systems, the release authority is dominated by the public sector and often follows narrow and rigid release criteria. Regardless of the degree to which the authority maintains a mandatory character, its representation must be significantly broadened to reflect (and encourage) the diversification of national seed sectors. The standards used to judge variety performance must also be broadened to include the range of characteristics important to farmers.

Table 5.5 *The evolution of variety performance testing*

Current status	Alternatives	Goals
Release authority		
○ The release committee is dominated by the public sector ○ Performance testing for all major crops	○ Broaden the representation of the release authority ○ Reduce the number of crops requiring mandatory testing ○ Allow pre-release while tests are conducted	○ Increasing reliance on the reputations of breeders and seed producers for distinguishing varieties ○ Any release authority has participation from breeders, seed enterprises and farmers
Performance standards		
○ Rigid release criteria based mostly on yield in experiment station tests	○ Decentralize variety testing and development ○ Base standards for release on actual farming conditions ○ Use adaptation rather than yield ranking for release recommendations	○ Increasing attention to the diversification of varieties ○ Variety development responds to farmer priorities
Data sources		
○ Standardized data from public variety testing system are used for release	○ Increase participatory variety testing with local groups ○ Use variety testing plots for popularization of both public and private varieties	○ A wide range of criteria are used to make judgements about variety release ○ Data are increasingly the responsibility of variety developers, through voluntary systems or through licensing
Farmers' role		
○ Farmers do not participate in performance testing ○ Farmers receive recommendations from extension, and publicity from seed companies	○ Promote stronger role for farmers in setting plant breeding priorities ○ Support *in-situ* conservation and local variety enhancement ○ Encourage local farmer organizations to sponsor performance tests	○ Increasing input by farmers to public breeding system ○ Increasing capacity of farmers to articulate requirements to private sector

The nature of variety development must also be reformed (see Chapter 4). Mandatory performance testing currently forms part of a rigid protocol for variety development that emphasizes broad adaptation and neglects performance under varied conditions and management. First steps towards improving this situation include strengthening public sector breeding capacity for decentralization and farmer participation. If standard performance tests are maintained initially, public and private variety developers need more of a voice in how they are conducted, and opportunities for wider 'market testing' through a pre-release provision should be considered.

If mandatory testing is retained, it is likely to be for a restricted number of important crops. This can provide a type of competition with the voluntary testing systems in place for other crops, and all parties should have an interest in strengthening these latter systems and showing how they can replace more restrictive ones. Equally important is the need for more attention to be given to using any type of testing system as an opportunity for popularizing new varieties.

The final goal for this evolution in the regulation of variety development is to allow public and private plant breeding to address the diverse needs of farmers and to place increasing responsibility with breeders and seed producers for maintaining the reputation of their products. Farmers' role in variety regulation must also be transformed. At the present time, farmers have little input in performance testing and are often the passive recipients of extension messages or seed company publicity about new varieties. Opportunities to participate in decentralized plant breeding will provide them with a greater say in the setting of priorities for public research systems. Initiatives by farmer groups to sponsor and organize performance tests of new varieties will provide them with a forum for articulating their requirements to variety developers.

Conclusions

It should be clear that the decisions required for establishing an effective set of variety registration, performance testing and release procedures go well beyond the issue of specifying a mandatory or voluntary regulatory system. More important choices have to be made regarding the diversification of regulatory responsibilities, the efficient provision of data and ensuring funding support for whatever system is selected.

No matter what degree of control might remain for public regulatory agencies concerned with variety release, much broader participation in regulatory management is required. Achieving this participation will require demonstrating to public and private plant breeders and the seed industry that a system of regulation is in their best interests, that it serves to promote the industry and that it is a source of consumer confidence and information. Breeders and seed producers will be more willing to

119

contribute to a regulatory system if they have a significant role in its organization and management. This implies sharing regulatory duties and altering the image of pervasive government control.

Just as importantly, farmers need to be provided with a stronger voice in variety regulation. The information provided by a regulatory system is, after all, meant for their benefit. Their participation can be enhanced by organizing more varietal testing at the farm level, through fora such as farmers' organizations that provide effective interchange between variety developers and users.

With a growing diversity of potential sources of crop varieties, it will be increasingly difficult for a public regulatory agency to maintain an adequate variety testing system. The choice is between using a declining public budget to prop up an increasingly irrelevant testing system, or using those public funds to provide incentives that allow a conversion to a more voluntary, more participatory, but widely subscribed system of managing information about new crop varieties. Such a system will offer useful information to farmers and strengthen the reputation of the formal seed sector.

There is no way of avoiding the conclusion that public variety regulation must make way for a wider array of variety and seed choice. Part of this challenge involves allowing private plant breeding and seed production to serve those farmers and situations that private enterprise is best able to address, and removing any regulatory barriers that prevent this from happening. Part of the challenge involves rethinking public breeding roles, and focusing on the support of breeding strategies that meet the needs of farmers less likely to be attractive to commercial breeding enterprises. And part of the challenge requires making a more effective link between public variety development and the seed production system. Parastatal seed companies must be placed on a more competitive footing, and small-scale seed production enterprises need to be explored as alternatives for providing seed of public sector varieties.

All of these changes imply a significant reorientation for public regulatory agencies. Even if variety release maintains a mandatory character, public agencies will have to devote relatively more of their efforts to strengthening breeder and seed producer responsibility, and developing mechanisms for farmer participation. The regulatory agencies will then devote correspondingly less of their efforts to actual control and policing and more to promoting the type of institutional environment conducive to dynamic and diverse crop variety development.

6   The conduct and reform of seed quality control

ROBERT TRIPP AND W. JOOST VAN DER BURG

Introduction

Seed quality control

SEED QUALITY CONTROL comprises two separate elements. One is the verification of genetic quality; this provides an assurance that the seed is of a specified variety and is sufficiently pure. This is the narrow meaning of the term seed certification, and is the responsibility of a certification agency. In addition, seed quality control includes attention to physical parameters such as analytical purity and germination capacity. These tasks are usually carried out by a seed testing laboratory, which may be separate from the certification agency. A certification agency includes the results of seed testing in its decision to issue certification labels. Table 6.1 summarizes the tasks and the actors involved.

The control of genetic purity begins with the earliest stages of seed production. Growing a quantity of seed sufficient for commercial distribution requires several cycles of multiplication from an original supply of seed of the variety provided by the breeder. Any genetic impurities introduced into the earlier stages of this process will be increased and amplified in later stages, and hence the maintenance of genetic purity requires careful

Table 6.1   *Actions and responsibilities in seed quality control*

Task	Agency	Actions
Control genetic quality	Certification agency	Verify seed source Perform field visits Keep track of seed lots Inspect facilities Perform post control
Control physical seed quality	Seed testing laboratory	Test analytical purity Test presence of weed seeds (Test varietal purity) Test germination capacity Test moisture content Test seed health
Certify seed	Certification agency	Check seed against norms Provide labels Check retail outlets

Table 6.2 *Major nomenclature for seed generation control*

Generation	OECD	AOSCA	Responsibility
1	Breeders	Breeders	Breeder responsible for producing breeder seed from original parental or nucleus material and for maintaining this latter to provide fresh releases.
2	Pre-basic	No direct equivalent	In the US system, the second generation may be a later multiple of breeder or an earlier multiplication of foundation seed.
3	Basic	Foundation	Selected growers produce this generation from supplies provided by the breeders and under their close supervision.
4	Certified 1	Registered	Produced on large-scale by seed organizations and sold for commercial crop production. Number of generations of multiplication depends on multiplication factor of particular species but should not be more than two.
5	Certified 2	Certified	Further multiplications outside this controlled generation system, or multiplications that failed to meet quality control standards, are not certified. To maintain this system of multiplication requires a regular release of breeder seed.

Note: OECD = Organization for Economic Co-operation and Development
      AOSCA = Association of Official Seed Certifying Agencies (US and Canada)
Source: Cromwell *et al.*, 1992

inspection and control throughout the course of seed production. The two major systems of nomenclature for seed generation control are shown in Table 6.2. Most countries have adopted the classification of one of these two systems. They both represent a progression from the seed produced by the breeder through a series of generations that ends in seed of defined genetic purity available for sale. Earlier generations have more stringent standards of genetic purity.

Control of genetic quality is carried out through a series of operations that include: verification of the source and identity of the parent seed, inspection of the field to be used for seed production, visits to the field at key periods during the growing season, post-harvest monitoring and control, and, in some instances, growing a sample of the seed to ensure that the progeny conforms to the characteristics of the particular variety. The standards vary by certifying agency and by crop. The level of purity is assessed by comparison with the characteristics of the original variety, which implies that the certification agency is in possession of a sample of that variety. If the certification is done by a public agency, the variety must be officially registered.

Physical seed quality inspection may include a number of parameters, including germination capacity, moisture content, seed vigour, purity (including freedom from weed seed and other impurities) and seed health. Standards for the various parameters included in seed testing are established by the inspecting agency, which may be an independent entity or the seed enterprise itself. An international body, the International Seed Testing Association (ISTA), develops and promotes uniform laboratory procedures for seed testing. Most industrialized countries and some developing countries have ISTA-accredited seed testing stations.

Seed quality control may also include attention to storage and marketing conditions. Certification agencies often take responsibility for inspecting retail seed outlets, sampling merchandise and licensing merchants.

Seed that is certified by public agencies meets a defined standard of genetic purity; it usually also meets several physical seed quality standards as well. A principal alternative to certified seed is 'truthfully labelled' seed; in this case the seed receives no official inspection, and the seed producer is responsible for the genetic and physical quality, certain aspects of which must be described on the label.

Origins of seed certification
It is very difficult for the purchaser of seed to judge its genetic purity, and often difficult to assess many physical quality characteristics as well, so it is understandable that these factors have long been the subject of regulatory activity. In the Netherlands, the government provided seed testing services as early as 1877, and a voluntary system of licensed seed dealers was also established. The seed industry set up several independent certification agencies, and it was only in the 1940s that the government took responsibility for certification. In Germany, a seed certification programme was established by the German Agricultural Society (DLG) in the late nineteenth century; the certification system became the subject of national legislation in 1934 (Rutz, 1990). An official seed certification system was established in Sweden in 1888, under the management of the Royal Swedish Academy of Agriculture (Kahre, 1990).

In the US, a large proportion of early seed production was in the hands of state land grant universities, which established their own certification programmes. As private commercial seed production increased, many states passed laws regarding minimum levels of seed purity and germination. Seed merchants resisted efforts at government control, however; indeed, the inaugural meeting of the American Seed Trade Association (ASTA) adopted a disclaimer to be used by all members which was intended to protect them from claims for damages (Kloppenburg, 1988:64). Seed certification remains voluntary in the US and is managed by private agencies, state departments of agriculture and universities.

In many developing countries, seed certification agencies were organized in conjunction with the establishment of public seed production enterprises. In India, for instance, the National Seeds Corporation was established in 1963 and it became the first official seed certification agency as well. In the 1970s public seed companies were set up in many states, accompanied by a transfer of seed certification responsibilities to independent state seed certification agencies, co-ordinated by a Central State Certification Board (Agrawal and Tunwar, 1990). In Kenya, a seed testing laboratory was organized in 1965, with assistance from a grant from the Netherlands. This was followed by the establishment of a Seed Unit in 1969 and the enactment of the Seeds and Plant Varieties Act in 1972. Further donor assistance led to the establishment of the National Seed Quality Control Service in 1978 which assumed responsibilities for seed testing, inspection and variety control (Kimenye and Nyangito, 1996).

Current practice of seed certification
The requirements for seed certification vary across countries (see Table 6.3). In the EU seed certification is mandatory for most agricultural crops, but not for vegetables. The process is managed in different ways. In Germany, for instance, certification authority is vested in the individual states and is often the responsibility of state chambers of agriculture (Rutz, 1990). In the UK, on the other hand, the Ministry of Agriculture licenses personnel from the seed industry and other private individuals to certify seed; the process is supervised by the ministry, which requires periodic renewal of certification licences (Kelly and Bowring, 1990).

In the US, seed certification is voluntary and seed may be sold subject only to individual state requirements of truthful labelling. When seed is certified, the process is managed by independent certification agencies, under the umbrella of the Association of Official Seed Certifying Agencies (AOSCA). Much of the commercial seed of crops such as wheat and soybean is certified, but very little hybrid seed of crops such as maize or sorghum is formally certified.

In most developing countries, seed produced by state enterprises is usually required to be certified, although in certain cases the parastatal may be allowed to market a second class of seed that has not been through the complete certification process. In countries where there is a private seed production capacity, the rules regarding certification vary. India has

Table 6.3 *Seed certification requirements*

Country	Requirements
EU	Mandatory. Certification responsibilities vary by country; may be carried out by government agencies or by independent inspectors licensed by government.
US	Voluntary. Certification carried out by independent agencies belonging to Association of Official Seed Certifying Agencies (AOSCA).
New Zealand	Voluntary. Ministry of Agriculture and Fisheries conducts service, but full costs charged to industry. Industry personnel licensed as samplers.
India	Mandatory for public seed companies. Voluntary for private companies, but truthful labelling enforced.
Pakistan	Mandatory for public seed companies. Voluntary for private companies, but truthful labelling enforced.
Nepal	Mandatory for public seed companies (but non-certified seed can be sold as 'improved seed'). Truthful labelling for private sector.
Philippines	Voluntary, but certification required for seed used in government programmes.
Kenya	Mandatory (for major crops).
Zimbabwe	Mandatory (for 10 crops). Some companies licensed to do certification.
Bolivia	Mandatory for all 'formal sector' seed, but two classes ('certified' and 'inspected') recognized.
Argentina	Mandatory for maize, sorghum, sunflower and potato. Optional for other crops. Certification done by public agency.
Mexico	Voluntary. National seed certification service inspects seed of parastatal seed company and offers service to other companies.

Sources: FAO, 1987a; FAO, 1994b; Jaffé and van Wijk, 1995; project case studies; authors' research.

allowed privately produced seed to be sold as truthfully labelled for many years, and Pakistan has recently established a truthfully labelled designation as well. In some other countries, all seed from the private sector must be certified; Zimbabwe has just introduced such a rule after previously allowing private seed companies to sell truthfully labelled seed. In Kenya, where a private seed sector is just beginning to be established, current regulations require all seed to be certified. In most developing countries the certification operations are directly managed by the public agency, but in a few cases there may be licensing of certain responsibilities. Some seed companies in Zimbabwe are licensed to carry out seed certification (but seed testing remains the responsibility of the public agency) (Rusike and Musa, 1996), while in Bolivia private seed testing laboratories have recently been allowed to operate (Rosales, 1995a).

Box 6.1   Problems with the management of seed quality control

Efficiency

Delays. Seed certification requires field inspections and tests at appropriate times. If agency staff cannot be efficiently mobilized, seed certification will be delayed and seed may reach the market late, or not at all.

Costs. Seed certification implies a very seasonal demand for technical staff. The costs of multiple field inspections, especially to dispersed sites, are considerable, and the costs of laboratory testing are rising as well.

Standards

Excessively strict management of certification standards is sometimes responsible for keeping appropriate seed from the market. On the other hand, public seed companies often sell seed that is below the established certification norms, or is produced in response to government requests that suspend certification standards. These practices call into question the relevance of current standards.

Participation

Commercial seed sector. When seed certification is mandatory, commercial enterprises rarely have the opportunity to participate in defining the management or standards that are used. There are few instances where private certification or seed testing is allowed.

Local-level seed projects. There are few instances where certification agencies are able to provide appropriate service or advice to local-level seed production projects. Certification requirements at times discourage such projects.

Transparency

Rent-seeking and collusion. Mandatory certification schemes provide opportunities for rent-seeking, the exercise of political or economic influence, and possibilities for collusion among public sector entities.

Uneven management. Seed producers may find themselves subject to varying interpretations of certification rules. The breadth of authority of the certification agency may not be clearly defined.

Inadequate enforcement at point of sale. Insufficient resources are available for monitoring seed quality at point of sale, contributing to farmer uncertainty regarding the nature and purpose of seed certification.

Challenges for the management of seed certification

The rapidly changing nature of seed production in most developing countries and the decline in public sector budgets both give cause for concern about the adequacy and responsiveness of current seed certification arrangements. Before considering possible options for reform, it will be useful to examine some of the principal problems that characterize seed certification in many countries. This section outlines the nature of these problems, which are summarized in Box 6.1. The problems can be divided into the following categories: *efficiency* (delays and costs), *standards, participation* (from commercial and local-level seed producers) and *transparency* (including problems with rent-seeking, uneven management and inadequate control at the point of sale).

Delays

Seed certification is characterized by its seasonal requirements for labour. Seed production fields must be inspected at specified stages of the growing season, and if the fields are widely dispersed this will imply the investment of considerable time and resources for the certification agency. In Malawi, for instance, field inspections account for 20 000 km of travel by the staff of Seed Services (Cromwell and Zambezi, 1993:66). Similarly, inspections done at harvest time or immediately post-harvest in the laboratory require a significant concentration of trained labour. The seasonality of seed certification is especially problematic if the certification agency is centralized while seed production is dispersed.

Delays in the certification process may cause serious losses. If a seed producer has to wait for the results of a test on harvested seed, this may delay getting the seed to market on time. In Indonesia, soybean is grown during different seasons, depending on the region. Because soybean seed is difficult to store, many farmers rely on purchased seed, and the seed to be planted in one region has usually been recently harvested in another region. Private grain traders handle an appreciable proportion of the soybean seed used, even though farmers are encouraged to buy certified seed. The traders are able to identify adequate sources of seed and move it into regions that are about to sow. The government Seed Control and Certification Service has difficulty in managing soybean seed produced by the parastatal seed company in an equally efficient manner, and this is one reason why state certified soybean seed is rarely used by farmers, apart from those who participate in special government programmes (van Santen and Heriyanto, 1996).

Delays are not only a problem with certification systems in developing countries; complaints about lost sales because of delays in testing or labelling are also heard in the US, for example (Barber, 1985). Any certification service must be able to offer its clients the ability to perform inspections at the appropriate times and provide results in a way that does not interfere with the requirements of seed marketing.

Costs

Multiple visits by certification agency staff to seed production plots and laboratory tests on large numbers of samples imply significant costs for seed certification and quality control. In addition, the seasonality of the work means that highly trained staff may have to be supported through significant slack periods. The question of how to finance and support a certification service must be addressed in considering realistic seed regulatory procedures.

In many developing countries seed certification is provided at little or no cost. In Nepal and Pakistan, for instance, no fees are currently charged for seed certification (which is largely directed towards public seed companies); in Kenya and Zimbabwe, there is only a small fee (even though in the latter case all seed is produced by commercial enterprises). In Bolivia, each regional seed office is able to set its own fees. The goal is to become self-supporting, although at the present time government funds and foreign aid still provide the majority of the budget for certification operations (Rosales, 1995a).

In some cases, however, regulatory agencies are self-supporting. India's state seed certification agencies charge fees that are sufficient to cover operational costs. Table 6.4 shows that the cost of certification accounts for between 2 and 4 per cent of the final price charged for the seed of most crops in India. In Argentina, seed regulation was reorganized in 1991 with the creation of the *Instituto Nacional de Semillas* (INASE), which is an entirely self-financing concern (Jaffé and van Wijk, 1995).

But even when government regulatory service is self-supporting, there may not be sufficient funds to address the necessity of continually keeping staff and equipment abreast of the latest technologies that allow the certification agency to offer an efficient service to its clients. The situation is even more critical when the certification agency relies largely on government budgets. In Malawi, an innovative attempt to decentralize seed production (the Smallholder Seed Multiplication Scheme) could not be covered by Seed Services because of a lack of funds (Cromwell and Zambezi, 1993).

In most industrialized countries seed certification and quality control are paid for by the seed producers. It is unlikely that developing country

Table 6.4 *Certification costs for crops in India*

Crop	Certification costs as % of seed sale price
Groundnut	1.8
Maize (hybrid)	2.7
Rice	2.1–2.7
Pearl millet (hybrid)	3.6
Pulses	3.5–4.5
Rapeseed and Mustard	4.2
Sorghum (hybrid)	2.6
Wheat	2.1

Source: Agrawal and Tunwar, 1990

governments will be willing to provide significant financial support to certification services in the future. As a wider range of seed enterprises emerges it becomes even more difficult for government regulatory agencies to provide their services on a limited public budget. The financing of seed certification is clearly a major challenge. If private seed enterprises have to pay for mandatory government seed certification and seed testing services, they will demand that the service provided is worth the investment. A poorly managed, but mandatory, certification service is a significant disincentive to diversifying national seed systems.

Standards

It is important that appropriate standards for seed certification be chosen. If levels are set too high they will discourage seed production enterprises, while levels that are too low may lead to inadequate quality control and unacceptable products (Srivastava and Jaffee, 1993:30). Standards for seed certification should be based on an assessment of the farming conditions under which the seed will be used and on the technical capacities of seed production and inspection.

There are a number of examples where two certification classes are established. In Pakistan, for instance, state seed companies are allowed to sell 'approved seed' which has been inspected but has not passed the standards for certified seed. Similarly, the Agricultural Inputs Corporation (AIC) in Nepal sells a class of seed denominated 'improved seed' which does not receive field inspection but does pass laboratory tests for physical purity, germination and moisture. There have been disputes with the public certification agency over the tendency of the AIC to sell 'improved seed' that has not even had laboratory testing. Indeed, there are many times when the AIC sells more improved than certified seed (Rajbhandary, 1995).

These instances of the use of two standards, or the weakening of a single standard, raise questions about the adequacy of the certification process. If, on the one hand, acceptable seed can be produced that does not meet stringent certification standards, should not more emphasis be placed on this type of seed as a way of reaching a wider range of farmers? On the other hand, if the differences between the two classes of seed are significant, is there evidence that farmers understand the differences and are able to choose freely which type of seed they will purchase? Certification standards may be set aside in most countries in cases of national emergency, but in many instances pressures from government development projects for large quantities of seed may also result in certification standards being compromised (e.g., Chaudhry et al., 1990:47). If such actions are acceptable, it may be argued that certification standards are too high; if, on the other hand, these arrangements lead to the provision of low quality seed, then farmers may be discouraged from using this source of seed again.

129

Strict certification requirements may also limit farmers' access to popular varieties. If certification is a requirement for seed sale, varieties that are not sufficiently uniform to pass DUS standards may not be eligible. The most commonly marketed groundnut variety in Zimbabwe, Natal Common, is actually a mixture of material whose seed is produced from multiplying purchased grain rather than from strict generation control (Friis-Hansen, 1992). Under the certification requirements now proposed for Zimbabwe, seed of this variety could probably not be marketed.

Standards used for seed physical quality should be based on evidence of seed performance under farmers' conditions, not on textbook prescriptions. In some cases, certification standards may require very high germination percentages (for example, above 90 per cent) or may severely limit the presence of off-type varieties even though there is no evidence that this will

---

Box 6.2   The performance of inspected seed in farmers' fields

One of the reasons for seed certification is to control the presence of plant pathogens. For crops like beans and potatoes these may cause serious yield losses. But the efforts devoted to providing clean seed may not necessarily pay off in the field, especially under the production conditions of the majority of farmers. Good field data on the impact of disease control are required before embarking on an expensive certification scheme. Relatively few cases are reported in the literature. The following summary indicates that variable results may be expected and that more work is required.

Impact of clean seed	Crop	
	Potatoes	Beans
Positive	In Peru, on-farm trials showed that an initial investment in purchasing clean seed potato was responsible for higher yields over several years, and a significant economic return. (Scheidegger et al., 1989)	Comparison of pathogen-free bean seed with farmers' bean seed in Rwanda showed a significant yield increase of 21 per cent for the clean seed. (Trutmann and Kayitare, 1991)
None	In Ecuador, several experiments comparing farmers' seed potato with certified seed showed that although farmer seed had higher virus levels, variety and location were more important than seed source in explaining yield differences. (Crissman and Uquillas, 1989:41)	A review of studies done in Latin America comparing clean bean seed with farmer-managed seed showed that in 10 out of 13 cases, no significant yield difference could be shown. (Janssen et al., 1992)

produce a significant yield advantage in farmers' fields. Such practices either add unnecessarily to the cost of seed or, more often, discourage commercial seed producers from attempting to serve more marginal farming environments. There is a great need for better on-farm data about the actual performance and value of seed of various types before deciding what type of quality controls are necessary for a particular seed provision system (see Box 6.2).

Commercial seed sector participation
Despite the growing presence of private seed enterprises in a number of countries, there is little evidence of their participation in the conduct of seed certification. In most cases where seed certification is mandatory for private companies, they have little opportunity to help define what standards are to be applied or how the certification process is to be carried out. Where seed certification is voluntary, private sector seed is often sold under a truthful labelling provision that implies little interaction with the regulatory agency other than perhaps the definition of minimum allowable standards for physical purity and germination. The recently established truthful labelling option in Pakistan has contributed to an expansion in the number of small seed companies and, although these are supposed to register with the Federal Seed Certification Department, the agency is hard pressed to maintain adequate monitoring of the seed that is brought to market (Alam and Saleemi, 1996).

Government seed certification agencies in developing countries usually include little representation from outside the public sector in their management. An exception may be the newly established *Instituto Nacional de Semillas* (INASE) in Argentina whose management board includes three representatives each from the private and public seed sectors, one representative from farmers' organizations and one from the Ministry of Agriculture (Jaffe and van Wijk, 1995:37).

There is also little evidence that public seed policy is encouraging the establishment of independent certification capacity. Several seed companies in Zimbabwe are licensed by Seed Services to carry out certification, with supervision from Seed Services, but only the largest company has a laboratory licensed to carry out seed testing (Rusike and Musa, 1996). There were 17 private seed testing laboratories operating in India in the late 1980s, but they were not allowed to be used for seed certification (Agrawal and Tunwar, 1990).

Interactions with local-level seed production projects
There are uncertain relations between many local-level seed production activities and the public regulatory system. Local seed activities are often initiated because of the failure of both public and commercial sectors to meet the seed requirements of resource-poor farmers. Public regulatory

131

agencies have an opportunity to contribute to strengthening these activities, both through the provision of appropriate quality control services and through training and supervision. The record, however, is mixed.

On the positive side, there are several examples of seed regulatory agencies providing training and advice to local-level projects. In Nepal, farmers in hill regions are effectively isolated from contact with the formal seed sector, and alternative seed provision schemes have been devised. In one project, the Department of Agriculture supported the emergence of 'private producer sellers', farmers who were trained in seed multiplication and provided with foundation seed and technical advice and were then responsible for marketing their own seed (Bal and Rajbhandary, 1987). A survey of current local-level seed activity in Nepal (Joshi, 1995) reveals a wide range of activities supported by NGOs and by public sector research and extension. The public sector institutions provide training and foundation seed, and help improve quality control through field visits and laboratory tests, but this role in supporting the local projects is supervisory rather than regulatory.

In many cases, however, public certification agencies do not have the resources or the motivation to interact with local seed production activities. A 'hands-off' attitude may prevail in which the agency assumes that local seed projects are beyond its reach, and any type of regulation is deemed inappropriate and supervision or training infeasible. In some countries, much NGO activity represents a tradition of opposition to, or at least suspicion of, the government regime, and collaboration with public regulatory agencies is unlikely. This would seem to be the case in the Philippines, for example, where there is a wide range of NGO-initiated seed production and variety improvement projects, but little evidence of collaborative interaction with public regulatory authorities. There are also cases of certification agencies thwarting the attempts of local seed projects; in Zimbabwe, Seed Services discouraged an NGO's attempt to organize a small production enterprise for seed of indigenous varieties (Rusike and Musa, 1996).

Rent-seeking and collusion

Whenever an activity is subject to mandatory government regulation there are always opportunities for rent-seeking and collusion. These deviations from regulatory principles are often difficult to control, but if left unchecked, they seriously threaten the integrity and effectiveness of the regulatory system. The conduct of seed certification presents three major examples.

First, there is the temptation for inspectors to demand payment or favours from seed producers or merchants in order to approve a seed lot. In India, although seed may be sold as truthfully labelled, certified seed is exempt from sales tax, so there is an incentive for companies to have their seed certified. Corrupt inspectors may sell certification labels, knowing that a company will be willing to pay in order to gain a tax saving (Singh *et al.*, 1995).

There is also the possibility that politically or economically powerful seed producers, or producer associations, may be able to influence the decision of inspectors. Delouche (1990) describes how rice seed producers in the Philippines are able to exert influence on seed inspectors. A similar situation is reported in Ecuador, where powerful seed potato producers can influence junior field inspectors (Crissman and Uquillas, 1989). This type of rent-seeking is not confined to government regulatory activity, of course, and may be found in completely 'privatized' seed systems as well.

Finally, where a government regulatory agency is charged with inspecting government seed production, the incentives for maintaining standards may be low, and opportunities for collusion may well exist. The problem was illustrated in Mexico in the 1980s when the public seed company, PRONASE, attempted to expand production to respond to the requirements of government rural development programmes. PRONASE seed quality declined, partly because the quality-control agency (SNICS) did not have enough qualified inspectors to accommodate the expanded production, and partly because it was not sufficiently rigorous in maintaining standards for public sector seed (McMullen, 1987:201). During this period it was not uncommon for mention of PRONASE's name to Mexican farmers to elicit the rhyming response '*No nace!*' ('Doesn't germinate'). Government regulatory agencies have the responsibility of ensuring that parastatal seed production is efficient and capable of competing with private sector alternatives.

Uneven application of certification systems

There are several problems with the transparency of public seed certification systems. Although certification standards may be described in considerable detail, it is not uncommon to hear that two inspectors interpret a rule differently, perhaps because of differences in training or experience. There are also cases where a government seed certification agency may have disagreements over jurisdiction or interpretation with the plant quarantine agency.

A problem of considerable concern for seed enterprise development is the extent of the coverage of certification rules. The limits of the regulatory agency's authority are often not clearly defined, and this uncertainty can affect the decisions of potential seed enterprises. A concern for seed certification in Pakistan, for instance, is the growing number of small companies that do not meet the standards set for truthfully labelled seed (Alam and Saleemi, 1996). Too strong a move to punish such enterprises might be a disincentive to further seed industry development, or if sanctions were ineffectually applied the authority of the regulatory agency might be diminished. But allowing clearly inadequate seed enterprises to operate may damage the reputation of the seed industry as a whole.

In China, the majority of seed production is carried out by over 2 000 county seed companies. All seed is theoretically subject to certification, but seed laboratories and personnel are often inadequate. In addition, certification is the responsibility of seed administration stations of the Department of Agriculture, but most of these stations operate within the seed companies themselves, using company equipment and technicians. This confuses internal quality control by the company with external certification, and contributes to the fact that there are many complaints about the quality of seed on the market (FAO, 1994a). This affects farmers' confidence in (so-called) certified seed, and efforts are under way to reorganize the certification system.

Control at point of sale

Seed certification is established to ensure that seed of adequate quality and purity reaches the hands of farmers. A potential problem is the fact that the vast majority of the resources for seed certification and testing are invested in monitoring and supervising seed production and immediate post-harvest conditions. Relatively less regulatory attention is directed to storage or marketing, even though these may be the sources of many of the quality problems encountered by farmers in developing countries. It is worth considering a redistribution of seed quality control resources to address the deficiencies in seed delivery common to many developing countries.

We have already seen that seed certification is characterized by a very uneven pattern of labour demand. It is difficult for inspectors to be everywhere during harvest and immediately after, and even though seed lots may be inspected and classified there are often opportunities for the seed production enterprise to mix lots and even alter identifying tags or markers before the seed leaves its premises.

Seed is sold through a wide range of outlets, and although in many countries all seed dealers are supposed to be licensed, the level of inspection at the point of sale is almost non-existent. Many seed dealers have little experience with the requirements of seed storage, for instance, and in any case do not have the resources to monitor the quality of the seed they offer for sale. Even in relatively well-developed seed markets there can be serious quality problems. A survey of seed of 14 vegetable species offered for sale in 61 retail outlets in Thailand showed that only half the samples tested met the minimum government standards for germination (Anonymous, 1994).

Seed dealers may open sealed containers of seed in order to distribute smaller quantities, which is understandable, but they may also adulterate inspected seed or alter labels. There was a severe shortage of maize seed in

Kenya in 1993 and in many cases rural traders copied or changed labels to allow them to sell uninspected seed or grain as certified seed, leading to many complaints from farmers about seed quality (Kimenye and Nyangito, 1996). The national certification authority (NSQCS) has few resources to prevent such practices or to follow up complaints. In Malawi, dealers have been found to re-sew labelled seed bags or even to dye commercial grain to make it appear as if it is fungicide-treated seed (Cromwell and Zambezi, 1993:67).

It may be argued that such practices can be detected by farmer clients, but unfortunately this is not always the case. A survey in Zambia found that only 3 per cent of farmers (and only 18 per cent of extension agents and input dealers) could understand all the information on a certification tag, despite the widespread use of certified maize seed (Andren *et al.*, 1991). Even when farmers can identify a problem, it is not always obvious how to proceed with making a claim, and the assignment of responsibility for defective seed is sometimes difficult to make, especially when the seed has passed through several hands before the final point of sale. Even in the well-developed seed markets of the US there are problems with liability procedures for defective seed (Centner, 1989).

Despite the significant problems that can arise after seed has undergone a post-harvest inspection, regulatory agencies often devote little attention to monitoring seed at the point of sale. To do so would require frequent visits and sampling at widely dispersed sales points, and this would put a strain on the resources of a centralized regulatory agency. There is often a requirement that seed dealers be licensed, but this may entail only a registration procedure and is generally not followed up by monitoring or inspection.

In some countries a separate agency is responsible for inspecting seed quality at point of sale; in India, for instance, inspectors are managed by the state governments and have the power to stop seed sales, seize stocks or initiate prosecutions (Agrawal and Tunwar, 1990). Such agencies are usually responsible for the inspection of other agricultural inputs as well, and therefore devote only a fraction of their time to monitoring seed sale.

Alternatives for managing seed quality control

There are no simple formulas for the reform of seed quality control regulation. Policy-makers need to address a number of separate elements and choose the most appropriate strategies for their own national seed system. This section outlines the principal issues and options. The issues are presented in a way that emphasizes the division of institutional responsibilities for setting standards, monitoring and supervising adherence to the standards, and enforcement. The discussion also emphasizes that the decision between a voluntary or mandatory system of seed quality control must be seen in the context of the broader strategies chosen for reforming regulatory procedures.

The management of standards

Regulatory agencies should review the standards they have set for genetic purity and seed physical quality to see if they are appropriate for the farming conditions and seed production capability of the country concerned. If significant quantities of seed are regularly rejected and kept from the market, this may be an indication that standards are unrealistically high. Judgements about the most useful standards should be based on data about the performance of seed of different quality levels under actual farming conditions. If, for instance, high genetic purity is not a priority for most farmers and is not a contributor to significant yield advantage, then standards for genetic purity may be relaxed. This is especially true if the alternative is a severely restricted flow of seed because of the inability of seed producers to comply with the current standards.

Seed certification requirements usually place strict limitations on the number of generations of multiplication for basic or certified seed (see Table 6.2). In some cases this represents a significant waste of resources. For example, the progeny of basic seed may be of adequate quality to be used again as basic seed, rather than being moved on to the next generation (i.e. certified seed). More flexibility in these rules would contribute to increasing the efficiency of seed production.

This is not to say that standards for seed quality should be unreasonably low, however. If a system of truthful labelling is instituted, for instance, the regulatory agency should be able to define useful minimum requirements that can set limits, at least until farmers are better able to understand and interpret seed tags. The seed producer then has some flexibility to adjust seed quality to production capabilities and farmer demand, while still being obliged to guarantee certain minimum standards.

Seed quality standards are subject to change, and regulatory agencies can guide this evolution. When Bolivia reorganized its seed certification service in 1982, a strategy was established to encourage better quality seed through a gradual raising of standards. In the early years of the new system, two intermediate types of certification were used: 'classified grain', which was produced without a record of its parental material and without field inspection, and 'inspected seed', which received inspections but no generation control (Garay et al., 1988).

The level and evolution of seed quality standards should be the product of open debate among seed producers and farmers and should reflect changes in market demand and production conditions. It is not uncommon to find that private seed companies establish higher standards than those used by the government certification service in response to market pressure. As farming conditions change, seed quality control standards must adjust. In some Asian countries there is a significant shift from transplanted to direct seeded rice, for instance, and this will require stricter control of weed seeds, and more attention to germination capacity, in the rice seed that is offered for sale.

Quality control authorities can help local seed production projects establish adequate standards, which may be different from those used in larger commercial operations. Farmers who had experience in testing new bean varieties as part of a participatory research programme in Colombia set up an artisanal seed production group to supply local demand for seed of the new varieties. Production is carried out in the farmers' own fields and seed conditioning takes place at home, while the group uses a common warehouse for storage and sale. The seed is packaged and labelled, and appropriate quality parameters are used that have been discussed and agreed with the state certifying agency (Lepiz *et al.*, 1994).

Coverage and clarity of standards

Although seed quality control theoretically includes everything from the certification of early generations in the seed multiplication process to the inspection of seed at point of sale, the vast majority of the resources of seed certification agencies are currently devoted to the supervision of commercial seed production. Given the possibilities for decreasing official responsibility for day-to-day supervision, which can be managed by the producers themselves, a complementary argument would propose a relative increase in regulatory attention to the beginning and the end of the production process.

An expansion in the number of seed enterprises in a country implies a growth in the capacity to provide high-quality basic or foundation seed that can be used to produce commercial seed. As producers improve their capabilities in quality control, it will be sensible to direct regulatory efforts towards ensuring the quality of the earlier generations of seed. Much of this seed is still the responsibility of public sector organizations, and it is sometimes argued that many of the certification problems that arise in commercial seed lots can be traced to inadequate basic or foundation seed (e.g., Chopra, 1986). As national seed systems evolve, a greater proportion of early generation seed will also be produced by private enterprises, and the regulatory agency should turn its attention to developing this highly specialized capacity.

At the other end of the spectrum, seed certification agencies are theoretically responsible for monitoring seed quality in storage and at point of sale, but, as discussed above, resource constraints currently prohibit most agencies from doing this. In China, for instance, despite comprehensive seed laws, the authorities are only now beginning to address the problem of there being no provision for any kind of point-of-sale inspection (FAO, 1994a). It can be argued that the resources devoted to point-of-sale inspection in most countries are not representative of the degree to which farmers' problems with seed quality arise after the seed has been packaged and shipped, and after many certification agencies consider their job to be finished. There are possibilities for enlisting other organizations that operate at the local level, such as extension services, to help with the task. In addition, farmer organizations can help monitor problems that their members encounter with seed quality and can help prepare and direct complaints.

There are often concerns about how widely seed quality standards should apply. We have already discussed how regulatory authorities can support local seed production activities by setting appropriate standards for their clients' needs, rather than insisting on a uniform standard. Regulatory authorities should also adopt a supportive stance towards grain traders who are sources of seed for farmers. There is increasing evidence that much of the seed provided in this way is of adequate quality, and that the traders are filling a niche created by either excessive state control of seed production or inadequate incentives for commercial seed production. Rather than condemn such activities or try to bring them under the standards of commercial seed enterprises, regulatory agencies should monitor the quality of the seed provided in this manner, understand the conditions that give rise to this situation and work towards developing more specialized options for seed provision.

Harmonization
The harmonization of seed quality standards for international trade is largely addressed by OECD certification standards and protocols. Much of the seed that enters international trade conforms to these standards. In addition, bilateral agreements between individual trading partners can establish standards for particular types of seed. Current efforts are under way in southern Africa to harmonize seed certification standards among member states of SADC (Commonwealth Secretariat, 1994).

In large countries with decentralized seed certification agencies, harmonization may also be a concern. Certain areas of a country often provide advantages for seed production for particular crops, and seed may be produced in one place, conditioned in another and sold in yet another. If this means that the seed enters several certification agency jurisdictions, there may be problems and restrictions if standards are not compatible. This is a cause of some inefficiencies in seed production in India, for instance (Chopra, 1986) and has also been observed in the US (Brown, 1985).

Responsibilities for monitoring
The responsibilities for monitoring compliance with regulatory standards may be divided between a public regulatory agency, on the one hand, and seed producers and merchants, on the other. Four principal options are

Table 6.5 *Options for monitoring seed quality control*

Option	Justifications	Concerns
Public certification		
Public sector regulatory agency	o Government control for main food crops	o Allows little flexibility in standards
	o Necessary with seed production monopoly (e.g., parastatal)	o High costs
		o Limited coverage and participation
	o Provides technical assistance, particularly if seed growers are dispersed and/or inexperienced	o Possibilities for corruption
	o Often required for seed export	
Independent certification		
	o Allows seed producers and consumers the option of certification	o Depends on consumer understanding of certification
	o Allows flexibility in standards	o Requires sufficient demand to pay for private certification service
Sharing quality control tasks		
Shared responsibility between regulatory agency, seed producers and merchants (through Quality Declared Seed, delegating authority or licensing)	o Encourages development of quality control capacity	o Requires good capacity for spot checks
	o Less expensive	o Requires clear enforcement strategies
	o Allows wide coverage	o Requires technical capacity for seed producers and merchants
	o Allows flexibility in standards	
Truthful labelling		
Seed producers and merchants monitor seed quality, with regulatory agency oversight	o Seed producer responsible for seed quality	o Needs strong, independent enforcement capacity
	o Allows standards to respond to market demand	o Assumes well-functioning market and competition
	o Encourages diversification	o Should not be confused with lower standards
	o Costs borne by seed producers	o Still requires supervisory oversight

summarized in Table 6.5 and discussed below. They include conventional seed certification, independent seed certification, sharing responsibilities between regulatory authorities and seed producers and truthfully labelled seed. The following discussion maintains that these options are distinguished by different monitoring strategies, not by different standards.

Public seed certification. Most seed quality control in developing countries is currently in the hands of public certification agencies which assume responsibility for virtually all of the supervision of seed production. This means that agency inspectors visit all producers to inspect seed plots and to sample, test and label seed. The early part of this chapter was devoted to an inventory of the problems that characterize this type of conventional certification, including inadequate standards, high costs, limited coverage and participation and opportunities for corruption.

Although one of the principal recommendations of this chapter is to move towards sharing more responsibility for monitoring with seed producers and merchants, there are a number of reasons why reliance on public certification agencies will continue in a number of countries for some time to come. Governments may insist that the seed of principal food crops continues to be inspected by the state regulatory agency, for example. This may be especially so when such seed is produced principally or exclusively by a parastatal. In situations where it is produced by grower co-operatives or by outgrower schemes where it is difficult to assign individual responsibility, some type of official supervision is often required. Some small-scale seed production projects may welcome the supervision of official certification and see it as a chance to develop their reputation. Official certification may be required for seed export as well.

Even if a public certification agency maintains the principal responsibility, there are a number of ways to make its work more effective and efficient. Previous sections have discussed the adoption of more realistic standards, for instance. This section will examine three specific elements related to the management of conventional seed certification in developing countries: the possibilities for decentralization, the control of corruption and the future of the parastatal enterprises that often receive the majority of regulatory attention.

DECENTRALIZATION. One of the principal causes of inefficiency in seed certification is the mismatch between a centralized regulatory agency and increasingly dispersed seed production. One way of supporting a more targeted regulatory system is to decentralize the regulatory agency. Decentralization implies establishing regulatory authorities at a sub-national level and giving them considerable independence to develop their own standards and procedures. This is the way the regulatory system in Bolivia

Box 6.3 Regionalized seed certification in Bolivia

Seed regulation in Bolivia has been regionalized since 1982. Each *departamento* has its own Regional Seed Council (*Consejo Regional de Semillas*). The regional councils are co-ordinated by a National Seed Council. The membership of each regional council must be balanced between public and private sector members, but the exact size and composition is left to the decision of the council. In the regional council of Chuquisaca, for example, there are five representatives from public institutions (such as the ministry, research institutes and the regional development corporation) and 10 representatives from NGOs, seed producer groups and educational institutions. Each private sector vote on the Chuquisaca council is counted as half a public sector vote, to maintain the balance.

The regional seed councils have a broad range of responsibilities, including:

o defining regional seed policy
o co-ordinating regional seed activities
o contracting technical staff
o enforcing regulations
o nominating the director of the regional seed office
o supervising the regional seed office

Each regional council is responsible for supervising a Regional Seed Office (*Oficina Regional de Semillas*). The staff of the regional offices are responsible for carrying out seed certification. Because of considerable socio-economic and ecological differences between the *departamentos*, the duties of the regional offices vary considerably. Each office determines its own salary structure for staff and sets its own certification fees. In no case do the fees currently cover all the costs, but the aim is to make the service completely self-financing.

All seed sold in the 'formal sector' must be certified, but regional councils decide which seed production activities (and which crops) are considered sufficiently formal to be brought within their purview. Two classes of seed are allowed to be sold: certified and inspected (*fiscalizada*).

Departamento	Regional seed offices		1994, Certified seed (metric tons)
	Technical personnel	Administrative personnel	
La Paz	3	3	105
Chuquisaca	4	3	645
Santa Cruz	12	10	24 960
Cochabamba	6	3	4 193
Tarija	3	2	683
Potosí	3	2	226
Gran Chaco	5	4	680
TOTAL	36	27	31 492

Source: Rosales, 1995a

is set up, for instance (see Box 6.3). Decentralization of regulation offers the possibility of providing closer contact with seed producers and users and more opportunities for targeting regulations. It also allows for closer interaction with other public and private agricultural institutions at the local level.

There are a number of cautions about decentralization, however. First, there is the danger of spreading the regulatory resources too thin. There must be adequate budgetary support for multiple offices, laboratories and other facilities, although this is partially balanced by the savings in travel costs. One of the problems detected in Bolivia's decentralized system is a sacrifice in co-ordination and the ability to keep agency staff trained and abreast of the latest techniques (Rosales, 1995a). In addition, if different regional standards are established, there must be some thought given to ensuring that these are mutually acceptable, unless seed is not likely to cross regional boundaries (see previous section).

Decentralization also involves political compromises. Many public agricultural services in the Philippines have been regionalized, and the Bureau of Plant Industry certification staff are now part of the regional agricultural offices. Although this represents an attempt to address local needs by integrating the actions of the various government agencies, seed inspectors have lost much of their financial and operational independence, without any obvious gain in precision or efficiency, and must report to supervisors who have little understanding of the nature of regulation (Turner, 1990). Local control may also imply involvement in local politics. In Bolivia, there is some concern about the potential political influence of the president of the regional seed council over the operations of the seed office staff, for instance (Rosales, 1995a).

CONTROLLING CORRUPTION. Farmers and producers must have confidence in the certification agency. One of the principal problems with govern- ment regulation in any field where inspectors have considerable discretionary power is the opportunity for rent-seeking and collusion. There are a number of principles for agency management to help reduce corruption (see Box 6.4). These include paying more attention to staff recruitment, establishing rewards and punishments to discourage corruption, improving internal monitoring and changing staff attitudes (Klitgaard, 1988). Rose-Ackerman's (1978) analysis of corruption implies that the problem of producers bribing officials to pass low quality seed might be addressed by establishing a sequential certification process that requires more than one step, or that involves several staff, while the problem of inspectors demanding bribes to pass legitimate seed can be countered by a system in which producers have several possible entry points to the certification process, either through a hierarchy or through alternative inspectors.

142

Box 6.4 Some methods for controlling corruption in public agencies

A. Select agents for honesty and capability
   o Screen out the dishonest through better use of past records and tests

B. Change the rewards and penalties facing agents
   o Reward specific actions and agents that control corruption
   o Use non-monetary rewards (transfers, training, publicity, praise)
   o Raise the level of formal penalties for corrupt behaviour
   o Use non-formal penalties (transfers, publicity, loss of professional standing)

C. Gather and analyse information in order to raise the chances that corruption will be detected
   o Improve auditing and management information systems
   o Develop 'information agents' (auditors, inspectors)
   o Use information provided by clients and the public

D. Restructure responsibilities to remove the combination of monopoly power plus discretion plus little accountability
   o Induce competition in the provision of service (private sector, among government agents)
   o Reduce agents' discretion (have agents work in teams, subject to hierarchical review)
   o Rotate agents functionally and geographically
   o Organize client groups

E. Change attitudes about corruption
   o Use training, educational programmes
   o Promulgate a code of ethics

Source: Modified from Klitgaard, 1988:94–95

THE FUTURE OF PARASTATAL SEED ENTERPRISES. Many of the justifications for state seed certification are related to the control of parastatal seed production enterprises. Although many parastatals will continue to be important, there are also many cases where they are being replaced by private production enterprises. It is thus important that the remaining parastatals be encouraged to become more efficient and competitive. One way of achieving this is to begin transferring more responsibility for seed quality control to the parastatal and to make it understand that its future depends on developing a reputation for delivering quality seed. The state certification agency should be seen increasingly as a source of technical advice and as playing an 'arm's length' rather than close role. At the same time, it should learn to treat the parastatal as simply another producer to which it applies the same standards as to equivalent private enterprises.

Independent certification. An alternative to public seed certification is the establishment of an independent certification service. Such a service may be a feature of a mandatory certification system, but most often it is voluntary. Seed producers may choose to contract the services of an independent certification agency if they feel this will add value to their product.

Most of the seed certification in the US is done by state-level independent agencies that have been formed by farmer co-operatives or associations. The earliest example of seed certification in the US was the activity of the Wisconsin Experimental Association which was formed to test public sector varieties and some of whose members began to produce and market seed. The association began a seed inspection programme for its members in 1913, and by 1918 seed inspection and field inspection were required for the issuance of its 'Purebred Seed' label (Norskog, 1995). The various state certification agencies are members of the Association of Official Seed Certifying Agencies (AOSCA). Seed certification is most common for public sector varieties of field crops such as wheat and soybean. The majority of commercial crop varieties are sold as truthfully labelled seed, without certification. In 1983 the US produced 1.9 million hectares of seed certified by independent agencies affiliated with AOSCA (McLaughlin, 1985).

Independent certification can be used when consumers require additional assurance about seed quality. It can be adjusted to meet various standards. Scottish seed potato growers have proposed establishing a private company to manage quality control procedures that go beyond the mandatory ones the government is able to provide, in order to help them compete in export markets (Young, 1990: 65).

Independent certification is, of course, most useful when farmers are aware of the meaning and value of certification. Mention was made earlier (p. 135) of the study in Zambia showing that only a small minority of farmers understood the information on a certification tag. Similarly, a study in Sri Lanka showed that farmers were able to recognize the label of Department of Agriculture seed (which they trusted), but were not familiar with the concept of seed certification (Pattie and Madawanaarchchi, 1993). In order for independent certification to function well, farmers must understand the value of careful seed production practice.

Sharing responsibility for seed quality control. There are several possibilities for beginning to transfer some responsibilities for seed quality control to producers and merchants. These include the 'Quality Declared Seed' system, the delegation of regulatory duties and licensing arrangements.

QUALITY DECLARED SEED. The concept of Quality Declared Seed (QDS) is described in a 1993 FAO Plant Production and Protection Paper (see Box 6.5). Although the scheme was originally designed to provide guidelines for establishing manageable standards and procedures for

Box 6.5 Quality declared seed

The Quality Declared Seed system is designed to provide seed quality control in a way that is less demanding of government resources than conventional seed certification systems.
The system has four basic elements:

o *A list of varieties eligible for seed production.* A variety is considered eligible if at least one national government has included it in a list of eligible varieties. An application for eligibility must be accompanied by a morphological description, a statement defining the conditions for which the variety is suitable and evidence of acceptable agronomic performance.

o *A register of seed producers.* Qualified seed producers must demonstrate that they have suitable land, access to seed for multiplication, qualified supervisory staff and access to appropriate equipment and seed testing facilities.

o *Spot check of seed crops by the national regulatory authority.* The authority will check at least 10 per cent of seed fields each season and compare them with standards described in the Quality Declared Seed system.

o *Spot check of seed offered for sale.* The national regulatory authority will sample at least 10 per cent of the seed offered for sale and test it for germination, purity and other parameters considered appropriate. The system provides minimum standards.

Registered seed producers provide a Quality Declared Seed declaration for each seed lot. The national regulatory authority is empowered to penalize anyone wrongfully using a Quality Declared Seed label.

Source: FAO, 1993

carrying out seed certification and testing with limited resources, it also offers a suitable model for the transition of current state regulatory systems to those that assume greater producer responsibility. It presumes that a government regulatory agency will maintain ultimate authority, but it offers suggestions for reducing the resources required for managing quality control activities.

One of the most notable features of this system is the suggestion that the regulatory agency should randomly sample 10 per cent of plots each year, rather than attempting to inspect all seed production plots. This considerably reduces the budgetary requirements for many regulatory agencies. In addition, the system envisages a 10 per cent monitoring at point of sale, which implies a larger investment in this activity than is currently the case for most agencies. But the important feature for our purposes is that such a system can begin to shift responsibility for quality control to seed producers and vendors. The system emphasizes the importance of using reasonable standards, and it could accommodate variable standards in purity and seed quality.

A shift to a quality declared system would require seed producers and merchants to be motivated and capable of taking on more responsibility for monitoring and controlling seed quality. It is important to understand that QDS does not imply any reduction in the standards of seed being produced, but rather a shift in responsibilities. Perhaps most important, the system requires a well-defined enforcement mechanism, because the almost constant supervision of conventional certification is replaced by less frequent monitoring. With a lower chance of detection, unscrupulous producers or merchants may not be motivated to play their part unless a clear enforcement regime is established.

DELEGATION OF RESPONSIBILITY. As an intermediate step towards devolving quality control responsibility to seed producers and merchants, regulatory agencies may find it more efficient to delegate some of their monitoring duties to other agencies. This is especially true for the management of small-scale seed production activities, where some technical supervision is required but it is unlikely that a certification agency could provide coverage (see Chapter 11).

In Nepal, support has been given to extension agents, research station personnel and NGO staff to supervise and control seed production in remote areas. In one project, responsibility for quality control is gradually being transferred from technical staff to the farmer and trader organizations that have been formed as part of the project (Box 6.6).

In Bolivia, the regionalized regulatory agencies have adopted a clear policy of only attempting to inspect seed where it is feasible to carry out a certification programme (Rosales, 1995b). The regional seed offices provide advice and support to the technical staff of NGO and other local-level seed production activities. These local enterprises are able to decide if and when they wish to enter the formal seed certification scheme managed by the regional offices, and several of the NGOs are represented on regional seed councils (Rosales, 1995a; Pavez and Bojanic, 1995).

One area of seed quality monitoring that is particularly suited to delegation is that of point-of-sale inspection. If regulatory agencies can enlist the help of farmer organizations or extension agents to sample, and perhaps even to test seed that is offered for sale, this would greatly increase the coverage of post-production monitoring, as well as developing farmers' capacity to appreciate seed quality.

It should be recalled, however, that the technical expertise required for quality control may not always be available at the local level. In one area of Nepal seed grower committees were formed to take responsibility for monitoring seed quality, but it was found that they did not have sufficient experience (Joshi, 1995). A similar problem occurred in Kenya when a

Box 6.6   Institutional participation in quality control in an NGO seed production project in Nepal

The Koshi Hills Seed and Vegetable Project (KOSEVEG), funded by the UK Overseas Development Administration (ODA) operates in four districts of Koshi zone, Nepal. The project focuses on seed production of cereals and vegetables. Production activities are in the hands of 96 seed production groups, each with 10 to 25 farmer members. The groups are formed to improve access to loans and production inputs and to provide a focus for training in seed production. The groups have been brought together in the Koshi Seed Entrepreneurs Association (KOSEPAN).

Seed production sites are selected by group members, staff of the District Agriculture Development Office (DADO) and technical staff of KOSEVEG. Basic seed is provided by government experimental stations, including Pakhribas Agricultural Centre (PAC), while later controlled generations of seed are maintained by the groups. Both government and project extension staff provide technical training in seed production techniques. Pre-harvest inspections have been carried out by the Seed Technology Section of PAC, but this responsibility is being turned over to KOSEPAN and representatives of the Seed Entrepreneurs Association of Nepal (SEAN) who purchase seed from the groups.

Source: Joshi, 1995

programme was organized to encourage small-scale seed potato production in dispersed areas of the country (Kimenye and Nyangito, 1996).

In addition, the advantages of sharing regulatory duties with personnel from various institutions must be balanced against the possibility that the division of responsibilities is ill defined and that no one assumes ultimate authority. Finally, the regulatory agency's provision of support and advice to emerging seed enterprises must be kept separate from its role as regulator.

LICENSING.   Another possibility for transferring quality control responsibility to seed producers is through licensing. In the UK, for instance, seed company technicians are often licensed to carry out seed certification. There are a few examples of this in developing countries as well; several seed companies in Zimbabwe are licensed to carry out seed certification. In South Africa, the management of seed certification was transferred to the industry association, the South African National Seed Organization (SANSOR) in 1988 (Rusike, 1995); seed inspectors are employed by individual companies, but report to SANSOR. As with QDS, however, a licensing system presumes that the public certifying authority has an effective system of spot checks which allows it to monitor the conduct of the licensed inspectors. If this is not possible, then it is better to consider the option of truthful labelling.

Truthful labelling. The most straightforward option for seed quality control is truthful labelling. The minimum standards (for purity, germination, etc.) for truthfully labelled seed may be determined by the regulatory agency, or may be left to the discretion of the seed producer. Consumers bear the major responsibility for monitoring adherence to standards and reporting complaints; regulatory agencies may play an oversight role and carry out spot checks. The enforcement of truthful labelling may be the responsibility of the courts or the regulatory agency. The principal distinguishing feature of this system is that the regulatory agency plays little or no role in the supervision of seed production. It is up to the producer to ensure that the seed meets the minimum standards described on the label. This system is to be distinguished from the sale of non-labelled seed or of uninspected seed without truthful labelling provisions. In these latter cases it may be very difficult for the consumer (or the regulatory agency) to challenge any deficiencies that are detected.

Truthful labelling is widely used in the US seed system. Most vegetable seed sold in both industrialized and developing countries is truthfully labelled; the small, dispersed plots characteristic of vegetable seed production would make formal certification unmanageable. Truthful labelling for agricultural crops is also found in several developing countries. India is perhaps the outstanding example, where private seed companies are able to market seed without depending on the state certification agencies. Companies that have developed their own hybrid varieties and do not wish to surrender the inbred lines to the government for registration sell their seed as truthfully labelled. Private companies that sell seed of public sector varieties may choose to have their seed certified or may sell it as truthfully labelled.

The truthful labelling system has a number of advantages. It does not require a large regulatory bureaucracy. It allows seed enterprises considerable flexibility in meeting specific seed demands. Companies can respond to particular requirements for varietal type and seed quality as long as their product meets the minimum standards and is marketed with an accurate description. The level of standards will be determined by the demands of consumers and the degree of competition in the seed market, and reputations are established through brand names. A truthful labelling system means that seed producers are controlled by the discipline of the market rather than by the intervention of a regulatory agency.

There are several concerns about the establishment of truthful labelling in developing countries, however. Most important, it requires the support of open markets and good information systems. This is probably a fair description of the current seed system of the US, but the early decades of the twentieth century were marked by a significant amount of questionable practice, where the sale of adulterated and mislabelled seed was common. One observer described the seed business as *'caveat emptor* with a vengeance' (Fowler, 1994:81). A number of states passed seed laws at this time to counter these practices. The establishment of seed certification in Europe also reflected farmers' concerns about confusion over variety names and seed quality during the early development of seed markets.

Truthful labelling therefore assumes the existence of adequate markets. In theory, a truthful labelling system allows consumers to 'punish' unacceptable quality by shifting to alternative sources. But if there are few alternatives, or if farmers are unable to identify whether the source of a problem is the characteristics of the variety, the procedures of the seed producer or the management of the seed merchant, the truthful labelling system becomes less effective. The development of brand names for seed enterprises and a stable and competitive seed marketing structure are essential if truthful labelling is to function. In addition, even if markets offer a number of choices for seed source, truthful labelling is most effective if farmers have access to a legal system that allows them to pursue claims of inadequate seed quality.

It must be emphasized that truthful labelling is not a 'second-best' type of quality control, but rather a conscious choice on the part of regulatory authorities and policymakers about how best to stimulate the growth of the national seed system. In some instances seed that has escaped formal certification procedures but is still marketed, say by a parastatal, is described as 'truthfully labelled', but this is misleading. Truthful labelling systems require legal backing, regulatory oversight and an effective enforcement regime.

Much of the success of truthful labelling depends on the nature and development of reputation and on access to third-party certification as an option. It is not surprising that hybrid maize is not certified in the US; it requires specialized production capacity and considerable investment, and farmers look more to the reputation of the company than to the certification tag as a sign of quality. When maize hybrid seed companies were being established in the US in the 1930s, however, much of their production was certified by crop improvement associations, until farmers were able to recognize and trust brand names (Fitzgerald, 1990).

Reputation is equally important for small-scale seed production projects. In the hills of Nepal there has been significant growth in the amount of vegetable seed produced by individual farmers and farmer associations which is purchased for resale by traders. The development of this relationship depends crucially on the trust that is established between seed producers and buyers. Currently there are often complaints from both sides about the assessment of seed quality (Joshi, 1995), and it may be that some third-party judgement would be useful until stronger commercial relationships are formed.

In Bolivia, NGO seed production projects have the option of obtaining official certification services (for a fee). In one case, a bean seed producers' association received training from the regional seed office and paid for certification services; as it established its reputation in the area, it found that many farmers were willing to buy its truthfully labelled (and hence lower-priced) seed. In another case, several small producer associations were formed by an NGO whose own technician managed the quality control; as one of the associations begins to consider marketing its soybean seed outside the area, however, it realizes that official certification will probably be necessary (Rosales, 1995b).

When seed is produced for local use, farmers' familiarity with the producers may be sufficient to monitor seed quality. This is the case with the 'neighbour certified' potato seed as described by Scheidegger et al. (1989) in Peru; small quantities of good quality basic seed are sold to certain farmers, who then multiply it and sell it to neighbours, without further inspection. Examples of this type of internal quality control are not necessarily small scale; in India, co-operative societies affiliated to the National Dairy Development Board organize the production of seed of fodder crops on the fields of society members (Turton and Baumann, 1996).

Links with popularization

Several factors related to seed certification are linked to the popularization of new varieties and the diversification of seed sources, including the development of farmers' responsibilities as seed consumers, the organization of extension and support for small-scale seed production. At several points in the discussion, reference has been made to the importance of developing farmers' capacities to recognize the value of seed quality and to demand quality standards appropriate to their circumstances. This does not imply that farmers are not aware of seed quality issues. Indeed, most of the evidence points to the fact that farmers' management of home-saved seed provides adequate quality (e.g., Wright et al., 1994). But as farmers come to use more external seed sources and are introduced to a wider range of varieties they need support in assessing seed quality and, equally important, knowing how to pursue complaints if the quality is inadequate. Knowledgeable and demanding consumers are the best stimulus for an expanding seed industry.

Extension can play a useful role in helping to broaden farmer appreciation of seed quality issues. It can also contribute to the popularization of a wide range of varieties by not using officially certified seed only in its programmes, if other acceptable sources are available. Extension recommendations should not be focused only on the use of seed produced by parastatals or public varieties if other alternatives are also available.

The future of public sector varieties will increasingly depend on the existence of agile, small-scale seed production efforts that can efficiently produce and market seed of these varieties. Training and advice from public regulatory agencies are crucial for the development of these enterprises. Examples from Nepal and Bolivia have been discussed above. In Ghana, the collapse of the state-owned Ghana Seed Company left the country with little formal production capacity for the public sector maize varieties that were available. The government Seed Inspection Unit has been supported by an NGO to provide advice and supervision to promote the development of small-scale, often family-run, commercial seed enterprises to take the place of the parastatal (Bockari-Kugbei, 1994).

Funding

The costs of seed quality control must be recognized. Public budgets will not continue to support a large certification system, and certifying agencies will have to charge the full cost of their services in most cases. If a mandatory certification system requires seed producers to use the certification service, they will demand value for money. If certification remains mandatory, seed producers and consumers need to be given a stronger voice in the management of the regulatory agency, through participation in boards and expanded opportunities for less formal contact as well.

The discussion above has suggested that public certification agencies can make considerable savings by assigning increasing supervisory responsibility to seed producers and merchants. The one factor that implies an increase in regulatory agency activity is the necessity of enhancing point-of-sale monitoring and seed testing. Some of this can be delegated to local agencies or farmer groups, however, and regulatory agency laboratory facilities can be used for point-of-sale monitoring during the off season(s), when seed is not being tested for certification.

The public certification agency will thus be able to cover the majority of its expenses by the fees that it charges. But activities such as point-of-sale monitoring and the training and advisory services it can provide to emerging seed enterprises require some investment of public funds.

Enforcement

Under a mandatory certification system, the public regulatory agency usually has primary responsibility for enforcement. Its ability to withhold certification tags is perhaps its main enforcement tool, but once seed is in the market, its powers of monitoring and enforcement are often seriously diminished. Arbitration committees with equal participation from producers and consumers are one possibility. In serious breaches of regulations the agency may be able to seize company seed or close down operations.

Rusike (1995) describes how government policy in South Africa was directed towards establishing a viable private seed industry. Enforcement played an important role. Visits by government inspectors to seed sellers increased between 1964 and 1974. The number of prosecutions under the Seed Act rose rapidly and then fell, as seed enterprises learned that violations were harshly punished. The number of inspections fell after 1974 as the rate of violations declined.

Responsibilities for enforcing seed quality standards can also be shared among organizations, especially as more supervisory duties are passed to producers and merchants. For instance, alternatives such as QDS or truthful labelling can enlist the co-operation of seed producer or merchant associations to discipline their members. Enforcement of standards in local-level seed production activities may be in the hands of technical staff from public sector organizations or NGOs who can withhold further resources or supervision if they detect persistent violations.

But more effort needs to be placed on developing farmers' capacities to use the markets and, when necessary, the courts to enforce seed quality standards. When farmers have a wide range of choices for seed sources they can use the market to punish unacceptable quality. Consumer courts are also useful. Farmers in India are able to pursue compensation for defective seed through small claims courts, and there has been an increase in this activity in recent years (Turner, 1994). It may take some effort to develop farmers' capacity to use the court system, however; Rosales, (1995a) reports that farmers in Bolivia are reluctant to initiate court cases to claim compensation for poor-quality seed. Newspaper reports and other publicity about successful legal cases against offending seed companies will help develop farmer confidence in the court system.

Voluntary or mandatory?

The preceding discussion has illustrated that the choice between voluntary or mandatory seed certification systems must be made in the light of decisions about several other factors. Indeed, once those other decisions have been taken, the voluntary/mandatory choice seems much less important. Regulatory reform should first pay attention to establishing standards for seed quality control that are appropriate to the needs of diverse seed enterprises. In addition, the development of seed producer and merchant capacity to take responsibility for an increasing proportion of the supervision of quality standards should be a priority under both mandatory and voluntary systems. Finally, a more diverse set of actors needs to be involved in the enforcement of seed quality standards.

The choice among conventional certification, shared responsibility, or truthful labelling is an important one, and should not be confused with the mandatory/voluntary decision. A system such as QDS could be established with either mandatory or voluntary participation, for instance, and truthful labelling can be accurately described as mandatory in most cases. Many mandatory certification systems are poorly managed and openly flouted,

Table 6.6 *The evolution of seed quality control*

Current status	Alternatives	Goals
Standards		
○ Single set of standards for seed genetic and physical quality ○ Standards are not necessarily appropriate for the needs of many farmers	○ Allow different standards for various types of producer ○ Establish minimum standards to guide truthful labelling ○ Place more emphasis on genetic quality control in early generations of seed production	○ Seed quality standards are set in response to farmer demand and producer capacity ○ General trend of increasing standards as seed system evolves
Monitoring		
○ All supervision of seed quality control done by official agency ○ Supervision implies inspecting all seed production	○ Decentralize some public quality control activities ○ Delegate some responsibilities to other agencies, NGOs ○ Devolve more responsibility to seed producers and merchants, through a QDS or licensing system, complemented by spot checks and monitoring ○ Allow truthful labelling ○ Encourage independent certification capacity	○ Increase in quality control skills of seed producers ○ Majority of quality control activities carried out by seed producers, with oversight by public agency
Enforcement		
○ Enforcement of seed quality standards is uneven ○ Little attention given to quality at point of sale	○ Establish clear enforcement strategy ○ Devote more resources to point-of-sale inspections; train or delegate others to do this ○ Encourage seed quality disputes to be addressed by consumer courts ○ Encourage more seed industry participation in enforcement	○ Seed producers and farmers understand penalties for faulty seed ○ As much enforcement as possible through commercial law and market mechanisms
Farmer role		
○ Farmers have little awareness of seed quality options ○ Farmers have no clear recourse for complaints or concerns	○ Use extension and NGOs to acquaint farmers with issues and options of seed quality ○ Encourage growth of brand names, use of media to stimulate seed producer reputations ○ Promote farmer associations to monitor/demand seed quality	○ Farmers have access to multiple sources of information about seed quality ○ Farmers can clearly identify seed producers and merchants and know how to pursue complaints

while successful voluntary systems may be widely subscribed and respected. Thus the important choice is not whether all seed enterprises must submit to a mandatory certification system, but rather how to select a strategy that enlists the comprehension and co-operation of the entire range of seed enterprises in a quality control system that meets the needs of the nation's farmers.

Strategies for the evolution of seed quality control

Table 6.6 summarizes the most important factors that deserve attention in reforming national seed quality control systems. They are divided into the management of standards, monitoring and enforcement and the farmers' role.

Seed quality control standards must be appropriate for the needs of all farmers and, as a consequence, must be more diverse. Regulatory agency duties should emphasize the definition and understanding of standards targeted to particular types of farmers and seed producers. There should be more flexibility in quality control for commercial seed production. On the other hand, there should be stricter controls on early-generation seed (such as breeder or basic seed) that is provided to an expanding number of seed producers. It is likely that the evolutionary path will first see a drop in some standards, followed by a diversification and a gradual increase in quality standards as farmers become more demanding and seed systems become more sophisticated.

The responsibility for supervision of much commercial seed production should pass from the regulatory agency to other organizations. Seed producers will assume increasing obligations for quality control, and the regulatory agency will perform more back-up and spot-check duties. For small-scale seed production, the technical supervision of the regulatory agency may be substituted by others, such as extension agents or NGO staff, until local capacity is adequate. QDS, licensing of certification to seed producers or independent agencies and the establishment of truthful labelling are all options for increasing the resources available for the supervision of quality control and reducing public sector regulatory investment.

Enforcement of seed quality will have to depend increasingly on farmers' capacities to act through the market or through commercial law. Any move towards the delegation of authority for monitoring or truthful labelling will, however, have to be accompanied by a well-conceived structure for enforcement by the regulatory agency and, more important, a system of spot checks that pays particular attention to point-of-sale monitoring.

Finally, it should be obvious that an adequate system of seed quality regulation depends crucially upon farmers' capacities to recognize and demand seed quality. An important part of seed regulatory reform is the development of these capacities and the strengthening of the media and the markets to transmit information between seed producers and farmers.

PART 3

INSTITUTIONS, ORGANIZATIONS AND REGULATORY REFORM

7 The dynamics of seed policy change: state responsibilities and regulatory reform

ROBERT TRIPP

The context of policy change

THE DISCUSSION IN Part 2 identified principles and options for regulatory management in national seed systems, but left open the question of precisely how regulatory reform is to be implemented. Regulatory reform is most commonly associated with specific changes in laws and rules, or their interpretation, and policymakers thus assume a leading role in bringing about changes in regulatory frameworks. But it would be incorrect to believe that policy changes that are effected 'on paper' constitute the whole of regulatory reform. After all, policy change does not appear out of the blue, but reflects complex pressures that are a product of the larger society. In this sense, policy change can be seen to follow from these forces, rather than to lead.

In their analysis of policy change in developing countries, Grindle and Thomas (1991) focus on the decision-makers they call 'policy élites', and attempt to trace the factors that influence their choices. Their analysis rejects theories based on simple, monolithic explanations for policy change, such as those that posit class, interest group or bureaucratic control of the decision-making process. Instead, they believe policy change is influenced by two sets of factors: the backgrounds of the policy élites (including ideology, professional background, experience and political commitments), and the broader societal context (including political pressure, historical precedent, economic conditions and the interests of foreign donors).

An understanding of regulatory reform thus requires attention to the cultural, political and economic context of policy change. We need to examine the traditions and ideologies that shape the regulatory debate, and to recognize the interests and capacities that determine the direction of regulatory change. In this chapter we examine some of the contextual factors relevant to regulatory reform. The discussion begins with a brief review of the concepts of institutions and organizations. This is followed by a summary of the institutional prerequisites of regulatory reform and an examination of the influence of national regulatory culture. The discussion then shifts to an examination of some of the particular interests and pressures that influence regulatory reform, and the concluding section offers a summary of the implications of seed regulatory reform for the actions of government organizations.

The following four chapters in this section offer a detailed examination of the implications of institutional and organizational changes taking place in the commercial and voluntary sectors for seed regulatory reform. Chapter 8 examines the growing importance of the commercial seed industry and argues for regulatory reform to support the development of entrepreneurial activity. One of the concomitants of expanding commercial interests in developing country seed systems has been the rise of plant variety protection, and Chapter 9 analyses the implications of this trend. Chapter 10 shifts the focus to the contributions of community-level initiatives and reviews progress in participatory plant breeding and variety testing. Chapter 11 presents a review of NGO and other local-level endeavours in seed production and provision.

Institutions and organizations

A useful guide for addressing the intricate context of regulatory reform is the distinction between institutions and organizations. Several definitions are possible, but North's (1990) is among the clearest. Institutions are 'the rules of the game' (ibid.:3), while organizations are the players, 'groups of individuals bound by some common purpose to achieve objectives' (ibid: 5). Uphoff (1994:202) describes institutions as 'complexes of norms and behaviours' while organizations are 'structures of recognized and accepted roles'.

Following these definitions, entities such as local markets, commercial law and rural land tenure are all examples of institutions, while a seed company, a farmer group or a plant breeding institute are organizations. It may be asked where regulation fits in this scheme. Regulatory bodies, such as a seed certification agency, would qualify as organizations, while the laws on which seed regulations are based are closer to institutions. But Uphoff (1994) points out that the distinction between institutions and organizations is not always clear-cut, and some organizations may also be considered as institutions. Whether an organization, such as the Ministry of Agriculture, can also be treated as an institution depends in part on its perceived legitimacy, respect and permanence. All of these are prerequisites for an influence on norms and behaviour that would qualify it as an institution. Seed regulatory frameworks, and the discussion of regulatory change, would thus seem to occupy an area of overlap between organizations and institutions.

This intermediary position for seed regulation that claims both organizational and institutional ground is relevant to our discussion of how regulatory reform is to be implemented. Is it to be achieved by first changing the basic laws and traditions that govern the transactions of seed systems, or is it preferable to concentrate first on organizational change, promoting the growth of alternative plant breeding and seed production strategies, and then exploring regulatory options? Although it may be argued that institutions determine the scope for organizational action, and are thus primary, the practical process of regulatory change will depend to a considerable extent on modifications at the organizational level. Indeed, organizational change serves to modify the institutional environment, as North (1990) explains. 'Institutions, together with the standard constraints of economic theory, determine the opportunities in a society. Organizations are created to take advantage of those opportunities, and, as the organizations evolve, they alter institutions' (ibid.:7). 'Change typically consists of marginal adjustments to the complex of rules, norms, and enforcement that constitute the institutional framework' (ibid.: 83).

Incremental changes in the organizations that comprise a national seed system are capable of leading to significant reform in regulatory frameworks. It is thus relevant to focus attention on the opportunities for commercial and voluntary seed initiatives and to test innovative forms of exchanging information, establishing reputations and defining priorities that will modify regulatory behaviour. But at the same time we must be aware that these efforts will take place within an institutional environment that sets parameters on possible courses of action. The following section looks at the basic institutional background that influences seed system development.

The institutional context of seed system development

The promotion of commercial and voluntary seed activities, and the search for innovative strategies for the management of public sector seed responsibilities, will be influenced by the institutional environment. Choices among specific organizational options will depend on the rules and norms of economic and political life. The prospects for commercial seed options will be conditioned by the status of market development, the infrastructure for communication and trade, and the capacities of commercial law. In contrast, a focus on community-based options presumes the existence of mechanisms that encourage widespread participation and that allow and encourage the development of independent organizations. Finally, the success of public sector contributions to seed system development depends in part on the presence of representative and responsive government.

A useful way of summarizing these institutional prerequisites is through Hirschman's (1970) concepts of 'exit' and 'voice'. Exit is associated with 'the availability of choice, competition, and well-functioning markets' (Hirschman, 1986:78), while voice is concerned with the capacity to articulate demands and concerns, through means such as trade unions, consumer organizations and political parties. Institutional development should provide increasing opportunities for both exit and voice. Exit gives people the option of withdrawing from a commercial relationship (by seeking an alternative supplier in the market) or from participation in an organization (by seeking an alternative employer, political party or form of association). The exercise of voice, on the other hand, provides the opportunity to stay within, and improve, a relationship by communicating concerns to commercial partners, helping define priorities for public organizations or influencing the direction or management of a voluntary association.

The concepts of exit and voice are closely linked. As Hirschman (1986:87) points out, 'most markets involve voice: commerce *is* communication . . .' When national political and economic institutions provide more opportunities for both exit and voice, the number of organizational options for developing seed systems increases, and a wider range of regulatory mechanisms becomes possible. The success of organizational innovations is strongly influenced by the more general development of national economic and political institutions.

A principal challenge for developing responsive national seed systems is the lack of access to either exit or voice by the poor (Brett, 1993). As long as economic and political institutions provide resource-poor farmers with little opportunity for exercising exit and voice, the range of options for seed system development (and regulatory innovation) will be correspondingly limited. Prospects for promoting the growth of national institutions to better serve the needs of the poor vary by country, but in no case is this an easy task, involving as it does fundamental changes in traditions, governance and division of responsibilities. These difficulties expose the weakness of many donor programmes for 'institution building' that fail to define their targets or strategies (Moore, 1995). A lack of patience with the long-term job of building effective organizations, combined with a misunderstanding of the nature of institutional change, has encouraged aid agencies to believe that changes in laws or policies (as evidenced in a superficial conception of 'regulatory reform') are all that is required to promote equitable development.

Evidence of this fallacy is found in the debates about appropriate seed regulatory models for developing countries. Agencies and consultants tend to promote either a US-style system that relies on market mechanisms, or a European alternative that places more regulatory responsibility in the hands of government agencies. The feeling is that once an appropriate set of rules is established then everything else will fall into place. The argument is misconceived on two counts, however. First, it is counterproductive to argue about whether markets or the state should command regulatory authority. Second, and more fundamental, the differences between the two systems are more apparent than real. The US seed regulatory system includes government oversight and a strong tradition of voluntary participation in seed testing. Similarly, most European seed regulatory systems in fact depend on participation and management from farmer groups and commercial interests. The most remarkable fact is not the contrast between the two systems but rather their similarities in the complexity and depth of institutional participation. This situation is to be contrasted with that of many developing countries, where public agencies, commercial interests and farmer organizations are all weak. Regulatory reform thus involves much more than selecting a model of regulatory performance and promoting the necessary laws or policies.

Regulatory cultures

Although the contrast between European and US seed regulation is not particularly useful for identifying strategies for seed system development, it does point to another aspect of the institutional environment that is relevant to regulatory reform. The seed systems of European countries and the US function effectively, but they are subject to very different regulatory traditions. It would be difficult to imagine a farmer in France being comfortable with US-style seed regulation, or a farmer in Iowa accepting French regulations. The fact that such differences exist is further proof that regulatory reform is not a unilineal process leading to a standard outcome.

Regulatory management is subject to the traditions, history and political organization of particular countries. For want of a better term, these factors will be summarized here as 'regulatory culture'. The following discussion seeks to explore some of the reasons for differences among countries that can explain divergent regulatory pathways.

An interesting example of differences in regulatory culture is presented by the appearance of the cattle disease BSE in the UK. The possible link of BSE to human health led to an EU export ban on British beef in early 1996. Although the disease was largely confined to the UK, declines in consumer confidence (and beef sales) were more marked in several other countries on the Continent, which contributed to the enactment of the ban. The strong UK government reaction to the ban led one observer to contrast

the culture of deregulation which has always been latent in British capitalism . . . [with] the regulatory culture associated with the social capitalisms of mainland Europe. On one side, the right of the property owner to do what he will with his own. On the other, conditional property, restrained by a web of reciprocal obligations (Marquand, 1996).

This contrast is drawn to make a political point, but it does lend credence to the notion of regulatory cultures.

Regulatory cultures are part of national traditions, and views on the appropriate degree of regulatory control will vary. Germany may be cited as an example of a strong regulatory tradition. When a common seed regulatory framework was devised for the European Union, many farmers and seed producers in Germany were concerned that they would be forced to compromise their standards (Neuendorf, personal communication).

161

Historical experience may also influence regulatory culture. The contrast between US and European approaches to seed regulation may be partially explained by differences in experiences with food supply. The US has never suffered from the food shortages that many European countries have experienced. In the UK, the National Institute of Agricultural Botany was established to stabilize seed supply after the food shortages of World War I, and the institute's seed production committees that were established during World War II became the basis for later variety registration and seed certification schemes (Kelly and Bowring, 1990).

Seed regulation is also consistent with a government's approach to economic management. The comparatively 'open-market' strategy for seed regulation adopted in Chile, compared with the more thorough government regulatory involvement of its neighbour, Argentina (Jaffé and van Wijk, 1995), should not be surprising to those familiar with the countries' economic traditions, for instance. In a number of developing countries, the state's extensive regulatory responsibility is consistent with a philosophy that may accommodate both protectionist and paternalistic instincts. The motivation for these instincts may be questioned, but they are often backed by widespread public acceptance. Both nationalistic and anti-commercial ideologies have had a strong influence on the conception of seed regulation in India and Mexico, for example (McMullen, 1987), where until recently regulation has been used to limit the diversification of the private seed sector.

There are certainly limits to the usefulness of the concept of regulatory culture, however. Cultures are not monolithic, and they often present their own internal contradictions. Although the US features one of the most open systems of seed regulation in the world, the country cannot be distinguished historically as particularly 'unregulated'. It led the way in establishing a stringent system of pesticide regulations which has been characterized as the most complex of any industrialized nation (Boardman, 1986:78). Any explanation of why US seed regulation is largely voluntary, while US pesticide regulation has habitually featured headlong confrontation between regulatory agencies and chemical companies, would certainly have to go well beyond the notion of regulatory culture.

The application of regulatory philosophies outside their national cultures may lead to interesting dilemmas. Pavez and Bojanic (1995) describe the efforts of an NGO in Bolivia to develop opportunities for resource-poor farmers to grow the traditional Andean small grain, quinoa, for export to Switzerland and Germany, where its exotic origin and high nutritional quality command attractive prices in shops specializing in natural foods. Independent certification agents verify that the quinoa for export is grown organically. Because production and processing requirements favour the use of a single, uniform variety, farmers are unable to use the varietal mixtures they traditionally depend upon. The NGO works with farmers to help achieve the varietal purity desired by the consumers. The paradoxical outcome of this application of 'green' consumer preferences, emphasizing a diversity of foods and ecologically sound production, is inadvertent pressure on the genetic diversity of a native crop in the highlands of Bolivia.

Regulatory philosophies are also subject to readjustment in order to accommodate new opportunities. Fowler (1994) relates how the US seed industry's disdain for European seed regulation in the 1960s became tempered by wistful appreciation of European capacity to promote its seed industry and to offer its companies plant breeders' rights. This led to pressure for the US Plant Variety Protection Act of 1970. Lobbying by the seed industry for varietal protection had to contend with Justice Department scepticism about the wisdom of exclusive protection for agricultural endeavours, however. In addition, the seed industry had to come to terms with opposition from major food processors who feared their costs would be increased. Such negotiation is typical of regulatory change, and this directs our attention to understanding how the interests of particular groups are expressed in regulatory debates.

Interest groups, policymakers and regulatory change

Regulatory cultures change over time, and their evolution can be marked by what Eisner (1993:1) calls the 'regulatory regime . . . , a historically specific configuration of policies and institutions which structures the relationship between social interests, the state, and economic actors in multiple sectors of the economy'. In order to understand some of the factors that influence shifts in regulatory policy it will be useful to make reference to Grindle and Thomas's (1991) analysis of policy change. They present four sets of factors or 'lenses' through which policymakers examine the implications of proposed changes. These include technical advice, bureaucratic implications, political stability and international pressure. We shall briefly examine the relevance of each of these to seed regulatory reform.

Technical advice
When policymakers consider regulatory reform, they should review the technical evidence associated with various regulatory options. Such evidence for seed regulatory reform has been presented in Part 2, which reviews the current status of the regulatory frameworks governing public plant breeding, variety release and seed quality control. The performance of these regulations was measured in several dimensions: efficiency (taking particular account of limitations in state resources), standards (and their relevance to diversifying seed systems), participation (the capacity to involve seed producers and consumers in regulatory responsibilities) and transparency (the clarity of the information transmitted to seed system participants).

The technical evidence assembled in Part 2 points overwhelmingly to the need for regulatory reform. But Grindle and Thomas's concept of policy lenses reminds us that regulatory reform, like all policy change, depends only partially on technical analysis. Bureaucratic, domestic political and external pressures will all contribute to defining its direction and scope.

Bureaucratic considerations

In order to function properly, regulatory systems depend upon a bureaucratic framework, but this state administrative apparatus may also present one of the most serious impediments to regulatory reform. Positions, procedures and careers become established within any bureaucracy and these may be threatened by regulatory reform. Regulatory authorities may look for ways to extend their reach and will often resist challenges to their routines. In addition, regulatory agencies establish relations with the regulated industry that lead to synergies that are difficult to alter. All of these tendencies can cause difficulties for a programme of regulatory reform.

Bureaucracies naturally defend their positions and attempt to expand their authority. Although US seed companies successfully resisted the establishment of federal variety registration or seed certification, the battle featured strong pressures from within the US Department of Agriculture for tighter controls on the seed industry and the lobbying of professional seed regulators, most of whom operated at the individual state level. They formed the Association of American Seed Control Officials (AASCO) in 1955 which pressed for compulsory variety registration (Fowler, 1994:100).

Regulatory routines are established that may be difficult to alter. A previous example, (p. 100) described the problems that commercial maize seed companies in Canada experienced when they had to enter their varieties in performance trials, the plant population management of which was designed for the public sector varieties that regulators were used to testing. Regulatory routines are not necessarily biased against the private sector, however. Jones (1994) points out that mandatory state performance testing for insecticides may include protocols that favour the chemical insecticides of established commercial firms and do not provide a fair assessment of the efficacy of newer, and safer, microbial insecticides.

There is a fine line between situations where the defence of such regulatory routines is merely a symptom of bureaucratic inertia, and when it represents regulatory capture, where the regulated industry gains the upper hand. Bernstein's (1955) analysis of the historical development of US regulatory agencies ends with their becoming increasingly routinized and ultimately compliant to the demands of the target industries.

Besides the gradual growth of influence that industries come to exert over their regulators, relations may also be established between individual bureaucrats and members of the regulated industry. Such relationships are often characterized as corruption, but as Tanzi (1995) points out, they may also be seen as part of the expected norms of behaviour in societies where personalized kinship and group obligations render an idealized Weberian bureaucracy unrealistic. The multiplicity of these ties may raise an additional challenge for regulatory reform. Scaling down the state's regulatory role may tackle some of these problems, but with respect to seed regulation, most nations depend on a relatively small number of seed professionals who have close relationships engendered by common education, group membership or (previous) government employment. A move to 'privatization', on its own, will not necessarily break through this web of privileged access to seed system resources and information.

Political opposition and support for reform

Besides having to contend with the interests of the public bureaucracy, policymakers must also consider the broader political implications of possible regulatory reform. These may be publicly debated and defended, or may be less explicit. Regulation 'is a contested political resource' (Harriss-White, 1996:38).

A common dilemma that agricultural policymakers must face is how to balance the interests of farmers and those of the larger society. Some seed regulation is established to protect national interests in export markets, for instance, and may place rather rigid restrictions on farmers' choices. Canada's Wheat Board defines the types of varieties that farmers can grow in order to maintain the standards for Canada's wheat exports, but Ulrich *et al.* (1987) argue that deregulation would be in farmers' interests. There have been debates about whose interests should be served by agricultural research almost since the beginning of scientific plant breeding. A private plant breeder in Kansas developed a wheat variety, 'Blackhull', in 1917 that farmers found attractive because of its early maturity and drought tolerance, but that millers found to be inferior. The release of this privately developed variety was not subject to regulation, but arguments were heard that are familiar to many variety release committees today.

Kansas enjoys a premium for her wheat in the world's markets, because of the splendid reputation which has been established. It would be very unfortunate for all citizens of the state if this reputation should be lost by the widespread use of a variety unsuited to the trade requirements of a large part of the milling industry. (Salmon, 1927, cited in Flora, 1988:191).

The process of balancing interest-group pressures is expressed in the 'public choice' theories of political economy that see governments maintaining power through the protection of particular interest groups. Bates's (1981) analysis of agricultural policy in Africa is one of the most familiar examples, where he argues that African farmers are paid low prices for their produce in order to control food prices for more politically powerful urban consumers and to protect industrial interests. Farmers simply do not have the political capacity to pressure for changes that are in their interest.

165

One of the most common concerns about seed regulatory reform is the fact that it may challenge the political power of established groups, in particular the state agricultural research and seed production organizations which may enjoy a virtual monopoly in the formal seed sector. This has certainly been the case until recently in a number of African countries. The Kenya Seed Company, for instance, wields considerable influence with politicians, many of whom are farmers, and it has a strong relationship with the Kenya Agricultural Research Institute. Until recently, the company enjoyed a monopoly for maize seed production. Such relationships are not confined to public seed companies, however. In Zimbabwe, the Seed Co-operative, a private company, enjoyed exclusive rights to produce new government varieties until the policy was finally changed in 1995.

Even when private enterprise is present, it may be part of an intricate system of government controls and obligations. Sadowski (1991) uses the term 'crony capitalism' to describe such a system in Egypt, where 'business-men and bureaucrats ally in cabals to seek mutual benefit by influencing the pattern of state intervention in the economy' (ibid.:140). Such examples of seemingly pervasive state control are deceptive, however, and often misrepresent the state's capacity to oversee a transition to more open and participatory regulatory regimes. In many cases Myrdal's (1970) concept of the 'soft state', characterized by an inability to implement or enforce policy change, is relevant. The state uses its power to defend (and to profit from) entrenched interests, but when policy change is forced upon it, often by external pressure, state agencies are incapable of asserting the appropriate authority or eliciting the respect of new participants.

Policy change may see highly restrictive seed regulatory systems collapse like a house of cards (or, more appropriately, certification tags). In the 1960s and 1970s, Mexico had a very rigid (although not particularly effective) seed regulatory system, favouring the national seed company and the crop varieties of the national research service. As internal and external political forces pressed for greater private sector participation in Mexican agriculture, government seed regulation found itself standing on the sidelines. Rather than being in a position to guide the development of a diversifying seed industry and to promote seed enterprises for less commercially oriented farmers (consistent with the populist tradition that motivated the strict seed regulation originally), the national seed regulatory agency Servicio Nacional de Inspección y Certificación de Semillas (SNICS) has become marginalized. Asociación Mexicana de Semilleros, A.C. (ANSAC), an association of large commercial seed companies, was originally formed to lobby for deregulation, and now that this has been accomplished, there is little expectation of much productive collaboration between state regulation and private enterprise. Such 'all-or-nothing' scenarios are likely to be repeated as national seed regulatory systems collapse from internal fiscal exhaustion and the external pressure of privatization dogma that pays little attention to the need for supporting the development of a diverse set of national seed organizations.

International pressure

The fourth set of factors identified by Grindle and Thomas (1991) as influencing policy choice is external donor pressure, which conditions access to aid or loans. This type of external influence often plays a powerful role in the development of state seed sectors and regulatory systems.

The public sector seed systems of many developing countries have benefited from the contributions of aid programmes, but the donors' philosophies and regulatory cultures have often been transferred to the recipient countries. Kenya's seed regulatory procedures have been described as 'a blend of British law and Dutch regulations' (Kimenye and Nyangito, 1996:14), reflecting the country's colonial history and the effects of several projects sponsored by the Netherlands government that strengthened Kenya's seed certification system. Similarly, Thailand's greater reliance on market forces for seed regulation can be explained in part by the influence of several US Agency for International Development (USAID) seed projects, beginning in the mid-1970s (McMullen, 1987:189).

More recently, there have been several cases where donor activities have helped develop innovative seed regulatory systems in countries where government seed production has failed. Bockari-Kugbei (1994) describes a project of Sasakawa Global 2000 that supported the development of small-scale commercial seed producers after the collapse of the Ghana Seed Company. The project provided resources to the Ghana Seed Inspection Unit to perform both regulatory and training functions. Similarly, a project funded by USAID in Bolivia provided a stimulus for private (commercial and NGO) seed production through the development of regional seed boards which replaced an ineffective national seed certification authority (Garay *et al.*, 1988). Such donor projects can provide assistance for the development of imaginative seed regulatory systems adapted to local conditions, but a primary challenge is to ensure that such systems are sustainable when project funding terminates.

The importance of sustainability indicates that donor-led projects for seed regulatory reform must go beyond the slogans of privatization or deregulation and acknowledge the institutional and organizational context of the reform programme. Ostrom (1990:22) is correct in finding that often 'policy prescriptions are themselves no more than metaphors. Both the centralizers and the privatizers frequently advocate oversimplified, idealized institutions'. Pressure for reform from donors and lenders needs to be accompanied by attention to continuing government responsibility. The observation that 'deregulation will not succeed in bringing about greater efficiency unless it is overseen by a capable administration' (Botchwey, 1995:247) is certainly true for the seed sector.

We now turn to a brief review of the implications of reform for several government organizations.

The responsibilities of the state seed sector

Regulatory reform presumes significant changes for various government agencies and institutes included in national seed systems. This section outlines some of the concomitants of regulatory reform for seed policy units, government regulatory agencies, agricultural research and extension and parastatal seed companies.

Seed policy units

Many countries have established national seed boards, councils or committees. For example, the Philippines has a National Seed Industry Council, Nepal has a National Seed Board, and Kenya has a National Seed Regulation Committee. These bodies have responsibilities that may include the management of seed certification and variety release procedures, the establishment of plant variety protection and the design of national seed policy. Such policy units are a step towards effective seed policy, but in many countries it would appear that insufficient resources have been allocated to enable them to fulfil their mandates. The responsibilities that could be assumed by a seed policy unit include the definition of seed regulatory frameworks, the protection of genetic diversity, the provision of information to guide seed system development, the assurance that seed systems address the needs of disadvantaged farmers and the identification of training and technical assistance requirements and opportunities.

Seed policies should provide clear guidelines for the management and expectations of the regulatory system, including a definition of the division of responsibilities for variety development, variety approval and seed quality control. In addition, seed policy should define the terms under which plant variety protection (PVP) is to be established. The PVP system needs to provide sufficient stimulus to the developers of new varieties who seek protection from commercial competitors, without affecting the management of the larger national seed regulatory structure, which protects and encourages the activities of organizations and individuals working with crops and farming systems not subject to the commercial systems that require PVP.

The pressure for PVP should be matched by policies that conserve and enhance the nation's plant genetic diversity (Crucible Group, 1994). Seed policy bodies need to define national strategies for ensuring that crop genetic diversity is adequately preserved, *in-situ* and *ex-situ*, and that it is available for variety development. Policies are needed to reward local communities for their own variety development, without instituting restrictive protection regimes that would further limit the use of genetic diversity (Brush, 1991).

The diversification of national seed systems will require a considerable amount of information about the availability of seed and varieties, the requirements of particular sectors of the farming community and the performance of current seed provision options. Seed policy must be able to stimulate the development and analysis of this information by the appropriate agencies. Some seed system information can be managed by the agricultural census and planning divisions of the Ministry of Agriculture. The extension service can provide further information, and agricultural universities and research institutes should increasingly include assessment of national seed system performance in their work. The challenge for the national seed policy unit is to identify the priorities for information and to encourage and co-ordinate other government bodies to obtain it. One of the primary responsibilities of seed policy analysis is to ensure that the national seed system is meeting the needs of all classes of farmers. This implies the ability to disaggregate data on seed system performance and to take particular responsibility for understanding the seed needs of the most vulnerable members of the farming community.

Seed policy units must also be able to identify needs for technical inputs and training to strengthen the national seed system. This may be directed towards seed producers, farmers, NGO staff or merchants. Widespread participation in seed regulation is an empty slogan if the participants do not have adequate resources and experience. The seed policy unit should be able to stimulate the provision of training by national organizations or attract such training from outside. An additional training need may be the requirement to strengthen the national legal system's capacity to understand and help enforce seed regulation as the seed system becomes more commercial.

There is thus a wide range of responsibilities for national seed policy units, but there are very few that currently have sufficient resources or expertise to meet these challenges. Seed policy units are often dominated by *ex-officio* members who may not have the time, interest or experience to contribute to seed system development; seed policy units would benefit from the participation of more individuals chosen for their commitment rather than their current office (Poey, 1991). They also need to broaden their membership in order to include the types of expertise required for policy analysis, and to establish effective relationships with the commercial and voluntary seed sectors.

Seed regulatory agencies

Part 2 has provided a range of options for seed regulatory reform. The implications for the reorientation of the mandates for government seed certification agencies and variety release authorities have already been outlined. This section provides only a brief review of some of the major conclusions.

Regulatory reform often meets with opposition from entrenched bureaucracies defending their positions and privileges. Seed regulatory reform, however, can be approached with some optimism because the principal challenge is not to eliminate the regulatory bureaucracy but rather to reorient it. In general terms it can be said that state seed regulation needs to become less concerned with policing the government and commercial seed sectors and instead turn its attention to encouraging the diversification of seed enterprises. This diversification involves the concomitant sharing of regulatory responsibilities among the state, seed producers and farmers.

It can be expected that seed certification agencies will spend less time on the day-to-day monitoring of seed production, and will devote increasing attention to strengthening the technical regulatory capacities of the producers themselves, at both the commercial and the community level. The seed certification agency will probably serve as the ultimate authority in regulatory enforcement and will help define appropriate standards, but will play a diminishing role in actual supervision. A strong regulatory capacity is required to bring about this shift in regulatory responsibility. The regulatory agency needs to be able to negotiate the transfer of duties to the commercial sector from a position of technical authority, rather than as the last act of a discarded bureaucracy. Similarly, it needs the capacity to work with emerging small-scale enterprises to develop their technical abilities.

Markets are not a panacea, however, nor can they substitute universally for state regulatory responsibility.

[Markets] create livelihoods but they cannot *ensure* them or limit exploitation . . . They require vast amounts of information to operate effectively, and they need strong regulatory mechanisms rather than participation (where weak, untalented or poorly asseted parties can have but token presence) in order to curb abuse. In market exchange it is not possible *not* to have this ambiguity and complexity (Harriss-White, 1996:40).

While some of the duties traditionally associated with state regulatory agencies are transferred, others require increased attention. As the number of seed producers expands, particularly those that rely on public sector varieties, the certification of foundation seed assumes greater importance. The current neglect of seed inspection and enforcement at point of sale needs to be redressed, in order to contribute to farmer confidence in a growing seed market. In addition, seed certification agencies should be able to make a strong contribution to the collection of data on the performance of the seed sector that can be used for policy analysis.

The future of variety regulation organizations is more problematic. Even within the confines of government agricultural research institutes, the variety release committees need to achieve a wider representation of farmers' interests. If private sector varieties must pass through a variety release authority, there needs to be broad participation from seed producers, merchants and farmer groups. Variety regulation must be the subject of considerable reorganization.

A particularly difficult challenge for state seed regulation is the establishment of PVP. Governments must decide how they will respond to the demands of World Trade Organization membership. In many cases the requirements of variety registration for PVP will imply the development of new technical capacities in the regulatory system. It will be necessary to decide how these capacities are to be financed. In addition, it will be necessary to ensure that whatever PVP system is established for commercial varieties does not overwhelm the capacity to encourage public sector and farmer development and utilization of genetic diversity.

Government agricultural research and extension

Seed regulatory reform also has implications for the direction of state agricultural research and extension. Public plant breeding programmes need to establish an efficient division of labour with the expanding commercial sector. It is sometimes suggested that public sector varietal research should specialize in the 'upstream' tasks of germplasm development, particularly for traits (such as tolerance to drought or low soil fertility) that the private sector finds less attractive, and leave the development of commercial varieties to the private sector. But this is not an adequate definition of public sector plant breeding responsibilities, and there will be many crops and types of farming system that attract commercial interest only slowly or not at all. Similarly, despite the possibility of productive links to commercial seed operations, it is important that public plant breeding not be seduced by the lure of earning royalties for its materials and not become distracted from its obligations to address the varietal needs of the more marginal and less commercial farming areas.

Public plant breeding must become more competitive and demand-driven. It is imperative that public plant breeding organizations do a better job of assessing demands for varietal characteristics and promoting the varieties they produce. This implies better links with local-level organizations that can collaborate in the conduct of plant breeding under representative conditions and in the testing and demonstration of new varieties (see Chapter 10). It also implies better links with seed production enterprises, both commercial and voluntary, that can provide expanded markets for public varieties.

The public extension service can also contribute to seed regulatory reform by helping create awareness of new varieties, providing technical assistance to small-scale seed producers, and helping monitor seed quality at the point of sale. Extension can help organize demonstrations and variety tests that include all of the public, private and farmer varieties that are relevant to a particular cropping system. There are examples from Nepal and elsewhere in which the extension service has played a role in training small-scale seed producers and helping with supervisory tasks normally associated with the certification agency. One of the problems that regulatory agencies face in monitoring the quality and movement of seed provided by local merchants is the difficulty of dispersing agents to distant communities; arrangements might be made with local extension agents to help provide samples and information.

Parastatal seed companies

The future of parastatal seed companies will depend on several factors. In a number of cases parastatal companies have already been closed, either because the government could no longer afford to support their losses or because private seed companies have been able to offer a superior service. But there are many situations where demand for seed will not be sufficient to attract commercial enterprise, yet seed will need to be available. In these cases, government seed production needs to become more efficient (perhaps through decentralization and more dependence on contract growers) or the government funds previously destined to support an inefficient parastatal should instead be used to establish a tendering process for private enterprise to provide seed for designated areas.

To the extent that state seed companies remain in business, a new relationship will have to be established with the regulatory agencies. The parastatal should be treated like any other seed company, and it should be expected to develop internal quality-control mechanisms similar to those of private seed companies.

Summary

The implementation of seed regulatory reform requires both institutional and organizational change. Major responsibility for guiding this change rests with the state, but it is not simply a question of establishing new policies or changing laws. It is a superficial view of regulatory reform that sees general policy declarations, such as those associated with movements towards 'privatization' or 'deregulation', as sufficient to bring about fundamental change in regulatory frameworks, or in seed system development.

Regulatory reform takes place within an institutional environment that determines the direction and tenor of change. Government policy can help make the institutional environment conducive to the diversification of the national seed system and supportive of broad-based participation in the management of seed regulation. This can be done by fostering the development of both 'exit' and 'voice' within the national seed system; efficient markets encourage the entry of diverse commercial enterprises and provide an effective interchange of information between buyer and seller; the growth of civil society allows farmers to participate in the direction of public sector agricultural research, to form associations for

172

local agricultural development and to have access to the national legal system.

Regulatory change is also conditioned by the traditions, expectations and rules that contribute to a national regulatory culture. Nations differ in their attitudes to regulation, a general trend towards diversification of the seed system and broad participation in regulatory decisions will nevertheless manifest itself in a variety of forms. There is no simple blue-print for the management of regulatory reform.

The implementation of seed regulatory reform also requires policy change that develops the capacities of organizations within the national seed sector. Policy change is a complex process, and policymakers are guided by technical information, bureaucratic considerations, political pressure and the interests of international donors and lenders. Part 2 of this book has outlined the technical justifications for seed regulatory reform. The position of the established bureaucracy must also be considered in any policy change; in the case of seed regulatory reform the principal challenge is to redirect the skills and experience of the seed regulatory bureaucracy away from a restrictive, policing strategy towards an enabling philosophy that supports wider participation in regulatory responsibility. The political pressures that affect the direction of regulatory change will vary from country to country, but a common theme is the necessity to remove any unfair protection afforded to state agricultural research or seed production entities. Finally, policymakers will also be influenced by the pressures of international donors regarding regulatory reform; it is essential that donor conditionality is characterized by a long-term commitment to help build the institutional and organizational environment that supports diverse and equitable seed systems.

Government organizations will continue to be key players in the development of the seed system. Seed policy units need to be strengthened and must attract members who are committed to building strong national capacity. Seed certification institutions will play a leading role in helping redistribute regulatory responsibility throughout the seed system. And national agricultural research, extension and seed production organizations must redefine their roles and comparative advantages *vis-à-vis* expanding capacity in the commercial and voluntary sectors.

The following four chapters examine opportunities for innovation led by commercial and voluntary organizations. They demonstrate the rich variety of organizational possibilities for promoting and supporting seed regulatory reform.

8 Private commercial varieties and seeds: opportunities and obstacles

DAVID GISSELQUIST

Introduction

The Bangladesh experience

DURING APRIL AND MAY 1996, more than half the districts of Bangladesh were visited as part of the author's research to evaluate the impact of the 1988–90 regulatory reforms regarding agricultural inputs. During these years, officials in the Ministry of Agriculture eased barriers to private trade in seeds, fertilizers, irrigation equipment and power tillers. For seeds, the key reform was to allow private companies to introduce new cultivars without prior government tests or approval.

In 1990, the designers of seed reforms in Bangladesh allowed government scientists in the national agricultural research system (NARS) to limit (via an approved list) permitted cultivars for five crops: rice, wheat, jute, sugar-cane and potatoes. This was done in order to reduce opposition to seed reform, since most NARS scientists worked on these five crops. Although arguments circulated at the time claiming that the production of major crops could be damaged if farmers nation-wide adopted poor or disease-susceptible varieties, they were not seriously debated, given the reluctance of public sector scientists to cede control over varieties.

Six years after the reforms, throughout large regions of the country, 20–40-hectare blocks of land (amalgamating plots from many small farms) were found to be planted to hybrid maize—which had been illegal prior to 1990. Following the seed reforms, two NGOs, the Grameen Krishi Foundation and the Bangladesh Rural Advancement Committee (BRAC), working with a private seed company, have taken initiatives to promote hybrid maize. In 1995/6, these two NGOs and independent private farmers bought a total of 70 tons of hybrid maize seed, which was imported by one of the larger local private seed companies. Hybrid sunflower was also found, another crop which had been illegal prior to the reform; in 1995/6, farmers planted 600 hectares with three tonnes of imported hybrid seed. Similarly, all sweetcorn seed (OPV and hybrid) was illegal prior to the reform; in the 1990s, however, growing sweetcorn for foreigners in Dhaka has become a lucrative business for a modest number of small farmers with market connections. In short, responding to opportunities created by regulatory reforms, a number of parties, including private seed companies, private agricultural product processing companies, NGOs and vegetable dealers have taken the initiative to introduce new cultivars for vegetable and field crops.

With regard to the five crops for which government retained the authority to limit permitted cultivars, it was found that a majority of jute farmers are planting seed of illegal Indian varieties, even in districts far from the border with India. Most often the seed is smuggled in from India, though some farmers multiply seed of Indian varieties in Bangladesh. The Indian jute varieties in question are public, but the seed is multiplied and distributed in India through private companies and smuggled into Bangladesh in packages prepared by private companies for the Indian market. A number of illegal Indian rice varieties were also found dominating irrigated rice fields in the border districts.

The widespread planting of illegal seed of unlisted varieties is clear evidence that government officials who retain authority to list cultivars for the five crops still do not respect farmer opinion. If the National Seed Board would simply allow popular and proven Indian varieties of jute and rice, the legitimate seed trade could expand into existing (illegal) seed markets and also extend Indian jute and rice varieties to more farmers in Bangladesh. Not only would this help farmers, it would also strengthen the seed industry. The varieties in question have been released by public institutions in India, but private companies could be expected to handle the seed production and sale in Bangladesh. They might want to buy breeder or foundation seed, but they could probably get along without any formal co-operation from the Indian government. The companies would be satisfying existing commercial markets for jute seed; in the case of rice, farmers can be expected to pay a small premium over and above the cost of farmer-saved seed for commercial seed of the new varieties.

Potatoes are another of the five crops with limited permitted varieties. A number of private seed companies have tested new cultivars, but the slowness of government approvals for many of these new cultivars delays sale of seed and technology transfer. One government scientist remarked that farmers already have two good varieties in Diamont and Cardinal (both old varieties, the production of which has been abandoned in the Netherlands other than to serve south Asian markets), so why do they need more?

One possible strategy to improve the access of Bangladeshi farmers to improved cultivars for the five crops excluded from the 1990s seed reforms is to ask government scientists to be more responsive and to pay more attention to farmer assessment of cultivars. This would entail a significant change in attitude on the part of many government agricultural scientists, who favour varieties released by Bangladeshi public sector research organizations and who support the current regulations that prohibit seed traders from giving farmers access to seeds of other popular varieties. Another strategy is to eliminate the authority of government scientists to control the introduction of new cultivars for these remaining crops. (The government would retain authority to limit cultivars on the grounds of environment and public health concerns, but not of performance.)

The regulatory issues

In Bangladesh, as in other developing countries, seed regulations can have an impact on the emergence and operations of a modern seed industry (comprising both public and private components) that is able to improve farmer access to the latest and best technology from public and private research throughout the world. Not only new cultivars but also other new agricultural technology can be embodied in seeds for sale to farmers. With a little investment in local trials, private companies can often introduce public or private cultivars from foreign countries that offer advantages over locally bred or traditional cultivars. Depending on the size of the potential market and on other factors, private companies (as well as public agencies) may breed for a specific country, though actual crossing may not be done in that country.

However, government regulations often discourage private seed companies from contributing to agricultural development through the sale of quality seed of established cultivars as well as through the introduction of new cultivars and other technology transfer. Here we discuss three of the major regulatory issues at stake: regulations governing the introduction of new cultivars, seed certification and seed company registration.

New cultivars

Regulations governing introduction of new varieties

How radical or dangerous is the proposal for governments to allow companies to introduce new cultivars without prior government performance testing and approval? First, let us look at what some developed and developing countries are doing in this regard. There are three basic patterns:

○ *No cultivar lists (voluntary cultivar registration).* In the US, India and many other countries, governments allow private companies to sell the seed of cultivars that have not been officially recognized, registered or tested. In these countries, companies may register a new cultivar if they wish, but they can sell the seed without registration. (This approach also allows companies to sell the seed of landraces, which may be too genetically diverse to qualify as varieties.)

○ *Multi-country cultivar lists (compulsory cultivar registration, but with automatic registration for cultivars registered in other countries).* This is the pattern practised in the European Union (for most seed). Before selling seeds in an EU country, a company must submit samples to the government for testing to establish that the seed does represent a cultivar (DUS tests for distinctiveness, uniformity and stability across generations) and that the cultivar performs well (VCU tests regarding value for cultivation and use). Tests in any EU country take two years. However, as noted in Chapter 5, once a cultivar has been accepted in any one EU country, within months it goes into an EU Common Catalogue, after which seed can be sold in any country throughout the EU without any further testing. (The EU requires that someone, normally a seed company, pays an annual maintenance fee for each cultivar listed; this discourages the registration of public varieties, which anyone can produce and market, and tends to leave the market to proprietary varieties.)

o *Single-country cultivar lists (compulsory cultivar registration based on in-country performance tests, without any provision for automatic registration)*. Some developed and many developing countries maintain single-country lists of permitted cultivars, and insist on government review of in-country performance tests before allowing seed of any new cultivar to be sold. Countries that follow this practice for at least some major crops include: Australia, Canada, Ghana, Egypt, Indonesia, Nigeria, Sri Lanka and many others.

Clearly, farmers in many developing countries have very poor access to the flow of new seed technology in world markets. Many of the developing countries with single-country lists of permitted cultivars are relatively small countries with only limited capacity in government research systems to breed or even to review cultivars, so that lists of authorized cultivars are very short, and new entries are limited.

Since the US and EU governments either have no cultivar lists or maintain multi-country lists, most farmers in developed countries have access to seeds of new cultivars without prior approval from their national governments. A significant proportion of farmers in developing countries (including farmers in India, Mexico, Argentina and Chile) are also able to use new cultivars without prior government approval. However, in many developing countries, governments still severely limit farmer access to improved cultivars.

Impact of limiting private introduction of new cultivars

Developing countries that limit the private introduction of new varieties leave their farmers with a narrow choice of improved cultivars, often no more than 5–10 for major crops and fewer for minor crops, and many of these approved cultivars are relatively old or unattractive to farmers. In contrast, the OECD's *List of Cultivars Eligible for Certification* added more than 400 new cultivars for maize and 100 new cultivars each for sugarbeet, wheat and sunflower in 1993 alone. Even in a relatively small country, farmers can use multiple improved cultivars for each crop for different planting dates, cropping patterns, soils, etc.

When countries enforce compulsory variety registration, and in particular when they maintain single-country lists of authorized cultivars, new cultivars face barriers to entry that commonly include: 1–6 or more years of multi-locational tests by government agencies; fees for testing; and evaluation of test results by government-run committees. Aside from the time and expense involved, the process is often not conducted objectively, so that managers of private seed companies fear that cultivars submitted will not be honestly evaluated. Even if the process works as planned, objective criteria for evaluating new cultivars may be designed so as not to approve those that farmers would prefer (for example, short-duration varieties whose yields may not be high enough to meet the criteria for registration).

Many seed companies build up their businesses around the introduction of improved cultivars (either from own-breeding or testing of cultivars from other public or private breeding programmes). When a government refuses to allow the introduction of new cultivars, many companies are unwilling to enter the market; they do not want to compete in a limited national market with other companies producing the same (often inferior) cultivars from a short list of government-approved cultivars.

The importance of new cultivars for private seed companies has major implications for policy-based strategies to encourage the emergence of private seed industries in developing countries. Governments that allow companies to introduce new cultivars are more successful in attracting new companies. Moreover, the same strategy promotes agricultural growth: governments that allow companies to introduce new cultivars give farmers better access to new seed technology from public and private foreign and national research.

A note on small countries and minor crops

Seed companies weigh the costs of overcoming regulatory barriers against potential profits. This means that larger countries can get away with more onerous regulations without discouraging the development of the private seed industry whereas smaller countries with smaller markets need to be relatively open to attract companies, private cultivars and other private seed technology.

A similar argument holds for minor crops. For example, in Zambia (with a population of 10 million) annual sales of hybrid seed for maize (a major crop) can be estimated at US$10 million, much more than annual sales of seed for wheat (a secondary field crop), which can be estimated at $250 000. Companies that expect to get 5 per cent of the market for 10 years with a new cultivar would anticipate cumulative gross sales of $5m for a maize cultivar but only $125 000 for a wheat cultivar. Companies must balance expenditures for seed production, interest, product development *and* overcoming regulatory barriers against these gross revenues.

Clearly, regulatory barriers can loom larger for crops with smaller markets. Hence, seed regulatory reforms are of particular importance for smaller countries and minor crops.

Risk with introduction of new varieties

The most common argument in favour of prior government testing and approval of new varieties is that farmers might lose from the introduction of a variety that does not perform well. There are a number of responses to such arguments, including the following:

o *The risks are not all on one side.* With the introduction of a new cultivar, there is the risk that some farmers will lose if the cultivar does not perform as well as familiar cultivars. On the other hand, regulations that delay or do not allow the introduction of new cultivars risk gains forgone when farmers are not able to realize their higher yields and profits attainable with new cultivars. The forgone gains can be substantial: in Turkey, for example, the 1980s seed reforms brought the introduction of new hybrid maize cultivars which boosted annual farmer incomes by almost $100m; these gains would have been forgone (lost or delayed) without the seed reform. Six subsidiaries of foreign firms have about 50 per cent of the market, and another six local companies have the remaining 50 per cent. Turkey is a significant net exporter of hybrid maize seed (Pray and Gisselquist, forthcoming).

o *Risks are limited to those who choose to plant seeds; there are no externalities to worry about.* In market economies, the standard practice for most sectors (for example, computers, consumer electronics and transport equipment) is for governments to allow private companies and consumers to manage the technology transfer so long as externalities (impacts on others) are not an issue. Companies adopt new technology (from their own research or acquired by contract from other companies), incorporate it into consumer goods, and offer it to customers. Governments that allow seed companies and farmers to introduce new cultivars are extending these common practices to seed markets, allowing the market to decide which technology (cultivars) works best.

o *Risks with new cultivars are familiar to farmers, and they are able to control and limit those risks.* Even without the introduction of any new cultivars, farmers deciding what to plant in any particular field have many choices to make: what crop to plant; what particular cultivar to plant among dozens of familiar (traditional and improved) cultivars; when to plant; what and how much fertilizer to apply, etc. Giving a farmer another improved cultivar adds to an already existing list of options, and does not change the fact that farmers have to make choices in the face of some risk or other. Before trying out a new cultivar, farmers can seek information from demonstrations, neighbours' fields and elsewhere, and they can limit their level of risk by the proportion of planted area put under a new cultivar. Those who are more risk-averse can avoid new cultivars altogether until they are well established in a community. Since farmers can adequately protect themselves from the

179

risks associated with new cultivars, governments can leave farmers to deal with these risks.

○ *Reducing the risk of poor performance in new cultivars is part of normal operations for seed companies.* In the normal course of operations, seed companies continuously introduce new cultivars as part of their efforts to increase their market share and boost seed sales. Companies typically identify promising cultivars from breeding or testing programmes, then introduce them to farmers over a period of years through an expanding series of on-farm trials and demonstrations. These trials and demonstrations are essential for seed companies to be able to estimate farmer interest and future sales, and to allow them to match seed production with demand. In other words, farmer participation in cultivar trials is business as usual for private seed companies. Cases of private companies selling inappropriate cultivars usually involve government agencies or NGOs as buyers. For example, around 1990 the Bangladesh Agricultural Development Corporation, a parastatal, bought sweetcorn seed that did not germinate, from a private company in Thailand. There are also numerous cases of NGOs importing inappropriate seed for distribution during emergencies (ODI Seeds and Biodiversity Programme, 1996). Such cases illustrate poor judgement on the part of governments and other non-commercial agencies, and undermine the arguments in favour of governments controlling the cultivars allowed in trade.

○ *In poorer developing countries, risks with new private cultivars are often limited by the small proportion of planted seed provided by private companies.* Some agricultural development experts favour cultivar tests and lists for poorer developing countries where seed companies and legal systems are not yet well developed. However, these are also situations where the risks are limited by the size of the private seed industry. In many countries in sub-Saharan Africa, for example, private seed companies provide seed for no more than 0–3 per cent of the planted area; often trade is limited to vegetable seeds. The small volume and value of the seed trade limits the potential damage that any seed company could cause by introducing an inappropriate new cultivar. Also, if the legal system is weak, the government's ability to enforce all aspects of seed performance is equally weakened, so that is not a reason for governments to limit private varieties. When a government cannot enforce basic commercial law, such as truthful labelling at the retail level, then any other regulation, short of suppressing private trade, is essentially ineffective, so that weak supervision is not an excuse for more regulation. Countries should not use the fact that the private seed sector is undeveloped as an excuse for maintaining the very rules that are responsible for this lack of development.

Seed certification and other seed quality regulations

Seed certification is the assertion by an agency that seed is from the cultivar it is claimed to be. Many governments require certification for the commercial seed of certain crops. Aside from certification, some governments require that samples of all commercial seed be tested in government (or government-approved) laboratories to ensure that the seed meets specific quality standards (for example, for germination and purity). Compulsory testing may be required as part of the certification process and may also be required for one or more non-certified classes of seed.

In some countries, such as the US and India, seed certification and testing are available but voluntary. In such situations, governments commonly recognize a class of truthfully labelled seed, requiring that seed packages be labelled with information about quality, then enforcing whatever claims seed companies make in their labels.

When and how do these quality regulations interfere with the development of a competitive private seed industry? The following are some of the main issues.

○ *Compulsory seed certification entails compulsory cultivar registration.* For seed to be certified (i.e. guaranteed to be from a particular cultivar) that cultivar must first be registered. Hence, compulsory seed certification entails compulsory cultivar registration, which often implies serious obstacles to the introduction of private cultivars, as discussed in the previous section.

○ *Compulsory seed certification and testing raise seed production costs.* When inspectors must go to seed plots or seeds to government laboratories, production costs are increased. Payments for certification and testing may be legitimate travel and testing expenses, but sometimes informal payments are also demanded and paid. For hybrid seeds, companies can boost prices (within reason) to farmers who do not have the option of retaining their own seed. However, for seeds of self-pollinated or OPV crops, seed from private companies competes with seed moving through informal trade and farmer-saved seed. At the limit, higher seed costs from compulsory seed certification and/or testing block the emergence of private commercial (formal) seed supply for relatively low-value seed for crops such as wheat, groundnut, millet, etc. When that happens, farmers are left with their own retained seed, seed available through informal trade or sometimes subsidized seed from parastatals. Arguments about how much value the certification process adds to seed can be left to the market. When certification is voluntary, farmers will buy certified seed if the added value is greater than the added cost; when certification is compulsory, the added cost can exceed the added value, and market mechanisms are not available for farmers to indicate that that is the case.

181

o *Compulsory certification and seed testing can be barriers to entry for new seed companies.* Large, established seed companies have an advantage over small, new companies in ease of contact with government officials, including not only officials in seed certifying agencies but also others in high office with influence over these agencies. For example, large companies are likely to have offices in the major cities where seed certifying and testing staff are stationed, whereas anyone hoping to launch a new seed company from a remote rural location would face greater expense in communicating with seed certifying agencies.

The risks to farmers from governments allowing private companies to sell truthfully labelled seed (i.e. seed that is not certified or tested in government laboratories) are similar in some respects to the risks from the private introduction of new varieties and arguments for and against compulsory seed certification are similar to arguments for and against compulsory cultivar registration, as discussed in the previous section.

Some people may argue that when countries have weak legal systems, governments are not able to enforce truthful labelling, so that compulsory certification and testing are required to ensure quality seed. However, if governments are not able to enforce truthful labelling, there is also no way to ensure that seeds labelled as certified or tested have in fact been properly inspected. Hence, a weak legal system is no excuse for excessive seed regulation.

Also, let us consider the risks with some of the other goods and services that private sectors in developed and developing countries supply with relatively little government intervention to ensure their quality. Private mechanics fix brakes on buses and trucks, where failure could kill in seconds; governments often license mechanics or garages, but generally do not review actual repairs. Private food stalls prepare and sell food, which could kill if it is unclean or adulterated; governments commonly license premises but neither approve recipes nor inspect all prepared food. In contrast, farmers can easily determine some aspects of seed quality (for example, from physical appearance and simple germination tests), and failure in quality seldom leads to more than partial loss of income because of using mixed varieties. There are risks with truthfully labelled seeds; but there are also risks with certified and tested seeds. Furthermore, these risks are significantly less than many other risks that governments leave to markets to control.

Finally, relaxing regulations to favour the development of competitive private seed industries may be the best way to ensure good seed quality. With many companies to choose from, farmers can be expected to patronize those with reputations for quality. Companies competing for market shares do not rely on government certification and testing, but rather make their own checks to ensure that their reputations are not damaged by poor seed quality.

182

Registration of seed companies

Many governments regulate the registration of seed companies in a way that limits entry and competition. Regulations can limit entry by:

○ setting objective conditions that are expensive to meet (e.g. ownership of land or equipment, employment of staff with formal degrees); or
○ leaving officials with authority to make subjective judgements about whether or not to allow a prospective company to enter the business.

On the other hand, regulations can favour entry by setting minimal objective criteria for registering new seed companies and by giving legal assurances that any prospective company meeting these objective criteria will be registered.

Whether or not a seed company is able to meet quality standards in the market is the real issue. When a company is able to satisfy truthful labelling regulations for seeds in retail markets, it clearly has adequate capability as a seed company. Beyond its performance in the market, other conditions about ownership of land or laboratories can be ignored. As Deng has said, it makes no difference what colour the cat, so long as it catches mice.

A country with a healthy private seed industry has a variety of seed companies specializing and competing in different sectors of the industry. Large research-based companies, often with formal international links, may dominate production for the hybrids of field crops. Smaller local companies, with lower overheads, can have an advantage in the production of seeds for OPVs and self-pollinated varieties. Some companies may specialize in vegetable seed production or trade. In Turkey, for example, after the seed reforms of the early 1980s, the seed industry expanded from fewer than five companies to more than 75 in the early 1990s; for hybrid maize and sunflower, subsidiaries of multinationals and large domestic companies dominate; for wheat, several larger private domestic companies compete with parastatal sales; other multinational and domestic companies specialize in potatoes, other vegetables and other crops. Healthy competition in a dynamic private seed industry entails the steady entry and exit of companies.

Priorities for seed regulatory reform

Seed regulatory reforms that allow greater scope for private initiative are the natural elements of strategies to support crop diversification, horticultural exports, homestead gardening and social forestry. Policymakers have many opportunities for strengthening national seed systems by means of greater reliance on the private sector.

Reforms often focus on privatizing a seed parastatal, but this does not give farmers access to any new cultivars (though it may save the government

183

money). Indeed, privatizing a parastatal may not even ensure private competition if the government continues to limit the private introduction of new cultivars or the registration of new private seed companies. This is not an argument against privatizing seed parastatals, but rather an argument for prioritizing seed reforms, with the primary emphasis on: (a) easing regulations restricting the private introduction of new cultivars; (b) making seed certification and testing voluntary; and (c) removing barriers to entry for new private seed companies. With these regulatory reforms, private companies can enter and compete with seed parastatals. Private companies have so many advantages that they can be expected to dominate many seed markets, even when parastatals offer subsidized seed. Parastatals in developing countries seldom supply more than 5–10 per cent of planted seed. Also, parastatal seed sales are often concentrated in markets for relatively low-value seed of OPV or self-pollinated crops, presenting little or no competition to private companies in markets for high-value hybrid seeds for vegetables and field crops. A private seed industry that begins with hybrids for vegetables and field crops can expand into OPVs over time, though different companies may be involved. Governments that allow private companies to operate and reduce parastatal subsidies on OPV seeds can allow seed markets to guide the pace and direction of parastatal reforms.

Government scientists in NARS often oppose regulatory reforms allowing private companies to introduce new cultivars. The opposition may be motivated by fears that private companies will take away the *raison d'être* for public research. This is a gross confusion and misunderstanding of the situation. Allowing private companies to introduce new cultivars adds openness and competition to national research systems, creating conditions that could lead to improvements in NARS performance over time. Along this same line of reasoning, politicians and senior officials making decisions about how much to allocate to NARS can be advised that private research is no substitute for public agricultural research in many situations, and that seed regulatory reforms are consistent with continued funding for NARS.

9 The impact of intellectual property protection on seed supply

JEROEN VAN WIJK

Introduction

INTELLECTUAL PROPERTY PROTECTION used to be a little-known legal discipline, handled only by specialized lawyers and patent offices. It is only in the past two decades that interest in patents, copyrights and plant breeders' rights has increased. Fundamental technological innovations in the area of informatics and biotechnology have speeded up technological development. The world is embarking on a new techno-economic paradigm in which 'knowledge', or, in more general terms, 'information', is the main factor of production (Freeman, 1988). As a consequence of this change, the industrial sectors with the most promising future in the leading OECD countries differ from those of the past. Rather than relying on cars, steel and grain, which are increasingly produced elsewhere, the technological lead of OECD countries is shifting to products such as computer technology, audio-visual entertainment and seeds of (often genetically engineered) plant varieties. For these information-intensive products, the traditional strategies for the protection of a company's interests or of national competitiveness have become insufficient. Severe international technological competition, the need to expand exports and the relative ease with which information can be copied, have resulted in legal protection of innovations becoming a top priority for OECD countries in international trade negotiations.

The major recent event in the area of intellectual property has been the agreement on Trade-Related Intellectual Property Rights (TRIPs), which has been signed by over 140 countries as a part of the new General Agreement on Tariffs and Trade (GATT, 1994). The TRIPs agreement, for the first time in history, obliges member states to provide the same minimum level of protection of intellectual property. With this obligation, the TRIPs agreement has introduced a change in the international system of intellectual property protection. Until now, the main existing conventions in this area, such as the Paris Convention for the Protection of Industrial Property and the Berne Convention for the Protection of Literary and Artistic Works, have been based on the so-called principle of 'national treatment', which means that the protection of the intellectual property of foreigners must at least be equal to the protection provided for the intellectual property of nationals. The 'national treatment' principle allowed countries considerable room for manœuvre in framing legislation for intellectual property rights (IPR), and resulted in a wide variation in the level of protection among countries. In developing countries in particular, protection of intellectual property has been much weaker than in OECD countries. Specific products, such as medicines, plant varieties and many innovations in information and biotechnology, were often not protectable; other products were protected only for a relatively short period of time; or the protection was, in practice, not enforceable (van Wijk and Junne, 1993). The TRIPs agreement has eliminated the principle of national treatment and considerably narrowed the room for manœuvre in national policy. With respect to biological material, the agreement obliges each member country to provide for patent protection of all types of plant material, except for plant varieties, which must be protected either by patents or by an 'effective *sui generis* system'.[1] The latter refers to the system of plant variety protection (PVP) or plant breeders' rights (PBR).[2]

The impact of intellectual property protection on the diffusion of plant varieties and seeds[3] in developing countries is the focus of this chapter. In view of the forceful attempts on the part of the OECD countries to conclude the TRIPs agreement, it can be assumed that the strengthened protection for planting material in developing countries increases the opportunities of the world's main biotechnology and seed companies to control the diffusion of their innovations. What will be the consequences for developing countries? Will IPR legislation result in better varieties becoming available on the market? Will it encourage local plant breeding or will it predominantly strengthen the market position of foreign seed companies? Will the diffusion of seeds and new varieties become restricted?

The chapter first provides an overview of intellectual property protection of planting material, with the focus on Latin America, because it is there that developing country experience with IPR is most advanced. The role of intellectual property protection on investment in plant breeding is then examined. The third section focuses on the functions of seed saving, and on the extent to which this form of seed supply is restricted by the introduction of plant variety protection. In the fourth section, some other legal mechanisms which restrict on-farm seed saving are briefly discussed. The final section contains some concluding comments.

1 At the time when the Uruguay Round began, in 1986, piracy of plant varieties was not considered to pose a serious trade problem that required negotiations in the GATT. Plant breeders' rights, as such, were therefore never formally included as a topic for negotiation. Consequently, the TRIPs agreement could only refer in general terms to a *sui generis* ('of its own kind') system for plant variety protection, leaving considerable flexibility for the definition of acceptable protection mechanisms.
2 The meanings of PVP and PBR are essentially the same and the two terms will be used interchangeably here.
3 In this chapter the term 'seeds' is broadly defined as all living materials used to plant a crop, including dry seeds, cuttings or vegetative parts.

Intellectual property rights for planting material in Latin America

Most Latin American countries have introduced plant variety protection (PVP) legislation or are considering its introduction (see Table 9.1). This development is in part a response to foreign pressure from subsidiaries of foreign seed companies which are demanding protection of their varieties and breeding lines before they will agree to enter the Latin American seed markets, and from foreign governments which want to see an overall strengthening of IPR protection in Latin America. Moreover, the World Trade Organization, under the TRIPs agreement, obliges all member countries to provide for legal protection of plant varieties. There is, however, also political pressure from domestic seed companies who wish to protect their own plant varieties, or domestic cultivators of fruit and ornamental plants who are under pressure from foreign breeders to improve legal protection in order to get better access to foreign breeding lines and varieties. Furthermore, in several countries the public agricultural research centres have been advocating PVP, because they see it as a way of acquiring additional income to compensate for budget cuts (Jaffé and van Wijk, 1995:30).

A PVP system has been in operation in Argentina, Chile and Uruguay for some time, but only in Argentina has it been effectively enforced. PBR

Table 9.1 *Plant Variety Protection in 11 Latin American Countries (situation May 1996)*

Country	Adoption and regulation	Start of effective enforcement of law	Accession to UPOV
Andean Pact countries (Colombia, Venezuela, Ecuador, Bolivia and Peru)	1993	In process	Colombia 1996 Other countries unknown
Argentina	1973/78	1990	1994
Brazil	PVP law in drafting process		Unknown
Chile	1977; new law in 1994	1994	1995
Costa Rica	PVP law in drafting process		Unknown
Mexico	PVP law in drafting process		Unknown
Paraguay	PVP law in drafting process		Unknown
Uruguay	1984/1987	1994	1994

Table 2   *Protection of Plant Material under Patent Law in Nine Latin American Countries* (situation 1996)

Argentina	The 1996 patent law excludes plant varieties from protection.
Brazil	The 1996 patent law refers only indirectly to plants. (Parts of) living material as found in nature, including their genome, are not patentable, even if they are 'isolated from nature'. On the other hand, all transgenic micro-organisms, including those 'auto-reproductive organisms' derived from plants and animals, isolated in laboratories, are patentable.
Chile	The 1991 patent law excludes from protection plant varieties and animal races.
Andean Pact countries	The common patent regime for Andean Pact (Decision 344, 1993) excludes from protection (among other things): a. inventions which are evidentially contrary to the health and life of persons or animals, the preservation of plants, or the preservation of the environment; b. animal species and races and essential biological procedures to obtain them.
Mexico	The 1991 patent law, amended in 1994, excludes from protection (among other things): a. essential biological processes for production, reproduction and propagation of plants and animals; b. biological and genetic material as found in nature; c. plant varieties and animal races.
Uruguay	The patent law of 1941 does not explicitly exclude plant material from protection. It is, however, not possible to patent such material because plant varieties of all genera and species can be protected under PVP legislation.

Sources: De Alencar and van Ree, 1996; Jaffé and van Wijk, 1995; Bureau of National Affairs International, 1996

are private property rights, and it is up to the individual rightholder to enforce and exercise their rights, i.e. to control the multiplication of their varieties and to collect royalties. It was not until 1990, when the Argentinian seed firms started to exercise their breeders' rights collectively, that PBR became an effective mechanism for protection against unauthorized multiplication and distribution of seed (Gutiérrez, 1996).

Many Latin American countries are also considering patent protection for planting material. The scope of patent protection is much wider than that of PVP. For example, patents protect plant-related inventions, while PVP only protects plant varieties; under PVP breeders may freely use a protected variety for further breeding, while under the patent system such use requires the authorization of the patentee.

There are basically two patent traditions in the world related to planting material. The US patent law does not exclude such material, while the European Patent Convention does. The latter tradition is followed by Argentina, Chile, Mexico and Uruguay, whose laws explicitly exclude plant varieties from protection (see Table 9.2). The five Andean Pact countries follow the American legislation and do not exclude plant varieties. No varieties have so far been patented, however. The Patent Office in Colombia says that patenting varieties is not being considered. The Mexican patent law of 1991 created an opportunity to protect plant varieties, but this provision was never instituted and was later repealed. Planting material, other than varieties, seems to be patentable in at least seven Latin American countries. It is excluded in Uruguay and possibly also in Brazil.

Plant variety protection and innovation

Whether or not intellectual property protection is a crucial determinant for innovation is still uncertain. The theory of intellectual property protection is fragmented and provides no robust answer to the question of the appropriate or optimal level of protection under various sets of real world circumstances, according to a literature survey carried out by the World Bank several years ago. In the same survey it was concluded, however, that market incentives alone tend to lead to under-investment in research and development (R&D) (Primo Braga, 1990:32). In other words, some state intervention is needed to increase investment in R&D to a desirable level. The state has several options for supporting innovation, among them the granting of intellectual property rights. What is of interest here is whether IPR legislation stimulates innovation in plant breeding.

Patents and PBR enable holders to prevent unauthorized commercial use of the protected innovation. These rights have an effect on innovation because they serve two basic functions: they increase imitation costs and time; and they define ownership and thereby enable diffusion of the innovation.

(a) Increase of imitation costs and time. One of the reasons for giving the innovator a temporary monopoly on the exploitation of his invention is to protect him against imitators, who may be able to produce the original innovation at lower cost and in a shorter period of time. The effect of patents and PBR is to increase the costs and time of imitation. As potential competitors are not allowed to copy the protected process or product without the innovator's permission, they must either obtain a licence to do so or invent an alternative process or product themselves. The innovator will naturally try to raise the highest possible barriers to imitation: some biotechnological companies have filed for patents with claims that are extremely wide in scope.[4] This also explains the introduction of the principle

4 See, for example, the patents granted to the firm Agracetus on all transgenic cotton and all transgenic soya bean in 'Sweeping Patents Put Biotech Companies on the Warpath' (Science, 5 May 1995; RAFI, 1995).

of essential derivation in PVP.[5] The higher the imitating costs and the longer the imitation time, the better are the prospects for the innovator to recoup his investment.

(b) Defining ownership enables diffusion of innovations. When an innovator is awarded a patent or a PBR, the innovation is considered to be his intellectual property. The right of exclusive exploitation of the innovation, combined with opportunities to enforce that right, make it less necessary for the innovator to keep the innovation secret. The formal recognition of his intellectual property opens the way for the diffusion of the invention through licensing. Firms that lack the capacity to scale-up or to market their innovation, or firms which do not want to enter the market themselves, may opt for licensing out their technology instead of supplying the market with the final product. This is precisely one of the reasons for developing countries to introduce patents and PVP. They hope that protection of intellectual property will increase the transfer of foreign plant varieties and other plant material.

The question is whether the legal mechanisms to increase imitation costs and time, and the assignment of PVP to plant breeders, do indeed stimulate innovation in plant breeding. Because the practice of plant patenting is of recent origin, it is only possible to explore answers with respect to the effects of PBR. Even in this area, the information is meagre: only a small number of studies have been carried out in the US and in Argentina.

In the US plant varieties can be protected under two systems: the Plant Patent Act (PPA) (1930) which protects asexually reproduced plants other than tuber-propagated plants, and the Plant Variety Protection Act (PVPA) (1970) which protects sexually reproduced plants. The effects of both acts on innovation have been limited. The PPA had little impact on private investment in fruit breeding because the Act only protects against competition from exact copies of the protected variety (this means that very close substitutes of the protected variety can be commercialized), and because enforcement costs are high (Stallman and Schmidt, 1987). The effect of the PVPA on R&D in breeding has also been limited, despite the claims of the seed industry. The PVPA has stimulated the development of new varieties of a few crops, such as wheat and soya bean, but there is little evidence that it has affected the R&D output for most self-pollinating crops (Butler, 1996:28). In Argentina, where PVP has been enforced since 1990, the system appears to have played a role in *preventing a reduction* in plant breeding in soya bean and wheat, rather than in *stimulating additional* R&D expenditure. Among seed firms in Argentina, a broad consensus exists that PVP has

5 Exploitation of an essentially derived variety, i.e. a new variety which retains the essential characteristics that result from the genotype of the source variety, requires the authorization of the rightholder of that source variety.

enabled domestic wheat and soya bean companies to increase their sales and royalty income and to survive difficult economic periods. As wheat and soya bean breeding is mainly carried out by domestic firms and institutes, it is the domestic seed industry, rather than foreign seed companies, which has so far benefited from PVP in Argentina. Foreign firms predominantly deal with hybrids and do not feel competition from unauthorized seed trade. These firms protect their inbred lines under PVP against unauthorized use by competitors. It is unlikely, however, that multinational seed companies in Latin America will increase their activities because of PVP. These companies' activities will presumably only increase when commercially viable hybrids for more crops are available (Jaffé and van Wijk, 1995:48–50).

In sum, PVP enables seed firms to get a better return on their investments. In Argentina and the US, however, there is relatively little evidence that the prospect of a better return has led to increased plant breeding. It remains difficult to assess the precise impact of PVP, because it is almost impossible to answer the question of what the R&D behaviour of seed firms would have been had PVP not been available.

Restrictions on seed saving by plant variety protection

Farmers have basically three options for acquiring seed: (a) they may obtain high-quality seed for every crop cycle from public institutes, seed companies or dealers; (b) they may save part of their own harvest as seed; or (c) they may buy or swap grain for seed with co-operatives, grain elevators or other grain dealers. They often use all three channels simultaneously. This chapter focuses on the latter two forms of seed supply, for the reason that in developing countries more than 80 per cent of farmers' seed requirements are met in this way (Srivastava and Jaffee, 1993; Heijbroek et al., 1996).

Self-pollinating crops, such as wheat and soya bean, or vegetative reproducing crops like potatoes and cassava, offer the best opportunities for seed saving. Only when the plants' vigour begins to decline, making them susceptible to insects and diseases or when a better variety is released, are the seed or vegetative parts of these crops replaced by fresh, certified seed from official seed distributors (Srivastava and Jaffee, 1993:3). Farmers growing crops under contract to the processing industry may be obliged to purchase fresh seed for every crop. In the three Southern Cone countries of Latin America the main commercial crops where seed saving accounts for a significant share of the crop include soya bean, some grains (notably wheat) and potato (Jaffé and van Wijk, 1995:70).

Benefits of seed saving
The benefits which farmers may derive from saved seeds are threefold: saved seed may (a) lower their seed costs, (b) contribute to an unofficial credit system and (c) serve as a check on the prices for commercial seed.

191

(a) Saved seed may lower seed costs.   The economic benefits of using saved seeds are difficult to assess, and may differ depending on the crop, year, country or even region. One factor which plays a role is the genetic deterioration of saved seed which may result in yield losses. Seed companies often mention this argument to stress the higher quality of fresh seed. On-farm seed saving may also result in another type of yield loss. By setting aside part of their land for propagation purposes, farmers lose part of their harvest which would otherwise be sold. The extent of this loss depends on the difference between grain and seed prices. The wider the gap between these prices, i.e. the higher the seed price in relation to the grain price, the more farmers will be inclined to use saved seeds. This is the reason why some farmers in Latin America even use second-generation seed of maize hybrids. It has been calculated that considerable cost savings can be achieved by seed saving: between 30 and 40 per cent in the case of wheat and soya bean in Argentina (Gutiérrez, 1994).

(b) Saved seeds as unofficial credit system.   In some countries, many farmers do not save their own seed, but swap their grain for seed with grain dealers (including grain elevators and co-operatives). This is a common practice for soya bean and several grains in Argentina, for instance (Gutiérrez *et al.*, 1995). In these transactions, grain is purchased from farmers, conditioned and subsequently handed over as a credit in kind to other farmers who use the grain as seed. Occasionally the dealer is informed about the origin of the grain, for example whether or not it is produced from certified seed and whether the field conditions were suitable. The grain/seed swap has certain advantages for farmers. They can obtain a bag of seed as a credit in kind during planting time. The credit is paid off at harvest time with a double quantity of grain. The final price for the seed is attractive, and the payments in kind provide farmers with some protection against currency fluctuations.

However, what farmers perceive as a credit system is to breeders a black market in seeds. Seed industry sources contend that it is not the farmer but rather the seed dealer who benefits most from the grain/seed swaps (Gutiérrez, 1996; Smith, 1996). In these transactions the dealer obtains two bags of grain for the price of one; he does not have to ask permission from the breeder for propagating a variety or to follow costly quality control procedures; royalties do not have to be paid, and taxes can be avoided. Taxes—VAT, municipality tax, income tax—constitute a far higher burden for dealers than royalties.

(c) Saved seeds control the prices for fresh seed.   By reason of the relationship between grain and seed prices, seed saving acts as a check on seed prices. When the prices for grain decrease, the seed industry has to lower its seed prices in order to prevent seed sales from dropping.

The farmers' privilege

Seed saving by farmers was formerly permitted by those countries which established the plant variety protection system and the International Union for the Protection of New Varieties of Plants (UPOV). This 'farmers' privilege' (or 'farmers' exemption') was not explicitly mentioned in the UPOV convention, but was derived from the wording in the convention on the scope of the breeder's right. PBR protected breeders against unauthorized 'production for purposes of commercial marketing' or propagating material of their varieties.[6] This implied that production of propagating material for sowing the private land of the farmer was not within the scope of the breeder's right, and thus was allowed.

The farmers' privilege has been disputed within UPOV ever since its foundation, because seed dealers and food processors have exploited the exemption for unauthorized large-scale seed production. International breeders' organizations, such as ASSINSEL and FIS, have argued that such an exploitation of the farmers' privilege has resulted in unfair competition for breeders who have to cover development costs and to comply with costly seed quality requirements (Van der Kooij, 1990:304). These strong demands from the seed industry finally resulted in explicit provisions in the 1991 act of UPOV (UPOV, 1991b). Article 14 of this act actually rescinds the farmers' privilege, since it stipulates that 'production or reproduction (multiplication)' of propagating material of a protected variety requires the authorization of the breeder. An additional optional clause, however, allows member states to exempt farmers under certain conditions.[7] In a specific recommendation made at the Diplomatic Conference in 1991 it is stated that the intention of this clause is to legalize the existing situation, not to enlarge the use of the farmers' privilege.[8]

Both in Europe and the United States, seed saving has become one of the most hotly disputed aspects of intellectual property protection in agriculture. US farmers were previously allowed to save and sell the seed of protected varieties, but the US Supreme Court and Congress have recently restricted the American farmers' exemption. In September 1994, Congress

6 Art.5, 1978 Act of UPOV (UPOV, 1991a).
7 Article 15(2): '[Optional exception] Notwithstanding Article 14, each Contracting Party may within reasonable limits and subject to the safeguarding of the legitimate interest of the breeder, restrict the breeder's right in relation to any variety in order to permit farmers to use for propagating purposes, on their own holdings, the product of the harvest which they have obtained by planting, on their own holdings, the protected variety or a variety covered by Article 14(5)(a)(i) or (ii).' (UPOV, 1991b).
8 'The Diplomatic Conference recommends that the provisions laid down in Article 15(2) ... should not be read as to be intended to open the possibility of extending the practice commonly called 'farmers' privilege' to sectors of agricultural or horticultural production in which such a privilege is not a common practice on the territory of the Contracting Party concerned' (UPOV, 1992:63).

repealed the farmer sales provision of the farmers' exemption when it amended PVP legislation. Some months later, in January 1995, in a ruling in the highly publicized case of Asgrow Seed Company versus the farming couple Denny and Becky Winterboer, the Supreme Court limited the farmers' exemption to the amount of seed a farmer needs to replant a crop, with allowable sales of any surplus of this saved seed (Hamilton, 1996:84).

Despite these restrictions, the American farmers' exemption remains broader than the farmers' privilege in the European Union. In Europe, farmers were allowed to save seed only to replant their own farm, but the establishment of a European PVP system has triggered an extensive discussion concerning this privilege. Because no agreement could be reached among farmers' and industry organizations, on-farm seed saving from EU protected varieties is now the subject of a complicated compromise. The farmers' privilege applies only to certain crops, and breeders must be remunerated for the seed of their varieties that has been saved on-farm. However, the royalty that must be paid for saved seed is lower than that for fresh commercial seed, and 'small farmers' are exempted from payment of royalties (Tiedje, 1996:82).[9]

In Latin America, the farmers' privilege is included in the PVP laws of all countries that have adopted such legislation. In Argentina, Chile and Uruguay, remuneration for saved seed is not required since these countries have acceded to the 1978 Act of UPOV. Nevertheless, the large-scale use

9 The EU Commission adopted Regulation No. 1768/95 on 24 July 1995 which implements rules on the agricultural exemption. This Regulation provides:
* In the absence of common ground between the breeders' and the farmers' organizations, it has not been possible to determine at present a specific percentage of the royalty usually charged for the licensed production of seed of a variety covered by a Community plant variety right. In consequence, the level of the remuneration is left to contractual arrangements between the holder of the Community plant variety and the farmer.
* The definition of small farmer in respect of cereals, oilseeds and some fodder plants was already specified in Council Regulation No. 2100/94. The necessary completion in respect of potatoes and other fodder plants has been achieved under the aforesaid Regulation No. 1768/95:
– Potatoes: Small farmers are farmers who grow potatoes on an area not bigger than the area which would be needed to produce at most 185 tonnes of potatoes per harvest. The area is calculated without taking into account areas on which plants other than potatoes are grown.
– Fodder plants other than those falling under the rule for cereals/oilseeds: Small farmers are farmers who grow these fodder plants for a duration of not more than five years on an area bigger than the area which would be needed to produce at most 92 tonnes of cereals per harvest. The calculation of the area does not include areas where plants other than those fodder plants are grown.
* Farm-saved seed may leave the farmer's holding for the purpose of processing only if the supplier of processing services has been registered or listed in the Member States and has undertaken to the farmer to take appropriate measures to ensure identity of the product throughout processing.
(Source: Tiedje, 1996)

of the exemption in these countries is controversial. In Argentina, as in Europe, on-farm seed saving is only permitted for the purposes of replanting. The Argentine PVP authority, *Instituto Nacional de Semillas* (INASE), established specific provisions for defining seed exempt from PVP:

a) seed that is propagated must have been legally acquired;
b) the seed must have been produced on the farmer's land;
c) the farmer must replant the saved seed on his own land;
d) the farmer must prove that the transport of saved seed to another place is for preparation purposes only.[10]

With these provisions, INASE attempts to draw a line between small-scale use by farmers and commercial trade in saved seeds. In Argentina it is estimated that only one-third of wheat and soya bean seed requirements are legally supplied through saved seeds. The remaining part of the unauthorized market is considered as constituting a black market in seeds. In order to reduce this black market, INASE and the breeders' organization, *Asociación Argentina de Protección a las Obtentores Vegetales* (ARPOV), joined forces and began to register dealers and the entire seed trade in wheat and soya bean. In four years, they have succeeded in reducing the unauthorized trade in wheat seed from 83 per cent of the total commercial market in 1990, to 22 per cent in 1994. In the case of soya bean seed, the unauthorized trade was 75 per cent in 1992, and 48 per cent in 1994 (Jaffé and van Wijk, 1995:38).

The attempts by breeders in Argentina to exercise their rights and to reduce the unauthorized seed trade may have been successful for them, but could be disadvantageous to farmers, for whom the black market in seeds functions as an unofficial credit system and a major channel for seed diffusion. When this segment of the seed market is officially registered, seed dealers have to pay royalties and taxes on their sales. These costs could be passed on to the farmers, with higher seed prices (and more on-farm seed saving) as a likely result. In Argentina, however, little seems to have changed in this respect. The grain/seed swap has so far survived the PVP enforcement. This channel for seed distribution is being legalized while prices have not increased: two bags of grain can still be swapped for one bag of seed. It seems that the increase in the cost of seed caused by PVP has been borne by the middlemen (Jaffé and van Wijk, 1995:74).

Restrictions on seed saving by other intellectual property systems

Plant variety protection restricts seed saving, although farmers who save seed for their own use are in most cases exempt. However, PVP is by no means the only legal mechanism for plant breeders to prevent

10 The Argentine Seed Law prohibits transport of seed outside the farmer's premises if it is not identified or certified.

unauthorized multiplication and trade in their varieties. At least three other mechanisms have a similar or stronger effect: (a) the breeding of hybrids, (b) patents and (c) purchase agreements.

(a) Hybrids. Historically, the seed industry in OECD countries has expanded by developing and selling hybrids. Nearly 40 per cent of the total global commercial seed business of about $15 billion is accounted for by hybrid sales in various crops (Seghal, 1994). Hybrids are available for many important commercial grains, such as maize, sunflower, sorghum, oilseed rape, various vegetables and (to a limited extent) rice. Hybrids for wheat and soya bean have not yet conquered the market. One of the characteristics of hybrids is that they do not breed true to type, making them unattractive for seed saving. This is one of the reasons why the private sector has developed hybrids. According to the director of Plant Genetic Systems (a Belgian biotechnology company), IPR legislation is neither necessary nor desirable to develop the hybrid seed industry (ibid.). As the yield potential of hybrids is held to be a solution to pressing food supply problems, their increasing use, rather than IPR, may prevent farmers from saving their own seed in the future.[11]

(b) Patents. Ever since the 1980s, plants have been eligible for protection under utility patent law, but this phenomenon has so far been limited to the main OECD countries. With the coming diffusion of genetically engineered varieties in Latin America, however, it can be expected that the first patents on plants or plant parts will be filed soon. What effect these patents will have on seed saving is not yet clear. In most Latin American countries all plant material, except for plant varieties, is or soon will be patentable in principle. If patents for plant parts are filed, they may trigger disputes on the scope of the claims of the patentee. Such disputes have been occurring for a number of years in Europe where companies have, for example, filed a patent for a process to alter the genome of a plant, and consequently claimed protection for all plants and seed resulting from that process.[12]

11 The use of F2 seed is not impossible, however. Especially for farmers who lack the opportunity to buy fresh seed each year, the lower yields of the F2 may outweigh the costs of obtaining fresh hybrid seed. In Argentina, in 1994, various sources mentioned that up to 20 per cent of the hybrid maize seed may consist of F2 seed. These statements could not be verified, however.

12 See, for example, the case of Greenpeace versus Plant Genetic Systems (PGS). In 1990, the Belgian biotechnology firm PGS obtained a patent on a method to produce herbicide-resistant plants. The patent claims covered all plants and seed that result from the method. Greenpeace opposed the patent. During the procedure, PGS withdrew six claims related to seeds and plants which had been granted in 1990. On 21 February 1995, the appeal board rejected the earlier decision by the European Patent Organisation because the examples provided by PGS concern mere plant *varieties*; varieties are excluded from patent protection under the European Patent Convention (Private communication with PGS).

196

The outcome of this dispute, however, is of more importance to breeders in Latin America than to farmers. Patenting plants may hamper innovation, as breeders will then be unable to use a protected variety for any commercial purpose without authorization from the patent-holder. Unauthorized seed saving of patented plants is also forbidden. As most patented plants are hybrids, the consequences for farmers are less visible.

(c) Purchase agreements. A relatively new development in the US which restricts seed-saving practices is the use of Purchase Agreements. Rather than plant variety protection, a number of American seed companies rely on contract provisions which enable the company to use breach of contract claims in local courts to enforce ownership of the seeds. Labels on the seed bags inform farmers that, by purchasing the seed, they enter into an agreement with the seed company. Such an agreement may provide, among other things, that 'Purchaser hereby acknowledges and agrees that the production from the Stine Brand Seeds herein sold will be used only for feed or processing *and will not be used or sold for seed*, breeding or any variety improvement purposes' (emphasis added) (Hamilton, 1996:96–7). The restrictions on the exploitation of protected varieties imposed by the breeder via such purchase contracts have a far wider scope than those ensuing from PVP. Farmers purchasing Stine's seed are not allowed to save seed, nor can the variety be used for further breeding by other breeders. These restrictions are in conflict with the provisions of UPOV, of which the US is a member.

Concluding comments

PVP may help the domestic seed industry in developing countries to restrict the trade in saved seed of its varieties and to increase its income. There is little evidence, however, that this additional income leads to more and better varieties becoming available to farmers. Seed multinationals work with hybrids and do not compete with saved seed. PVP may have importance for foreign seed multinationals in protecting their inbred lines against unauthorized use by other foreign competitors. In this way, PVP may be an additional stimulus for these seed firms to transfer their inbred lines to developing countries.

The practices of on-farm seed saving and local seed exchange are likely to decline in many countries and the introduction of PVP will play a role in this development. Under PVP, seed saving is considered to be a 'privilege' which may be restricted, as PVP regulation in the European Union shows. However, an increased use of hybrids in the developing world will probably have a more significant impact on seed saving than PVP.

10 Participatory plant breeding: emerging models and future development

LOUISE SPERLING AND JACQUELINE A. ASHBY

Introduction

PARTICIPATORY PLANT BREEDING (PPB) is distinguished by the involvement of end users—particularly farmers—in plant breeding and variety selection. These methods are participatory because farmers help define the priorities, beginning with the early stages of varietal development, and because both farmers and formal breeders have well-defined roles which allow them to take advantage of their respective skills and experience.

The following discussion employs the term PPB to cover a wide range of activities. It includes both farmer participation in testing stabilized varieties as well as farmer selection (and at times crossing) of materials that are still segregating. Although some authors (e.g., Witcombe and Joshi, 1996a) reserve the term PPB for the latter type of activities, this chapter will focus on the common participatory elements that distinguish all of these innovations in variety improvement. The chapter provides a review of the alternatives for farmer participation in plant breeding, to foster the decentralization of public sector variety testing advocated in Chapter 4.

The PPB approach is the product of a critical assessment of the strengths and weaknesses of classic breeding programmes. Centralized, research-driven breeding (or supply-driven research) has been extremely effective in higher-potential uniform environments, and for those farmers who can afford external inputs to modify production systems. It has been less effective in difficult environments, in reaching farmers with fewer resources, and in reaching users with specialized concerns, such as those found in sophisticated marketing systems featuring rigorous product quality requirements. Classic plant breeding can deliver productive technology when the target is widespread and relatively uniform. It is less successful in dealing with variable environments, diverse clients and differentiated product criteria.

PPB has also been encouraged by a growing appreciation of farmers' varietal selection skills. Studies of local production systems reveal that farmers' expertise in germplasm management can be very precise— especially in regions with broad varietal diversity (Richards, 1985; Sperling, 1992; van der Heide *et al.*, 1996; Voss, 1992). Farmers have been selecting varieties over generations, promoting the better adapted and higher quality entries, and matching cultivars to particular production niches. Documentation of local experimentation methods also indicates that farmer variety testing is widespread and dynamic in most rural communities. PPB aims to benefit both from farmers' insights on criteria for variety development and from farmers' ability to lead the way in site-specific testing.

The fundamental rationale of a PPB programme is that joint scientist-farmer efforts can deliver more than if each side works alone. Ultimately, justification for PPB will depend on combining indigenous and scientific knowledge in a way that maximizes genetic diversity and increases productivity, developing a greater number of usable products, more quickly and at less cost, than conventional plant breeding.

Basic elements of participatory plant breeding

The greater involvement of farmers in formal breeding research programmes is a development only of the last 10 years. Experimental PPB programmes are being designed for a range of crops and regions: for instance, pearl millet in India (Witcombe and Joshi, 1996b), barley in Syria (Ceccarelli et al., 1996), common beans in Brazil (Zimmerman, 1996), rice in Nepal (Sthapit et al., 1996). Farmer participation in these formal efforts spans a broad set of activities ranging from involving farmers in developing the plant ideotype to decision-making about the release of varieties or seed production. While PPB organizational forms and methodologies are still very much in the testing stages, and vary significantly by research programme, there are several basic features which should be central to PPB and which are characteristic of participatory R&D in general.[1]

First, PPB has to be client-driven. This means that knowledge, needs, criteria and preferences of farmers (that is, the principal clients) have weight in decisions about varietal development. More fundamentally, it implies that farmers are actively involved in decision-making about innovation early in the process, when the agenda for breeding research is set and when varietal traits are given their relative importance. In practical terms, before the initial germplasm pool is prepared for screening and, before crosses are made, research programmes should have a clear idea of what farmers want and need. The initial aim is to construct a 'client-sensitive germplasm pool'. During the subsequent experimental phases, research must also have a sharpened capacity to modify plans in response to client critique.

Client-driven agendas differ markedly from those geared towards basic, long-term plant breeding research. Clients have differing needs, specific to their own agronomic and socio-economic situation. Farmers always select varieties in a given locality, and with particular constraints and opportunities in mind. Addressing client needs means that the varietal development process itself must be sufficiently decentralized to meet diverse

1 This section draws extensively on Ashby and Sperling, 1995.

farmers' goals, and to allow for site-specific, local adaptation. Such de-centralized varietal technology development suggests other features central to PPB.

To anticipate diverse client needs, applied research must produce an increased range of technology options that farmers can adapt to their particular needs. National research programmes and regional experimental stations need no longer aim at final recommendations. Instead, researchers should think in terms of 'prototype designs', which would then be shaped or contextualized to fit specific niches. This second feature of PPB, the development of prototypes, rather than finished products, may involve clients throughout the varietal development process. To pre-screen or create prototype designs, farmers have been taught to make crosses themselves (Kornegay *et al.*, 1996); they have been involved in screening segregating populations (Sthapit *et al.*, 1996); and they have been brought directly on to experimental stations (Sperling *et al.*, 1993) and farm sites set up for screening pre-released lines (Weltzein *et al.*, 1996a). Such early involvement can help to target a new variety, re-orient research on an unacceptable one or stimulate farmers to offer new ideas for further breeding work.

Effective decentralization of varietal testing is a task beyond the resources of most public sector research services, however. The requirements for testing many different 'varietal menus' tailored to different preferences and localities imply the third major feature of PPB: the devolution to farmers of major responsibility for adaptive testing. Farmers take the lead in organizing experimentation, evaluating results and transmitting local recommendations. Such devolution potentially allows for increased scale of testing, better targeting of varieties and more realistic variety evaluation. As will be discussed below, devolution is best managed through organized groups of farmers.

Finally, the fourth important feature of any truly client-driven agricultural programme, including PPB, centres on the sharing of accountability. Those involved in research (state research and extension programmes; NGOs; producer organizations; local communities; informal farmer groups) share responsibility for the relevance and quality of the technology on offer. One of the biggest obstacles to institutionalizing participatory programmes in the public sector is that the staff of most agricultural research systems are neither penalized for producing technologies which farmers cannot use, nor rewarded for having reached particular clients. A necessary feature of PPB is that clients must have the right to support or reject a research programme via their control over a significant proportion of the programme's resources.

Is the PPB approach really distinct from an effective conventional plant breeding system? Haven't formal breeders always promoted varieties with farmers' interests in mind? Figure 10.1 suggests that there are important

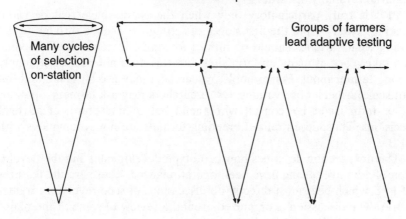

Modified from Sperling and Berkowitz, 1995; and Ceccarelli *et al.*, 1996

Figure 10.1   *A comparison of classic plant breeding and participatory plant breeding*

conceptual and practical differences. In the conventional model, researchers make all the major decisions on germplasm creation and promotion, from the initial stages when germplasm choices are wide through to the restricted stage of on-farm testing. Screening criteria, of necessity, focus on areas of breeder expertise—principally yield and adaptation in controlled experimental plots, and tolerance to important diseases. If researchers do assess client opinion, it is only immediately before varieties are to be released for diffusion. At this stage, farmers' only option is to accept or reject a few finished cultivars. Finally, formal breeding research usually seeks these opinions from a few individual, and often unrepresentative, farmers.

As Figure 10.1 shows, a PPB approach enhances farmers' involvement and responsibilities. The initial germplasm pool is directly shaped with strong client input. Screening criteria include quality concerns and local production requirements, for example the maturity or plant architecture characteristics required to fit varieties into multi-cropping systems. As farmers screen or help develop subsequent prototype pools, they are generally exposed to a more diverse range of germplasm and, to meet their different needs, the PPB format has to be decentralized very early on. This farmer leadership role can potentially shift some of the costs away from the formal research system, with farmers effectively integrating experimentation into their ongoing farm management. Group work early in the technology development process also produces important spin-offs: promising entries are multiplied and exchanged among farmers, variable entries are shifted to fit more appropriate production niches and unpromising material is rapidly discarded.

PPB is truly participatory only when the clients have real decision-making power—from the first stages of setting the agenda through to deciding what varieties should be moved forwards. Decentralized breeding can take place at many on-farm sites, but this does not necessarily imply strong farmer input. For example, researchers may use farmers' land but not seek farmers' observations. Or researchers may ask farmers' opinions of on-farm trials, i.e. consult with them, but retain control of all final decisions. Thus, decentralized breeding formats are not synonymous with PPB.

The next section describes how prototype development and the devolution of adaptive testing have been operationalized. These are the features of PPB which bear most directly on discussions of seed regulatory frameworks. The discussion is organized around a review of some of the major examples of PPB that have been developed.

Participatory breeding: select case studies

Prototype screening and development
A major feature that distinguishes various types of PPB is the status of the entries used for testing. In several examples of PPB, much of the prototype testing has focused on advanced, pre-released entries. This strategy can be easily integrated into ongoing national breeding programmes and it allows breeders to control their materials and to screen for factors such as disease susceptibility that may not be readily apparent to farmers. But in many cases the initial germplasm pool of advanced lines will hold little of client interest, and researchers and farmers will have to collaborate during the earlier stages of crossing and screening segregating material. This more labour-intensive collaboration has been practised most widely in very marginal environments, for example, drought-prone areas, where it has been difficult to introduce any new varieties through conventional breeding.

A range of cases illustrates the promising involvement of farmers in varied forms of prototype testing. The examples below are ordered along a continuum: from screening of released lines developed for other locales to working with farmers in the crossing stages. In these examples farmers have worked with anything from one up to 100 different materials.

Rice (and other crops) in India   (Witcombe and Joshi, 1996a, b). The formal research system in India has released a relatively large number of rice cultivars: 525 in all, and 88 in the period from 1988 to 1993. Despite this relatively diverse choice, the two most popular cultivars across India are IR36 and Rasi, released in 1981 and 1977, respectively. A PPB effort was initiated in the belief that variety replacement rates were low, not because released material was unacceptable to farmers but because farmers had never been exposed to a range of choices. In India, many crop varieties are released and used in only a single state (although a state may encompass tens of millions of farmers). Researchers believed that simply by moving released material from one state to another, a more relevant choice of varieties could be presented to farmers.

In 1992, the Crops Programme of the Krishak Bharati Co-operative Indo-British Rainfed Farming Project (KRIBP) launched a process to: a) identify farmers' varietal preferences, and b) find matching suitable material. To increase the basket of choices, pools of released and pre-released lines available from Indian public breeding programmes were screened. In subsequent on-farm trials, farmers were randomly assigned to grow a single variety alongside their local one. Using this very simple technique, two varieties of rice, one of maize, three of chickpea and two of blackgram were identified as being markedly preferred by farmers. These results were achieved in only three years.

A strategy of working with released varieties has significant advantages in India's well-developed public plant breeding system. Any organization working with farmers can, in principle, readily procure seeds of a released variety in sufficient quantities for testing. Further, if such varieties prove to be acceptable, they should be able to be shifted across state boundaries, and could be fed into the conventional, large-scale seed multiplication channels and extension systems.

Of course, such a programme would have enhanced results only if the researcher-constructed pool contains entries of potential interest to farmers. In many countries, this approach of screening finished varieties is similar to a well-conducted programme of on-farm trials. Advanced lines are tested on farmers' fields, under farmer management and with comprehensive farmer evaluations.

Common bean in Rwanda (Sperling *et al.*, 1993; Sperling and Scheidegger, 1995). Rwandan farmers have considerable experience in managing local bean diversity: some 550 varieties exist countrywide and farmers adjust mixtures of varieties for specific soil types and crop associations (Scheidegger, 1993). Despite such diversity, the selection sequence of the national agricultural research institute (ISAR), following Western models, sharply narrows the range of varieties on offer: some 200 entries are initially screened, but only 2–5 enter on-farm trials, the sole means of client feedback. An experimental programme, conceived by the International Centre for Tropical Agriculture (CIAT) and ISAR from 1988 to 1993, sought to draw on farmer experience early in the selection process, when

Table 10.1   *On-farm performance of varieties selected from on-station trials by Rwandan farmers versus varieties selected by breeders*

Season	No. of trials	Trials where new variety out-performed local mixture (%)	Yield increase of new variety over local mixture (%)
Farmer Selection—Central Plateau			
1989A	11	73 ns	3.9 ns
1989B	19	89 **	33.4 **
1990A	36	64 ns	12.9 ns
1990B	18	83 **	38.0 *
Breeder Selection—Central Plateau			
1987A	32	34 ns	−8.8 ns
1988A	45	49 ns	−18.9 ns
1988B	15	53 ns	0.7 ns
Breeder Selection—Countrywide			
1987A	131	51 ns	6.7 *
1987B	83	41 ns	−6.0 ns
1988A	204	50 ns	2.6 ns
1988B	204	50 ns	7.6 *

ns = not significant * $P<0.05$ ** $P<0.01$

Source: Sperling *et al.*, 1993

varietal options were still extensive. During a first phase, local farmer experts evaluated 15 cultivars in on-station trials 2–4 seasons before normal on-farm testing. These evaluations revealed that women experts select bush beans on preference and performance criteria, with many of the attributes not easily anticipated in a formal breeding framework. On-farm trials also showed the farmers' ability to extrapolate from experimental station fields to their own home plots; farmer selections out-performed their checks with average production increases of up to 38 per cent, while breeder choices in the same region showed insignificant gains (Table 10.1). During a second phase of the programme, participants screened a broader range of cultivars earlier in the breeding process: 80–100 entries were placed in on-station trials 5–7 seasons before conventional on-farm testing. Longer-term results suggest some of the advantages of offering these options to farmers. The number of varieties adopted from the first phase of the work, 21, matched the total number of varieties released by ISAR in the 25 years previous to this programme. In the subsequent trials of the second phase, 26 varieties were selected for home testing during the first two seasons alone (Sperling and Berkowitz, 1995). The experiment suggests several benefits of prototype screening: enhanced and diversified production in heterogeneous environments and significant savings in on-station research time.

Rice in Nepal (Sthapit *et al.*, 1996). Chilling injury and Sheath Brown Rot (ShBR) are serious problems for rice production in the hills of Nepal and significantly limit the area planted under rice and the length of the potential growing season. Of the 39 cultivars recommended by the National Rice Research Programme (NRRP), only two have been released that are suitable for the high hills (>1 500m). Screening of international cold-tolerant materials has failed to identify productive varieties. In 1993, the Lumle Agricultural Research Centre (LARC) decided to test F_5 bulk seed of select lines with farmers, directly on their fields. This radical departure from the standard practice was motivated by a series of very practical concerns. LARC did not have the land or resources to do such breeding on station; researchers felt they did not have the means to address the high variability of farming systems and management practices via the conventional centralized testing approach; adoption levels of formerly released varieties had been low; and researchers were concerned about the future possibility of reducing genetic variability on farmers' fields through the promotion of uniform varieties. The PBB programme has had promising results in only two years. Two populations, selected independently by farmers in two sites, are showing unusually high yields, even in researcher-managed trials. The entries have very good resistance to the two major stresses, ShBR and chilling, and the straw yield is judged by farmers to be superior to that of the local varieties. Both populations are spreading quickly and the lines have been entered in the formal testing system in anticipation of official release. Researchers emphasize that the success of their programme has hinged on identifying expert farmers (i.e. not all farmers have skills in variety selection) and on identifying a problem relevant to the farming community. The LARC experiment focused only on white rice varieties—the type highly preferred by the local farmers.

Common bean in Colombia (Kornegay *et al.*, 1996). 'If farmers were taught the basics of plant breeding, would the varieties they develop be higher yielding and more acceptable to other farmers within the region?' This question formed the basis of a PPB study undertaken by CIAT in Colombia in the early 1990s. Eighteen F_2 populations were grown in five environments—two research station sites and three farms. A simple breeding strategy was used by CIAT bean breeders and farmers to advance segregating populations to homozygous advanced lines. While the segregation of different traits within each population was pointed out to the farmers, they were instructed to use their own criteria in making selections.

The results showed that farmers can indeed follow a breeding methodology recommended by researchers and successfully develop advanced lines. However, differences were found between breeder-selected and farmer-selected lines. Farmers tended to focus on commercial qualities, and their selections had more attractive seed colours, patterns and desirable sizes.

The farmers' most preferred lines did not have the highest yields or best disease-resistance combinations, traits on which breeders' had put emphasis. Interestingly, all the advanced breeding lines developed, whether by farmers or breeders, had yields as high or higher than the local check.

This Colombian case differs from the preceding ones in that it took place in an area of very demanding consumer preferences. It shows that participatory approaches can be highly effective for delivering varieties that are acceptable to commercially oriented farmers. The range of materials that these farmers chose was very narrow, however, and this may be an outcome of PPB (Voss, 1996). PPB *per se* does not necessarily lead to wider varietal diversity on-farm.

Reflections on prototype screening   One of the challenges of each PPB programme is to find the most efficient division of labour between breeders and farmers. Scientists should be challenged to offer a diversity of varietal options, rather than finished products. In many contexts, their comparative advantage lies in generating new options and screening for disease susceptibility or anti-nutritional traits which may not be immediately apparent to farmers.

A related goal of PPB programmes should be to identify the stage in prototype screening which is most cost-effective. For example, if the selection of finished varieties proves to bring significant results to a range of farmers, it may not be necessary to pursue direct collaboration during earlier stages of the plant-breeding process. (This point is also emphasized in Chapter 4.)

Much of the debate on prototype screening has focused on whether the early involvement of farmers and early access to varietal material increase risks. Fears are expressed that disease incidence may rise or that yields may decline. In addition, there are concerns that farmers may lose confidence in formal agricultural research or that they may receive materials that are not uniform. In fact, disease incidence should decline, as materials will be screened in the actual environments where they will be used. In terms of yield, the empirical results are already suggesting that a more acceptable product is developed when farmers and breeders collaborate. The other concerns raised show how much PPB may demand important attitudinal shifts. Researchers no longer take sole responsibility for delivering solutions: failures, as well as successes, are shared enterprises. And varietal uniformity is not a reasonable strategy for improving production in low-input farming.

Devolution of adaptive testing to farmer groups
Recent experiments suggest that decentralization of testing may be a technical as well as a logistical imperative. Genotypes selected under optimum conditions simply do not perform well under low-input

conditions: there is a 'crossover effect' (Ceccarelli et al., 1994). To have an impact in heterogeneous environments, and to address a broader range of client preferences, a genepool has to be screened under multiple actual farming conditions (ibid.). But allowing technologies to be shaped in many locations can easily multiply the demands on scarce formal sector professionals, so PPB programmes aim to shift the responsibility of adaptive testing towards farming communities themselves. Experience has shown that such participatory activities are most effectively organized through farmer groups. PPB may have to develop farmer groups or work with existing ones. The following cases provide examples of each option.

CIALs in Colombia (Ashby et al., 1995). One strategy for devolving adaptive testing has been to establish community-based organizations of experimenting farmers expressly for this purpose. From 1990 to 1994, the IPRA (Participatory Research in Agriculture) project of CIAT acted as the catalyst for such an approach in the Cauca Department of Colombia. Considerable effort was devoted to identifying principles for durable farmer research committees (*Comités de Investigacion Agropecuria Local*, or CIALs). CIAL members were trained to carry out diagnoses, set priorities and use the basic tools of scientific experimentation.

Eventually some 55 CIALs were formed, with many building up independent capacity to diagnose problems, design and implement trials, analyse the results and deliver a community report. The themes of experimentation within and across CIALs were broad, including agronomic practices, the composition of feed mixes, the integration of green manure and varietal experimentation. In four years, the farmer committees had tested some 1 000 varietal materials of crops such as beans, maize, peas and groundnuts.

The involvement of farmer groups also had direct spin-off effects in terms of seed production. Six of the CIALs set up small seed production enterprises to multiply the varieties selected, with the groups having received training in simple seed production, processing and quality-control techniques. More than 10 000 farmers have purchased CIAL seed, which over one season has generated a gross value of over US$2.5 million. In terms of the direct value to participating farmers, on a per capita basis, earnings from the seed multiplication were equivalent to a month's income (Ashby et al., 1995).

The capacity-building indicators of the CIAL programme have been particularly promising. The results of the majority of trials, independently conducted by farmer groups, were interpretable (75 per cent of the experiments were statistically analysable, while 90 per cent generated useful knowledge according to farmer criteria). Devolving an on-farm trial to a fully trained CIAL also costs 60 per cent less in labour costs than running

Table 10.2 *Labour requirements of an on-farm trial managed by CIAL and by extension*

Trial management	Days required	Total cost of salaried labour (US$)
Extension research	8	62
New CIAL	11	46
Fully trained CIAL	5	23

Source: Ashby et al., 1996

the same trial with an extension agent (see Table 10.2). Some CIAL members are now spurring the formation and training of new CIALs.

The close monitoring of the CIAL experience has also suggested some of the limitations of group work – even in the most carefully controlled of circumstances. CIALs were designed primarily to promote experimentation; the participating farmers were to build up community capacity to test technology and develop products which could then be used by neighbours. Distribution of knowledge about the CIAL activity, rather than direct participation in it, served as an important indicator of whether broader community interests were being served. Studies showed no significant differences in knowledge about CIALs along wealth parameters; the very poor were as aware of the experiments as the better-off. However, women seemed to have removed themselves from direct participation in many of the CIALS and, therefore, from setting community research priorities. Several options are now being proposed, including stimulating the formation of women-only CIALs, and allowing women's groups to evaluate trials they themselves may not have the time to manage.

Building on existing organizations: Rwanda (Sperling and Scheidegger, 1995). Another option for devolving variety testing is to build on existing farmer groups. The potential for this strategy, and the pitfalls of relying on hastily formed *ad hoc* groups, are illustrated by experience in Rwanda, where researchers sought to institutionalize and scale up the promising results of earlier farmer involvement in variety selection. From 1990 to 1993 several types of local groups of women bean farmers were involved in variety selection. These included members of groups that had been formed by NGOs for specific development projects, as well as farmers who belonged to a Rwandan administrative unit known as a 'commune'. The contrast between the two experiences is instructive.

In other countries in the region, such as Zaire, PPB has been conducted with well-organized farmers' co-operatives. Unfortunately, Rwanda has a limited tradition of co-operatives or indeed of any rural grassroots organizations that might represent farmers' interests. There were, however, several farmers' organizations that had been established with the backing of

NGOs that participated in the attempt to diffuse PPB methods. In one case, a women's co-operative, supported by a Belgian NGO, took charge of the work. Five experts were sent to the experimental station to select varieties for further testing. These were subsequently tested on the plots of designated group members, and an evaluation was completed by means of a walking tour of the plots (PAMU, 1993). The NGO produced a written evaluation of the results for the Rwandan national bean programme.

The experiment with the co-operative was successful because the women managed it themselves and because they saw themselves as truly representing a larger community. Once the varieties had been chosen, the co-operative multiplied and distributed over a ton of seed for its members.

The experiment within the 'commune' units was conducted in a more formal manner but without the benefit of a well-established group. The local agronomist took control, station researchers designed a standard trial (varieties sown in lines, at given densities) and some local farmers were invited to evaluate the plot and select varieties for home use. One advantage of the centralized format was that more farmers were exposed to a greater range of cultivars than in the first example, and, due to their greater involvement in commune evaluations, researchers received feedback more quickly. Such a top-down research strategy at the community level is not atypical of many local grassroots groups who collaborate with trained technicians. But the limitations of the approach were obvious, as there was little progress towards adaptive testing on individual plots and very restricted diffusion of promising varieties.

Some of the weaknesses of trying to conduct PPB through an *ad hoc* group were evident in this example. Within the communes, the male power structure distorted the expansion of the experiment at several key points. In the selection of farmer representatives to screen on-station trials, some of the so-called community-selected experts were neither very well informed nor very representative of community interests. For instance, one community was represented by the sister of the government agronomist and the wife of the sector head. The local government agronomists also sometimes fell short on their obligations to community participants; the community plot was planted and the evaluations were completed, but seed of selected varieties was never distributed to evaluators.

Devolution: reflections. Whether it creates new farmer groups or builds on existing farmer organizations, PPB opens up a range of issues that must be addressed. Fundamental issues include the quality of on-farm testing achievable with farmer participation and the representativeness of groups involved.

When farmers are involved in trial design and management, data sets can be heterogeneous within and among locations, although such results may represent the variability of actual farming practices. Should participating farmers be encouraged to follow more standardized experimental designs? Should farmers be taught to internalize and manage Western scientific methods, or will this hamper their creativity and independent insights? The costs and benefits of different approaches need to be addressed empirically (see Ashby, 1986).

The basis on which farmer groups are involved in PPB also raises important issues. If PPB is to be institutionalized, significant attention has to be paid to exactly who is involved. Groups need to cover the range of potential beneficiaries and to be able to show accountability to their own constituents. In some cases PPB may be able to rely on existing groups to articulate demands and orient formal research. In other cases, special groups will have to be created. The issues of who participates and who benefits are certainly not unique to PPB, but they take on special importance, given the biases and inefficiencies of formal plant breeding systems that have led to this search for alternative methods.

PPB: future directions

Participatory Plant Breeding is still in an incipient stage. Many programmes are taking a step-by-step approach, testing one or two innovations at a time. ICRISAT's work on diagnostic methods for breeding pearl millet in India, for instance, has been unusually rigorous in detailing the range of farmer preferences and selection practices (Weltzein et al., 1996b). Other programmes are seeking to understand the logistical boundaries of PPB better; scientists at ICARDA are proposing to screen over 200 lines, including some F_2s, directly on farmer-managed and -evaluated plots (Ceccarelli, personal communication). While PPB is sometimes perceived by outsiders as heretical, those actually involved in such efforts feel they have proceeded with caution: propositions are being tested and a small but growing literature is reporting the results and providing guidance for further experiments.

Additional work is needed on understanding both the technical and organizational issues related to PPB. With respect to technical breeding itself, the Consultative Group on International Agricultural Research (CGIAR) is proposing a programme with its national research partners and NGO collaborators to take a critical look at PPB methodology. Frameworks are being designed to make controlled comparisons between PPB programmes and their conventional breeding counterparts. These comparisons would examine cost-effectiveness, the most appropriate technical breeding strategies for PPB and the role of participation in upstream as well as adaptive research. Three to four field projects should help clarify how, and under what circumstances, PPB programmes should be institutionalized (Systemwide Programme on Participatory Research and Gender Analysis, 1997).

With respect to the organizational dimensions of farmer participatory research, and particularly the issue of devolution, the Overseas Development Institute and the International Service for National Agricultural Research (ISNAR) have been conducting a series of studies looking at local-level research partners, NGOs and farmers' organizations (Farrington *et al.*, 1993; ISNAR, 1994; Carney, 1996). These examine the institutional environment which successfully fosters NGO and farmers' organizations as well as the internal organizational features which enable such groups to serve their members effectively. Critical concerns include how farmer organizations can better identify and aggregate their constituencies' technological demands; how they can more effectively work as partners with formal research agencies; and how they can provide the necessary support services required by location-specific technology development. It is important to reiterate that participatory breeding can only take place if testing can be decentralized, and testing can only be decentralized if local groups take the lead.

PPB: current implications for national variety testing, variety release and seed systems

Beyond understanding the organizational and methodological dimensions of PPB, there are a series of regulatory issues which need to be addressed if PPB is to link with existing national testing programmes, variety release committees and seed systems effectively.[2] The implications of PPB for the organization of formal plant breeding programmes have been discussed in Chapter 4. The following points relate to the implications of PPB for variety release and seed production.

Varietal release systems
The increasing use of PPB for developing useful varieties will involve serious conflicts with most conventional variety release systems. A number of adjustments will have to be made in order to take advantage of the results of PPB.

Utilization of PPB data. A PPB approach implies that data on farmer acceptability should be an important basis for varietal release. Some practitioners have also suggested that data generated from farmer-designed and managed trials should be considered as legitimate evidence in variety release decisions. Mechanisms need to be developed for aggregating and communicating community-level assessments to variety release authorities.

2 This section draws heavily on a discussion among PPB practitioners at an IDRC/IPGRI/FAO/CGN-sponsored workshop on Plant Breeding, 26–29 July 1995 (Eyzaguirre and Iwanaga, 1996).

Uniformity. A PPB approach does not necessarily lead to uniform varieties. On the contrary, segregating populations, evolving in different locales, take on diverse characteristics. Release criteria need to accommodate this notion of heterogeneity.

Release recommendations. An important advantage of decentralized variety development is the resulting site-specificity of adaptation: varieties are targeted to suitable production niches. Variety release recommendations need to be able to respect this diversity.

Release system capacity. PPB systems can result in the identification of many farmer-acceptable varieties, particularly in heterogeneous environments with diverse farmer groups. Formal variety release systems need to be able to handle a relatively larger number of varieties than is currently the case.

Rewards for variety development. Within conventional plant breeding programmes, breeders are rewarded for finished products and officially released varieties. A PPB perspective encourages breeders to make available unreleased varieties or segregating materials that farmers can use for further selection and development. Reward systems need to be developed that recognize this early breeder contribution and the subsequent impact it has for specific groups of farmers. Similarly, farmer breeders should be given due recognition for their work. If a variety produced by PPB is accorded some type of plant variety protection and is subject to royalties, then farmer participants should share these rewards.

Seed production and PPB
Innovative variety development is of little use if seed of the new varieties is not easily available to farmers. Both formal and farmer-level seed systems need to establish better links with PPB.

PPB and public seed enterprises. PPB leads to the development of products that fall outside the public research system's links with supporting seed multiplication services. Procedures need to be developed that allow the finished products of PPB to be produced by public seed enterprises.

Strengthening local seed channels. It is well known that farmer seed systems often produce the majority of seed for many crops. Their effectiveness needs to be scrutinized more carefully and, if appropriate, selected features might be strengthened. Procedures need to be made explicit as to how the products of PPB can move into a range of local channels. For instance, should traders be encouraged to package and sell them in local markets, or are farmer-to-farmer seed exchange mechanisms sufficient?

Decentralized production. The site-specificity of PPB efforts suggests that complementary seed systems (whether formal or informal) need to have strong decentralized multiplication and distribution capacity. Seed production projects and enterprises will have to be capable of multiplying many different varieties and targeting the distribution of these varieties to the appropriate locales.

Conclusion

The incorporation of participatory methods into plant breeding began in the mid-1980s by involving farmers in the evaluation of pre-release varieties. The gap between users' and breeders' criteria for acceptability of new varieties identified through this type of participatory research has stimulated plant breeders to introduce user participation at earlier stages in applied plant breeding research. As experience accumulates, participatory methods are perceived by some plant breeders as comparable to biotechnological techniques in opening up new frontiers in breeding (Kornegay *et al.*, 1996; Zimmerman, 1996; Iglesias and Hérnandez, 1994).

However, this brief review of PPB programmes suggests that an effective participatory strategy still has a number of challenges to address. The scientific division of labour itself—what scientists should do, what farmers should do—has been brought forward as a researchable question. On-farm research methodologies are being scrutinized for their reliability, usefulness, interpretability and useability. Most fundamentally, PPB touches the heart of the breeding decision-making structure. The approach suggests that demand-driven rather than supply-side models can best deliver useful products to farmers.

Is it all worth it? The answer should become clearer in the next few years. Initial PPB results suggest that there may be options for greater cost-effectiveness in breeding, opportunities to achieve greater production impact and the prospect of reaching a greater range of resource-poor farmers.

11 Local-level seed activities: opportunities and challenges for regulatory frameworks

ELIZABETH CROMWELL

Introduction

THE PURPOSE OF this chapter is to examine how regulatory frameworks could be adapted in order to enable local-level seed activities to make their full contribution to the diversification of the seed sector in developing countries. As we shall demonstrate below, local-level seed activities are increasingly important in seed-sector development, but their potential contribution is constrained by the regulatory frameworks in which they operate.

The arguments presented here are derived from analysis of information about local-level seed activity collected for the ODI 1991/2 study of the role of NGOs in seed supply (Cromwell *et al.*, 1993), supplemented by information collected for the ODI/CAZS study of seed regulatory frameworks that forms the basis of Part 2 of this book.

For the 1991/2 study, 18 agencies supporting local-level seed activities were examined in nine countries in Africa, Asia and Latin America. These agencies were selected for examination because they were working with local seed systems at a practical level, their focus was on seed production for staple food crops and they had reasonably well-documented project experience. Beyond that, they were chosen to represent different types of agency (North-based NGOs, South-based NGOs, donor agencies) and development strategy; have experience with different types of seeds (of landraces, modern varieties, etc.) and agro-ecosystems; and operate in countries with different macroeconomic and policy contexts. One-third were North-based NGOs directly involved in local-level seed production; one-third were North-based NGOs supporting seed activities being carried out by local organizations; and one- quarter were multi- and bilateral donors or technical support agencies supporting local seed systems through government projects. The remaining two were South-based NGOs.

The ODI/CAZS study of seed regulatory frameworks consists of a review of the relevant literature and the development of a model for analysing different country experiences, followed by seven commissioned country studies in Africa, Asia and Latin America. The case studies include attention to local-level seed provision alternatives and their relations with formal seed regulatory systems.

Before proceeding further, we should draw attention to three dimensions of our analysis. First, as regards farmers, in most developing countries

Box 11.1 Small farmers' seed needs—a summary

○ **Varieties**: farmers may use a large number of varieties of each crop and in addition many look for intra-varietal variation rather than uniformity and stability. Non-yield attributes (taste, storability, straw yield, etc.) are important. Demand for local farmers' varieties can be as strong or stronger than for modern varieties. The specific characteristics required in any given situation will depend on the function of each crop in the local farming system both agronomically and economically.

○ **Seed quality**: seed that meets formal quality standards may be unnecessary but seed has to be of proven and reliable physiological quality for it to be demanded by small farmers. Providing seed of superior physiological quality to that which farmers are currently saving themselves can be more valued than providing new genetic material.

○ **Quantity of seed**: the quantity of seed an individual farmer requires depends on prevailing seed replacement and sowing rates (which are not necessarily the same as those recommended by the research and extension services). The quantity required each year for a given crop may be extremely small and farmers often want to be able to buy seed in small packets.

○ **Timeliness of seed delivery**: seed from outside must arrive in good time for farmers' preparation and planting timetable. Again, this may differ from that recommended by the agricultural services. This is one of the most important small farmers' seed needs—because their labour-intensive production methods mean that planting at the right time is critical.

○ **Accessibility of seed delivery points**: farmers are often willing to travel some distance to acquire seed, so long as it is known to be of good quality. But they can have strong preferences for different kinds of seed delivery points (government crop authority, private seed company, general trader, other farmers, etc.), which vary between crops.

○ **Retail seed prices**: all but the poorest and most insecure families are able to buy seed, so long as it is of proven good quality, because seed purchases make up a relatively small proportion of total production costs. However, many families find it difficult to pay cash for seed and will seek alternative methods (labouring, in-kind loans, etc.) to acquire seed.

○ **Support services**: the potential benefit of using seed of certain varieties often depends on the use of fertilizer or some other external input. In this case, there will be no demand for the seed unless there is a service providing these complementary inputs.

Source: Cromwell *et al.*, 1992

small-scale resource-poor farmers operating in complex, diverse and risky (CDR) environments (Chambers, 1991) constitute a majority in terms of area cultivated and proportion of the agricultural population. Therefore, this chapter focuses on the needs of these farmers which are summarized in Box 11.1.

Second, as regards crops, we focus on cereal and legume crops propagated by true seed. This is because these are the crops of greatest importance in most small-farm farming systems in developing countries. Vegetatively propagated crops, such as potatoes and cassava, are very important in a number of countries but they present quite different technical seed production and distribution issues and they therefore receive less consideration here. Similarly, specific issues related to the production of vegetable or pasture grass seed are not discussed in any detail.

Third, as regards type of seed we use the following definitions. The seed produced by government and private sector seed organizations is often referred to as 'quality seed' or 'improved seed', but the implication of this—that it is better than the seed which farmers can save for themselves—is not always justified in practice. By the same token, although such organizations are usually described as producing seed of 'high-yielding varieties', these varieties do not always yield well in the complex, diverse and risky environments in which the majority of farmers in developing countries operate.

Two distinctions are useful for our purposes. First, the seed that these organizations produce are generally modern varieties (MVs), i.e. varieties produced using formal scientific plant breeding methods with the aim of being genetically distinct from others, and uniform and stable. Second, the seed has usually been through a formal quality control process, albeit sometimes imperfectly because of mechanical breakdowns or logistical problems. In this chapter we refer to the product of government and conventional private sector seed organizations as 'formal sector seed'. We call the seed that farmers save on-farm and circulate amongst themselves 'farmer seed'. This includes seed of landraces, farm-saved MVs and mixtures of the two resulting from farmer selection and breeding. These materials are generally less distinct, uniform and stable than MVs. In addition, farmer seed does not go through a formal quality control procedure in the same way that formal sector seed does, although—as we shall show later—farmers' own selection and handling skills can produce seed of good genetic and physiological quality.

An overview of local-level seed activity

Local-level seed activities and voluntary agencies
A country's seed sector can be defined as a set of institutions involved in the multiplication, processing and distribution of seed. Two different parts

to the sector have been distinguished in the previous section. On the one hand, there is the formal sector, which includes government seed companies or parastatals, and private commercial companies, which may have domestic or multinational origins. On the other hand, there is the informal sector, consisting of both individual farmers saving seed on-farm and the various informal means by which communities share seed amongst themselves.

This division between formal and informal seed sectors is not adequate, however, to address the increasing amount of local-level seed activity that draws on resources from both the formal and informal seed sectors. Local-level seed activities include a range of endeavours, from those that simply try to improve the infrastructure of farmer access to seed of local varieties, to those that attempt to link organizations and varieties from the formal sector to local seed production. Local-level seed activities, as defined here, are distinguished by a combination of elements from the formal and informal sectors in order to strengthen local seed capacity. These local-level activities may occasionally be the products of government programmes, but most often they are initiated by voluntary agencies or farmer organizations.

Voluntary agencies include not only formally constituted Northern- and Southern-based NGOs but also a wide range of grassroots organizations. These latter organizations range from relatively structured membership co-operatives seeking to promote the welfare of their members through an agreed set of activities, to church groups and other community development organizations, to more spontaneous and loose groupings of individuals responding to particular problems.

The formally constituted NGOs often control all resources and operations in the local-level seed activities that they initiate, and effectively act as an intermediary in the production and distribution chain of the formal seed sector. The more informal organizations may start seed activities out of a desire to help communities to become more self-sufficient, in which case farmers themselves may control activities. These activities may be relatively unstructured and have farmers' own seed, rather than MVs supplied by the formal sector, as the focus of operations.

In this chapter we consider the various types of local-level seed activities that have been initiated in the past decade, examine their strengths and weaknesses and ask how seed regulatory reform can contribute to improving their effectiveness.

Deficiencies of the formal sector

In many parts of Asia there are numerous formal sector seed organizations, both government and private sector, providing a wide range of MV seed through relatively well-developed distribution systems to various types of farmers. But in Africa, less than one-third of the countries surveyed by the FAO Seed Improvement and Development project in the mid-1980s had established formal seed production and distribution facilities for major food crops and less than 10 per cent of the total cropped area was under MVs (FAO, 1987b).

Overall, some 60–70 per cent of seed used by small farmers in developing countries is saved on-farm.[1] Of the remainder, seed sourced from the public sector and commercial companies constitutes at most 10 per cent and often as little as 2 per cent (CIAT, 1982). The remaining 20–30 per cent is obtained off-farm from what we call local-level sources.

Although there is now considerable pressure on the formal seed sector to become more efficient and more participatory, and to supply varieties that are more useful to farmers in CDR areas, there are various reasons why it can be unable or unwilling to meet CDR farmers' seed needs. One important reason is high transaction costs. There are high costs associated with assessing the complex seed requirements of farmers in CDR areas. Formal sector costs are further increased by the extra transport and storage costs incurred in satisfying CDR farmers' seed requirements: namely, having to produce seed of many crop varieties that will generally be sold in small amounts, and carrying stocks of seed sufficient to meet uncertain and fluctuating demand. In addition to steep transaction costs, formal sector seed suppliers have found it difficult to supply CDR farmers with useful and appropriate modern varieties. Formal sector plant breeding is usually focused on producing a limited portfolio of varieties that will produce high yields in response to inputs. These are more suited to farmers in areas of good soils and good access to irrigation water and chemical fertilizer, than to farmers in CDR areas. Supplying CDR farmers with modern varieties of self-pollinated crops is particularly unattractive to the formal sector because of the possibility of farmers only buying small quantities infrequently, and in the interim maintaining the varieties on-farm.

Local-level seed activity: comparative advantage

This section describes the principal motivations for the establishment of local-level seed activities and then presents a brief overview of some of the major types of activities that are currently being promoted in developing countries. The section concludes with an examination of the major strengths and weaknesses of current local-level seed activities.

Rationale for involvement

Voluntary agencies become involved in the seed sector for a variety of reasons. In some cases, they undertake *relief* seed distribution after emergencies such as war or drought. In other cases NGOs may be seeking to act as a *substitute* source of supply for MV seed to farmers who are not

1 Author's estimate based on various published country-level calculations.

served by other types of seed organization—because they are poor or remote, or because the government system is not operating effectively. Some voluntary agencies may be trying to *empower* communities by helping them to multiply seed of local varieties and landraces, thus conserving genetic diversity at the local level. This is becoming increasingly popular with many South-based NGOs, who consider such a strategy to be important for the sustainability of small farm systems, given the increased dependency and risk that the use of MV seed can involve. Or, voluntary agencies may be acting as *advocates* for disadvantaged groups, by lobbying on their behalf nationally or internationally and providing information and analytical support to them.

The organization of local-level seed activities involves a range of seed production and distribution systems. Some of the more important examples are outlined in the following section.

Types of local-level seed activities

There is great variation in the types of local-level seed activities that have been initiated by voluntary agencies and others, and any classification will necessarily be imperfect. Nevertheless, it is worth attempting to describe and categorize some of the major examples before proceeding with the analysis. The following discussion concentrates on activities that are designed to be sustainable, hence seed for emergency relief is excluded. It also focuses on activities that go beyond single communities, so seed banks and similar attempts to improve a single community's seed security receive less attention.

Farmer improvement and dissemination of crop varieties. There is growing interest in strengthening the capacity of farming communities to manage and develop their own crop genetic resources. Some of this interest is reflected in the various types of participatory plant breeding that are analysed in Chapter 10. In most of these cases, farmers are working at least partially with varieties or breeding materials from the formal sector, and are selecting materials that are immediately useful for their conditions or contributing to the development of MVs that are better targeted to local needs.

In addition, there are several efforts initiated by NGOs that focus on the utilization and improvement of local varieties. Cordeiro (1993) describes how a network of NGOs in Brazil has helped communities identify and preserve local maize varieties. Many of these materials have been included in national trials organized in collaboration with the public agricultural research institute (EMBRAPA); farmers have selected varieties from these trials and further improved them. In Zimbabwe, ENDA (an NGO) has worked with farmers to identify preferred local varieties of sorghum and pearl millet, to establish experiments for selecting superior types and to exchange seed of these varieties among communities (Mushita, 1993). There are several NGOs in the Philippines that are working with communities to preserve and enhance local rice varieties; farmers are encouraged to participate in breeding and selection activities, and seed of the locally improved varieties is distributed to other communities (Salazar, 1992).

Seed multiplication at the local level. One of the most common seed activities initiated by NGOs is the establishment of local seed multiplication capacity in order to improve farmers' access to seed of either modern or local varieties. In Ecuador, the NGO CESA works with farmer groups to identify preferred potato varieties and to establish community plots where the seed will be multiplied. CESA supplies the initial seed and chemical inputs and then recovers its investment in harvested seed. Farmer group members are given part of the harvest in return for their labour and the rest is sold to local farmers. In The Gambia, public sector agencies are no longer able to produce all the seed needed nationally; instead, several NGOs help to identify local farmers to multiply foundation seed of MVs and the NGOs help with distribution. The growers are also able to sell some of their seed directly to other farmers. A seed programme initiated by an NGO in Bolivia is described as *refrescamiento* ('refreshment'), where fresh seed of MVs of rice and maize is provided to selected local growers every three or four years; the growers then sell the multiplied seed to neighbours who want to renew their seed stocks (Rosales, 1995b).

Establishing farmers as commercial contract growers. In certain cases, NGOs have helped to identify and establish local farmers as contract growers for commercial seed operations. The Aga Khan Rural Support Programme (AKRSP) has been working in high-altitude areas of northern Pakistan that are ideal for seed potato production. The AKRSP helped village organizations initiate seed production and attracted funding for the establishment of a seed testing laboratory under the management of the Federal Seed Certification Department. The seed potato is purchased by private companies which send it for sale to farmers in the Punjab (Alam and Saleemi, 1996). In Bangladesh, the Mennonite Central Committee (MCC) undertook a large project to promote soybeans that included research, seed production, extension and market promotion. As part of this effort, they contracted growers to produce seed that was sold to farmers through the MCC's agricultural programmes.

Local-level commercial seed production. A growing number of local-level seed activities attempt to establish commercially viable production enterprises. Many of these activities represent a shift in focus from simply increasing the availability of good quality seed to addressing the sustainability of local seed provision options. Several seed activities in the hills of Nepal (run by NGOs or established as components of foreign donor agricultural projects) have trained local farmers in seed production for food crops and vegetables. In most cases, the trend has been to establish local mechanisms that make seed marketing independent of the NGO or the project; individual farmers or farmer groups may take charge of marketing, or the seed producers may contract with seed merchants (Joshi, 1995). In Ghana, Global 2000 and the Ghana Seed Inspection Unit train and support small-scale seed entrepreneurs to produce and market seed of maize, cowpea and other crops (Bockari-Kugbei, 1994). In Colombia, several farmers' co-operatives took advantage of demand for seed of new bean varieties to begin production and marketing activities (Janssen *et al.*, 1992). Rosales, (1995b) describes the growth of an association of co-operatives in Bolivia, supported by the local university, an NGO and the regional seed board, to produce and market bean seed.

There is evidence that a number of NGOs are placing more emphasis on establishing commercially viable seed operations. The latest step in the MCC's 20-year involvement with the promotion of soybeans in Bangladesh is to guide the establishment of an independent private seed company that will assume many of the functions previously managed by MCC (Chakraborty and Schroeder, 1996). Similarly, a CARE seed project in Sri Lanka that was initially concerned with general seed provision has changed its focus to the establishment of independent commercial seed enterprises, run by co-operatives or individual entrepreneurs (R. Tripp, personal communication).

These examples illustrate the fact that the distinction between local-level seed activities and those of the formal sector is not clear-cut. Seed initiatives that begin as local-level activities supported by external agencies may evolve to become fully-fledged commercial seed enterprises that can be considered part of the formal seed sector. Correct classification is, of course, not the issue; attention should rather be focused on the conditions that allow the maximum diversity of seed provision endeavours to serve local needs.

Strengths

Local-level seed activities have a clear advantage in meeting CDR farmers' variety needs as they typically deal with relevant farmer varieties as well as adaptations of MVs. Farmers have for many centuries been actively involved in variety maintenance, and these skills are highly developed within many community seed systems. For example, when seed banks were established in Eritrea in the late 1980s in response to drought and war, the agency involved was able to capitalize on farmers' finely-tuned selection skills which allowed them to maintain a large diversity of varieties of different crops, including small-seeded ones such as tef and millet (Berg, 1992).

The limited evidence which has been collected (Wright *et al.*, 1994) suggests that there is also a considerable amount of indigenous knowledge within farming communities about solutions to on-farm storage problems using locally available materials. Local skills and technologies appear consistently to produce seed of equal or better quality than formal sector seed at the point of sale. For example, the CIAT Great Lakes Regional Programme in east Africa recently conducted experiments to measure the comparative quality of bean seed saved by farmers and seed obtained from the local agricultural research station and found 'no statistical difference . . . in terms of vigour, emergence and yield' (CIAT, 1992:4).

Local-level seed activities are often able to deal effectively with some of the quality control and marketing problems that plague the formal seed sector. There is no 'moral hazard' involved in obtaining seed locally because farmers usually know the person supplying seed to them. The individual quantities of seed exchanged are often very small compared with the amount formal sector organizations typically deal in, and because seed is available at community level, farmers do not have to travel far to source it.

Most local-level seed activities are initiated and supported by voluntary agencies, which are conventionally thought of as having a range of strengths in the development process (Farrington *et al.*, 1993). Their more flexible and independent approach, compared with public sector agencies for example, is believed to allow them to reach disadvantaged groups and farmers in marginal and variable environments, and to respond more quickly to their needs. Indeed, nowadays they often fill a gap left by the withdrawal of the public sector as a result of budget cuts. Furthermore, it is believed that their integrated approach allows them to pay attention to the institutional and economic context of development, as well as to technical factors, and their use of participatory methods is believed to increase the sustainability of their development activities.

It is certainly true that voluntary agencies often act as bridging organizations between the formal seed sector, which may not be very effective at reaching farmers in CDR areas, and farmers who may be experiencing problems in accessing the seed that they need. There is a misperception, however, that all local-level seed activities are necessarily small-scale. Several project profiles contradict this image, and present large-scale operations. In The Gambia and Nepal, for instance, voluntary agencies are in fact replacing formal sector seed activity in the regions in which they operate. The evidence from Mozambique (Cromwell *et al.*, 1993) suggested that all the voluntary agencies there could do the same, if the institutional barriers to this were removed.

Weaknesses
The ODI study on local-level seed alternatives revealed a number of weaknesses characteristic of voluntary agency involvement in the seed sector.

One of the principal concerns is that not all agencies have the time and resources to develop the necessary technical capabilities for organizing seed production and distribution (Osborn, 1990). Few of the agencies had surveyed their project area in advance in order to identify the appropriate range of technical seed services to be supported. It appears that most of the agencies made these decisions based on their own interests and policy agenda.

Furthermore, many voluntary agencies have relatively little understanding of the genetic and physiological attributes of the seed they work with. For example, one-third of the agencies reviewed in the ODI study did not test varieties for local adaptability before promoting them, or satisfy themselves that this had already been done by another agency. A similar proportion did not use seed from formally accredited sources. However, about half the agencies maintained rigorous quality control procedures in harvesting, treating, storing and testing the seed they produced. They obtained good test results and would have had little problem in getting the seed formally certified. Obtaining certification was, however, quite difficult: the government testing authorities often did not have sufficient resources to reach all the scattered production plots in order to carry out the necessary field inspections and laboratory tests in time for marketing the seed.

Although many of the local-level seed activities reviewed for the ODI study were closely associated with attempts to empower local communities, and two-thirds of the projects involved some degree of community control, none of the agencies investigated traditional community seed systems in any detail. It was much more common for voluntary agencies to set up new structures for seed multiplication and distribution than to build on practices already existing within communities. This meant that agency structures were often not well established or understood within the community. This problem is compounded by the fact that in some cases Southern NGOs are perceived as élitist by the local communities with whom they work (Fowler, 1991).

Similarly, few agencies had attempted to trace how far project seed had spread and to which social groups. Comments made by agency staff and the limited literature on this subject (see, for example, Green, 1987; Cromwell, 1990; Sperling and Loevinsohn, 1992) suggest that diffusion of seed through local-level networks may be less equitable than is generally assumed.

Although most of the agencies surveyed aimed to work with poorer groups, only in a few cases did they target poorer farmers within their areas of operation. Consequently, the relatively better-off and more powerful, with their extra resources and easier interaction with outsiders, were in most cases the first to benefit from the introduction of local-level seed activities. Moreover, where the agencies' seed activities involved multiplication as well as distribution, farmer multipliers inevitably had to be selected on the basis of their skill and resources, thereby favouring the better-resourced growers. This highlights the difficulties of attempting to make local-level seed activities provide both an income-generating activity for seed growers and a cheaper seed service for small farmers.

Most local-level seed projects assume that seed transactions will be cash-based. This has potentially severe implications for the social impact of their activities, because all the evidence shows that a significant minority of most farming communities do not have the resources to pay cash for seed. Supporting local-level production would therefore appear to achieve little in terms of wider access to seed for the most disadvantaged groups, unless it includes non-cash methods of distribution.

There were also significant problems with the economic viability of many of the local-level seed projects examined. The economic costs of seed produced with voluntary agency support were typically about 3.5 times more than the price at which it was sold. Added to this, staffing and administration overheads are usually absorbed elsewhere in the agencies' budgets. It is only externally funded NGOs, which are usually independent of local revenues for continued activity, that can bear these high costs.

As regards sustainability, there are few recorded examples of local-level seed activities operating for more than five years at a time, and most of these have been the subject of radical reorganization during their lifespan. Most of the agencies surveyed were experiencing problems in handing over activities to community control, despite their expressed desire to do so. For half of them, this was due to continued harvest failures threatening seed production or seed bank replenishment; for the other half, it was because of problematic links between their seed activities and the wider national economy, including problems with supplies of complementary inputs and with making links with government extension and seed certification services. The cost of compensating for the failure of these links is high and pushes up the cost of seed produced at the local level.

Institutional requirements for effective local-level seed activity

We have seen that local-level seed activities can replace or complement, public and private sector seed provision, depending on the situation. But the discussion in the previous section has pointed to significant weaknesses that must be addressed; deficiencies have been noted in both the economic viability and the institutional linkages of local-level seed projects. This means that both internal management structures and external relations merit examination.

Internal management
The voluntary agencies that initiate local-level seed activities are typically independent and flexible in their work, information sources, communication

methods and organizational structure. But there can also be disadvantages in voluntary agencies' organization and method of working. They are often small, many have relatively unskilled staff, and their programmes can be chosen somewhat unsystematically and distributed unevenly among and within countries. This can limit their effectiveness and long-term impact.

In relation to seed activities, voluntary agencies can quickly become subject to the same rigidities of organization and operation as formal sector seed organizations. Thus opportunities for farmer participation may be severely limited, which is one of theoretical advantages of local-level seed activities.

Most of the agencies surveyed for the ODI study had the necessary internal administrative systems in place to be able to plan and implement their work effectively, and they achieved significant results in terms of output and farmer contact. However, a number achieved this at the cost of having to absorb substantial overhead expenses.

Furthermore, it was not always clear that they had a good grasp of what their local-level seed activities were achieving. In particular, routine record-keeping and formal monitoring were not always in place. Often the outputs of the agencies' non-seed activities were easily visible—wells, schools, etc.—and so monitoring consisted of little more than physical verification. Seed activities tended to be monitored in the same way, focusing on the number of hectares under seed multiplication, quantity of seed harvested, etc. Questions about the quality of seed and its impact on local farming systems, and about its use and distribution, were often not addressed systematically.

External relations
Although there is an increasing realization that the internal management and economic viability of local-level seed projects deserve attention, there is still insufficient acknowledgement of the degree to which successful local-level seed activities are dependent on external links, with similar activities elsewhere and with organizations in the formal seed sector.

In some cases examined for the ODI study, networking between voluntary agencies involved in local-level seed activities was highly successful. For example, the On-Farm Seed Production Project, which networked and provided technical support to voluntary agencies active in seed activities in The Gambia and Senegal, was commended by both voluntary agencies and government organizations. However, in other cases inadequate time and resources and poor co-ordination reduced the effectiveness and sustainability of local-level seed activities. Collaboration with other voluntary agencies and government was often weak: agencies frequently found themselves competing for resources or setting up parallel, duplicate seed activities. For some agencies, particularly the smaller ones, this was because they had insufficient resources to allocate to forming links, while in other cases poor links were simply due to unfamiliarity with other agencies' operating procedures, or to differing aims and objectives.

Agencies tended to learn by experience as a substitute for getting relevant advice and support from other organizations. As a result, there were often problems in co-ordinating with other seed organizations—particularly those operated by the government—and with national seed policy, regardless of the degree of effort invested in trying to achieve this by the agencies involved. Where problems were encountered it was difficult to disentangle those caused by pressure on government budgets from those caused by public sector antipathy towards voluntary agencies.

Attitudes of voluntary agencies also affect their ability to form wider links. In a number of countries, local NGOs have served as a focal point of opposition to unpopular regimes; the situation in the Philippines in the early 1980s is an outstanding example (Miclat-Teves and Lewis, 1993). In these instances, it may be particularly difficult to form links with government organizations in the seed sector. In certain cases, voluntary agencies can develop their own expertise in seed technology and plant breeding, or can draw upon sympathetic university staff for advice. But where possible, stronger links with the government seed sector will help strengthen local-level seed activities.

There are several key links that agencies must address to ensure the sustainability of local-level seed activities. These include the exchange of information about local varietal needs, the identification of a reliable source of foundation seed, the access to technical advice on plant breeding and seed production and the development of effective marketing channels for project seed.

Farmers will only buy seed of varieties that are relevant to their needs. Local-level seed projects can further their own cause by making sure that the varietal requirements of farmers in CDR areas are made known to national plant breeding institutes. This will increase the probability that new and useful varieties will be produced that merit a seed-production project.

For those local-level activities focused on producing seed of MVs, a key factor is access to source seed that can be used for multiplication. If a project is to be sustainable, representatives of the seed-producing farmers must know how to obtain this seed from the government research organization (or other sources) and must establish a means of paying for it. When projects produce seed of local varieties, technical advice may also be necessary for maintaining an adequate quality of the source seed used for multiplication.

Access to technical advice on seed production is also essential for the viability of local-level production. Voluntary agencies can help establish relationships with government agencies. There are already several examples of this type of relationship: local extension agents and researchers provide advice to seed production projects in Nepal (Joshi, 1995); the

Ghana Seed Inspection Unit helps train seed producers in Ghana (Bockari-Kugbei, 1994); and regional seed boards in Bolivia provide advice to NGO seed projects (Rosales, 1995b).

Finally, no seed-production activity can be viable without an adequate marketing structure. Some voluntary agency seed projects have assumed that the seed would be sold locally, by individual farmers to their neighbours, but this strategy has had limited success. Often more formal and widespread market links are required. This has occupied considerable attention for several seed projects in Nepal, for instance; in some cases independent seed marketing groups are established, and in other cases relationships are developed with a national association of seed merchants (Joshi, 1995).

The role of seed policy and regulatory agencies

As demonstrated above, there are still defects with the local-level approach that need to be corrected, and most activities are still relatively small scale and costly. Some of the defects are the result of internal factors and can only be addressed by the voluntary agencies themselves, but a number arise from current seed policy and regulatory frameworks. We outline below some of the changes in government policy and support which could strengthen local-level seed activities.

Seed policy

Seed-sector institutions. In many countries there are restrictions on the types of institutions allowed to operate in the seed sector. In many African countries, for instance, there has been traditional discouragement of voluntary agency activity except in the provision of emergency aid. It is only since economic liberalization began in the mid-1980s that the role of voluntary agencies in development has increased and diversified. These restrictions could usefully be modified to allow public sector plant breeders and seed quality-control services to work with voluntary agencies, and to ensure that farmers in CDR areas are better represented in the client focus for these breeding and quality control organizations.

As we saw above, linkages with external institutions supplying plant breeding expertise and quality control services are essential for voluntary agencies. It is possible to minimize the need for such linkages by using low-input seed production and distribution systems, but external advice and collaboration will still be needed to some extent. Such links can provide valuable feedback for government organizations, based on voluntary agencies' direct contact with farmers.

The *nature* of the linkages between government and voluntary agencies is also important: these linkages should be supportive of local management and control of resources. Governments could include local-level seed activities in national seed-sector planning and policy. The limited scale on which this has been done so far reflects the fact that relationships between governments and local-level seed activities are still evolving. So far, governments have tended to share discrete tasks of implementation with voluntary agencies, but they have not encouraged agencies to contribute to policymaking and other forms of innovation. This could bring significant benefits. Thus government organizations could benefit from being more open and flexible, in order to capitalize on what voluntary agencies have to offer. Changes in the attitude of governments to local-level seed activities and the agencies that support them will become increasingly necessary as economic reform emphasizes market mechanisms and the role of the private sector in development.

Another aspect of institutional policy that has an important influence on local-level seed activities is the degree of co-ordination between the different government organizations involved in formulating seed-sector policy. In particular, the policies set by national seed boards or seed policy units within the Ministry of Agriculture often conflict with policies for the conservation and sustainable use of biodiversity set by government institutions charged with implementing the International Convention on Biological Diversity and Agenda 21. Local-level seed activities can provide an important bridge here, as they emphasize private initiative, on the one hand, but support the maintenance and enhancement of local varietal diversity, on the other.

Seed pricing policy. One of the main limitations on the long-term economic viability of many local-level seed activities is government intervention in price setting, where official seed prices do not reflect the full costs of production. It is not uncommon for there to be intense competition with farmers' varieties promoted by voluntary agencies, from seed provided at subsidized prices by government companies or extension programmes. Another aspect is the tying of agricultural subsidies and credit programmes to the use of public sector seed of MVs: this can artificially promote their use and severely restrict the viability of local-level seed activities geared to supplying farmers' varieties. A further problem is the policy whereby crop marketing authorities buy only MVs: this gives farmers thinking of buying seed of local varieties little prospect of selling the resulting produce on the official market.

Cultivar improvement and variety release
Local-level activities may need to provide access to seed of a new crop, to seed of new varieties of a crop that farmers already grow or to fresh seed of varieties already in use. In general terms, it is usually most helpful to provide a diverse range of varieties. It is also usually beneficial to

concentrate on material which has low requirements for external inputs and which meets farmers' needs in terms of non-yield characteristics. This implies a decentralization of government plant breeding and a re-orientation of plant-breeding objectives to serve the needs of farmers in CDR areas (see Chapter 4 of this volume).

As Biggs (1981) points out, it is relatively simple to identify an 'ideal' institutional model for formal sector agricultural research. However, exter-nal factors—such as the professional objectives of scientists, the interests of international donors and of different client groups and national develop-ment goals—have a critical influence on the actors within this model and thus on the relative strength of the key linkages. In many cases, this has meant that the ideal model has not worked in practice. The type of on-farm client-oriented research approach described by Kaimowitz (1990) is one way of reducing these imperfections, but much more needs to be done to make agricultural research genuinely adaptive and participatory.

For example, farmers' capacity for plant breeding needs to be investi-gated properly: few objective investigations of this have been undertaken so far, although the available evidence suggests that farmers have consider-able capacity to develop new varieties (Chapter 10 of this volume). This implies that the formal agricultural research sector should supply advanced material for selection at farm level and not only finished varieties. The possible impact of an increased application of plant variety protection (PVP) by public sector research institutions on the availability of advanced breeding material requires attention, however.

Thus formal sector agricultural research institutions should be encour-aged to allocate resources and tools to strengthening local-level innovation in breeding and plant genetic resource conservation. However, the formal research system should also continue with basic plant breeding for the crops and environments of most relevance to farmers in CDR areas, as this tends to be neglected by private sector research institutions.

Seed quality control

Farmers are often adept at maintaining physical seed quality, and local-level seed activities may not require much support in this area. However, there may be specific problems in certain areas. Assistance with pest and disease identification and with simple improved storage techniques and technologies are often among the main requirements.

Alternative quality-control systems need to be developed that can be used by remote, scattered farmers. The experiences of seed quality-control agencies in Bolivia and Nepal (see Chapter 6 of this volume) in supporting local-level seed activities are instructive. However, the high standards ad-hered to by many quality-control agencies are often not relevant to farmers in CDR areas. Therefore, one important way in which governments could encourage local-level activities is to introduce flexibility in seed quality standards, retaining emphasis only on those aspects that are of real relevance to farmers in CDR areas. In this way, local-level seed activities could officially trade the seed that they produce, enabling them to increase sales and charge realistic prices, as well as to reduce production costs (through not having to observe all the in-field inspection and subsequent testing that is at present often required).

Conclusions

There has been a significant growth in the number and types of local-level seed activities in the past decade. Considerable experience has been gained, but much remains to be learned about how effectively to organize seed-provision strategies that draw on the strengths of both informal and formal seed systems. Government seed policy must take full account of the potential of local-level activities; it must be willing to call upon them when they offer clear advantages, and it must direct resources to address weaknesses and deficiencies in current programmes. The voluntary agencies and others that support local seed activities must redouble their efforts to make them as economically viable as possible. They must also ensure that they are linked to formal sector seed organizations and to community modes of production and distribution. The future of local-level seed activities depends on establishing both economic and institutional sustainability.

Bibliography

Abeygunawardena, P., Reusche, G. and Suraweera, E. (1990) 'Relative Efficiency of Government Farm Seed Production versus Private Sector Seed Production in Sri Lanka', *Sri Lankan Journal of Agricultural Sciences* 27: 138–47.

Agrawal, P.K. and Tunwar, N.S. (1990) 'Seed Certification and Quality Control in India', *Plant Varieties and Seeds* 3(3):165–71.

Akerlof, G. (1970) 'The Market for "Lemons": Quality Uncertainty and the Market Mechanism', *Quarterly Journal of Economics* 84:488–500.

Alam, Z., and Saleemi, A.R. (1996) 'Seed Regulatory Frameworks in Pakistan', unpublished paper prepared for ODI/CAZS Seed Regulatory Project.

Almekinders, C.J.M., Louwaars, N.P and de Bruijn, G.H. (1994) 'Local Seed Systems and Their Importance for an Improved Seed Supply in Developing Countries', *Euphytica* 78:207–11.

Andren, U., Nkomesha, A., Singogo, L.P. and Sutherland, A. (1991) *National Seed Availability Study: Seed Problems, Practices and Requirements among Small-scale Farmers in Zambia*, Lusaka: Ministry of Agriculture, Adaptive Research Planning Team.

Anonymous (1994) 'Survey of Retailed Vegetable Seed in Thailand Reveals Low Germination Rates', *Asian Seed* 1(4):13–14.

Arora, R.S. (1995) 'Considerations Leading Towards Formulation and Introduction of Plant Variety Protection in India', paper presented at Asian Seed '95 Conference, New Delhi, 27–29 September.

Ashby, J.A. (1982) 'Technology and Ecology: Implications for Innovation Research in Peasant Agriculture', *Rural Sociology* 47(2):234–50.

Ashby, J.A. (1986) 'Methodology for the Participation of Small Farmers in the Design of On-farm Trials', *Agricultural Administration* 22:1–19.

Ashby, J.A. and Sperling, L. (1995) 'Institutionalising Participatory, Client-driven Research and Technology Development in Agriculture', *Development and Change* 26:753–70.

Ashby, J.A., Gracia, T., del Pilar Guerrero, M., Quiros, C.A., Roa, J.O. and Beltran, J.A. (1995) *Institutionalizing Farmer Participation in Adaptive Technology Testing with the CIAL*, Agricultural Administration (Research and Extension) Network Paper No. 49. London: Overseas Development Institute.

Ashby, J.A., Gracia, T., del Pilar Guerrero, M., Quiros, C.A., Roa, J.O. and Beltran, J.A. (1996) 'Innovation on the Organisation of Participatory Plant Breeding', in P. Eyzaguirre and M. Iwanaga (eds) *Participatory Plant Breeding*. Rome: IPGRI.

Ayres, I. and Braithwaite, J. (1992) *Responsive Regulation. Transcending the Deregulation Debate.* New York: Oxford University Press.

231

Bal, S.S. and Rajbhandary, K.L. (1987) 'A Model for Seed Production in Remote Areas of Nepal', *Seed Science & Technology* 15:625–32.

Balogun, P. (1996) 'An Empirical Evaluation of Financial Losses due to Failures Within National Seed Regulatory Frameworks', Unpublished paper prepared for ODI/CAZS Seed Regulatory Project.

Banerjee, S.K. (1995) 'Report on Regulatory Framework for Seed Production and Quality Control in India', unpublished paper prepared for ODI/CAZS Seed Regulatory Project.

Bantilan, M.C.S.B., Subba Rao, K.V., Rai, K.N. and Pray, C. (1996) 'Use of ICRISAT-bred Pearl Millet Cultivars, Improved Germplasm and Parental Lines', paper presented at International Workshop on Joint Impact Assessment of NARS-ICRISAT Technologies in the Semi-Arid Tropics, 2–4 December. International Crops Research Institute for the Semi Arid Tropics, Patancheru, A.P., India.

Barber, G. (1985) 'A Seedsman's Views of Seed Certification', in M.B. McDonald Jr. and W.D. Pardee (eds) *The Role of Seed Certification in the Seed Industry*, Crop Science Society of America Special Publication Number 10. Madison, WI: CSSA.

Bates, R. (1981) *Markets and States in Tropical Africa.* Berkeley, CA: University of California Press.

Bellon, M.R. and Brush, S.B. (1994) 'Keepers of Maize in Chiapas, Mexico', *Economic Botany* 48(2):196–209.

Berg, T. (1992) 'Indigenous Knowledge and Plant Breeding in Tigray, Ethiopia', *Forum For Development Studies, Number 1.*

Berg, T., Bjoernstad, A., Fowler, C. and Kroeppa, T. (1991) *Technology Options and the Gene Struggle*, NORAGRIC Occasional Papers Series C.; Development and Environment No. 8. As, Norway: Agricultural University of Norway.

Bernstein, M. (1955) *Regulating Business by Independent Commission.* Princeton, NJ: Princeton University Press.

Biggs, S. (1981) *Institutions and Decision-making in Agricultural Research*, Agricultural Administration (Research and Extension) Network Discussion Paper No. 5. London: Overseas Development Institute.

Boardman, R. (1986) *Pesticides in World Agriculture: The Politics of International Regulation.* London: Macmillan.

Bockari-Kugbei, S. (1994) 'The Role of Small-Scale Enterprises in African Seed Industries', unpublished PhD thesis, University of Reading.

BOF/OGA (British Organic Farmers/Organic Growers Association) (1994) *Organic Certification*, Technical Note 3. Bristol: BOF/OGA.

Boster, J. (1986) 'Exchange of Varieties and Information among Aguaruna Manioc Cultivators', *American Anthropologist* 88:428–36.

Botchwey, K. (1995) 'Sustaining Recovery and Development in Economic Transitions: The Role of Deregulation in Ghana's Experience', *Public Administration and Development* 15:245–7.

Bould, A. (1992) 'Models for Plant Variety Registration and Grant of Plant Breeders Rights in the European Community and the Developed World', in ICAR, *Proceedings of the Group Discussion on Management of Change in All India Co-ordinated Crop Improvement Projects.* New Delhi: Indian Council of Agricultural Research.

Bray, F. (1986) *The Rice Economies: Technology and Development in Asian Societies.* Oxford: Basil Blackwell.

Brennan, J. and Byerlee, D. (1991) 'The Rate of Crop Varietal Replacement on Farms: Measures and Empirical Results for Wheat', *Plant Varieties and Seeds* 4:99–106.

Brett, E. (1993) 'Voluntary Agencies as Development Organizations: Theorizing the Problem of Efficiency and Accountability', *Development and Change* 24:269–303.

Brown, D.E. (1985) 'Seed Certification: a Seed-control Official's Views', in M.B. McDonald Jr. and W.D. Pardee (eds) *The Role of Seed Certification in the Seed Industry,* Crop Science Society of America Special Publication Number 10. Madison, WI: CSSA.

Brush, S. (1991) 'A Farmer-Based Approach to Conserving Crop Germplasm', *Economic Botany* 45(2):153–65.

Brush, S., Bellon, M.R. and Schmidt, E. (1988) 'Agricultural Development and Maize Diversity in Mexico', *Human Ecology* 16(3):307–28.

Bureau of National Affairs International Inc. (1995) *World Intellectual Property Report 1995,* Vol. 9. Washington, DC: BNA.

Bureau of National Affairs International Inc. (1996) *World Intellectual Property Report 1996,* Vol. 10. Washington, DC: BNA.

Busch, L., Lacy, W., Burkhardt, J. and Lacy, L. (1991) *Plants, Power and Profit.* Cambridge, MA: Basil Blackwell.

Butler, L.J. (1996) 'Plant Breeders' Rights in the US: Update of a 1983 Study', in van Wijk and Jaffé.

Byerlee, D. and Heisey, P. (1990) 'Wheat varietal diversification over time and space as factors in yield gains and rust resistance in the Punjab', in P. Heisey (ed.), *Accelerating the Transfer of Wheat Breeding Gains to Farmers: A Study of the Dynamics of Varietal Replacement in Pakistan.* Mexico, D.F.: CIMMYT.

Carney, D. (1995) 'The Changing Public Role in Services to Agriculture: A Framework for Analysis', *Food Policy* 20:521–8.

Carney, D. (1996) 'Research and Farmers' Organizations: Prospects for Partnership', Draft Summary. London: Overseas Development Institute.

Ceccarelli, S., Grando, S. and Booth, R.H. (1996) 'International Breeding Programs and Resource-poor Farmers: Crop Improvement in Difficult Environments', in P. Eyzaguirre and M. Iwanaga (eds) *Participatory Plant Breeding.* Rome: IPGRI.

Ceccarelli, S., Erskine, W., Grando, S. and Hamblin, J. (1994) 'Genotype x Environment Interaction and International Breeding Programmes', *Experimental Agriculture* 30:177–87.

Centner, T.J. (1989) 'Imposition of Liability and Allocation of Damages for Defective Seed', *Agribusiness* 5(6):597–606.

Chakraborty, S. and Schroeder, R. (1996) 'Building the Foundation for a Private Seed Enterprise', in H. van Amstel, J. Bottema, M. Sidik and C. van Santen (eds) *Integrating Seed Systems for Annual Food Crops.* Bogor, Indonesia: CGPRT Centre.

Chambers, R. (1991) 'Farmer First: A Practical Paradigm for the Third Agriculture' in M. Altieri and S. Hecht (eds) *Agroecology and Small Farm Development.* Boston, MA: CRC Press.

Chaudhry, M., Heisey, P. and Ahmad, M. (1990) 'Wheat Seed Production and Marketing in the Punjab and NWFP', in P. Heisey (ed.) *Accelerating the Transfer of Wheat Breeding Gains to Farmers: A Study of the Dynamics of Varietal Replacement in Pakistan.* Mexico, D.F.: CIMMYT.

Chopra, K.R. (1986) 'Problems in Seed Production, Certification and Quality Control', in *Proceedings of the First National Seed Seminar, Seed Association of India, New Delhi, 27–28 December.* New Delhi: SAI.

CIAT (1982) *Proceedings of the Conference on Improved Seed for the Small Farmer, 9–13 August, Cali, Colombia.* Cali, Colombia: CIAT.

CIAT (1992) Farmer Participatory Research and the Development of an Improved Bean Seed Strategy in Rwanda', paper prepared for workshop on Farmer Participatory Research, 17–19 February, Addis Ababa, Ethiopia.

CIMMYT (1993) *World Wheat Facts and Trends. The Wheat Breeding Industry in Developing Countries: An Analysis of Investments and Impacts.* Singapore: CIMMYT.

CIMMYT (1994) *CIMMYT 1993/94 World Maize Facts and Trends. Maize Seed Industries Revisited: Emerging Roles of the Public and Private Sectors.* Mexico, D.F.: CIMMYT.

Clunies-Ross, T. and Cox, G. (1994) 'Challenging the Productionist Paradigm: Organic Farming and the Politics of Agricultural Change', in P. Lowe, T. Marsden and S. Whatmore (eds) *Regulating Agriculture.* London: David Fulton Publishers.

Commonwealth Secretariat (1994) *Harmonization of Seed Laws in the SADC Region.* London: Commonwealth Secretariat.

Cordeiro, A. (1993) 'Rediscovering Local Varieties of Maize: Challenging Seed Policy in Brazil', in W. de Boef, K. Amanor, K. Wellard with A.J. Bebbington (eds) *Cultivating Knowledge. Genetic Diversity, Farmer Experimentation and Crop Research.* London: Intermediate Technology Publications.

Cotterrell, R. (1989) *The Politics of Jurisprudence.* London: Butterworth.

Cox, T. (1991) 'The Contribution of Introduced Germplasm to the Development of U.S. Wheat Cultivars', in H. Shands and L. Wiesner (eds) *Use of Plant Introductions in Cultivar Development.* Madison, WI: Crop Science Society of America.

Crissman, C.C. and Uquillas, J.E. (1989) *Seed Potato Systems in Ecuador: A Case Study.* Lima: International Potato Center.

Cromwell, E. (ed.) (1990) *Seed Diffusion Mechanisms in Small Farmer Communities: Lessons from Asia, Africa and Latin America*, Agricultural Administration (Research and Extension) Network Paper No. 21. London: Overseas Development Institute.

Cromwell, E. (1996) *Governments, Farmers and Seeds in a Changing Africa.* Wallingford, UK: Commonwealth Agricultural Bureau International.

Cromwell, E. and Zambezi, B. (1993) *The Performance of the Seed Sector in Malawi.* London: Overseas Development Institute.

Cromwell E. and Wiggins, S. with Wentzel, S. (1993) *Sowing Beyond The State: NGOs and Seed Supply in Developing Countries.* London: Overseas Development Institute.

Cromwell, E., Friis-Hansen, E. and Turner, M. (1992) *The Seed Sector in Developing Countries: a Framework for Performance Analysis*, Working Paper No. 65. London: Overseas Development Institute.

Crucible Group (1994) *People, Plants and Patents: The Impact of Intellectual Property on Biodiversity, Conservation, Trade and Rural Society.* Ottawa: IDRC.

Cuevas-Perez, F., Amezquita, M.C. and Lema, G. (1995) 'Diffusion Patterns of Individual Rice Varieties in Colombia and Southern Brazil', *Plant Varieties and Seeds* 8:9–15.

Curnow, I. (1961) 'Optimal Programmes for Varietal Selection', *Journal of the Royal Statistical Society* 23:282–318.

Dale, B. (ed.) (1994) *Managing Quality.* New York: Prentice Hall.

Dalrymple, D. and Srivastava, J. (1994) 'Transfer of Plant Cultivars: Seeds, Sectors and Society', in J. Anderson (ed.) *Agricultural Technology: Policy Issues for the International Community.* Wallingford, UK: Commonwealth Agricultural Bureau Internationl.

De Alencar, G.S. and van Ree, M.C. (1996) '1996: An Important Year for Brazilian Biopolitics', *Biotechnology and Development Monitor* 27, June.

Delouche, J.C. (1990) 'Seed Industry Development in Asia—Selected Case Studies', Draft Report to USAID/Bangladesh. Mississippi State: Seed Technology Laboratory, Mississippi State University.

Douglas, J. (1980) *Successful Seed Programs. A Planning and Management Guide.* Boulder, CO: Westview Press.

Due, J. (1990) 'Tanzania Seed Release, Multiplication and Distribution Systems', *Seed Science and Technology* 18:187–94.

Echeverria, R. (1990) *Public and Private Investments in Maize Research in Mexico and Guatemala*, CIMMYT Economics Working Paper 90/03. Mexico, D.F.: CIMMYT.

Eisner, M.A. (1993) *Regulatory Politics in Transition.* Baltimore, MD: Johns Hopkins University Press.

Evans, L. (1993) *Crop Evolution, Adaptation and Yield.* Cambridge: Cambridge University Press.

Eyzaguirre, P. and Iwanaga, M. (eds) (1996) *Participatory Plant Breeding.* Rome: IPGRI.

FAO (1987a) *FAO Seed Review 1984–85.* Rome: FAO.

FAO (1987b) 'Evaluation of the Seed Improvement and Development Programme', paper presented to 24th conference session, Rome, November.

FAO (1993) *Quality Declared Seed*, FAO Plant Production and Protection Paper 117. Rome: FAO.

FAO (1994a) *China Seeds Industry Commercialization Project*, Project Brief and Working Papers. Rome: FAO.

FAO (1994b) *FAO Seed Review 1989–90.* Rome: FAO.

Farrington, J. and Bebbington, A. with Wellard, K. and Lewis, D.J. (1993) *Reluctant Partners? Non-Governmental Organizations, the State and Sustainable Agricultural Development.* London: Routledge.

Ferguson, J. (1994) 'El Proceso de Liberación de Nuevos Cultivares de Forrajeras: Experiencias y Perspectivas', in J.E. Ferguson (ed.) *Semilla de Especies Forrajeras Tropicales. Conceptos, Casos y Enfoque de la Investigación y la Producción.* Proceedings of the 8th Meeting of the Advisory Committee of RIEPT, November, 1992, Cali, Colombia: CIAT.

Fitzgerald, D. (1990) *The Business of Breeding. Hybrid Corn in Illinois, 1890–1940.* Ithaca, NY: Cornell University Press.

Finney, D.J. (1958) 'Plant Selection for Yield Improvement', *Euphytica* 7: 83–106.

Flora, J. (1988) 'History of Wheat Research of the Kansas Agricultural Experiment Station', in L. Busch and W. Lacy (eds) *The Agricultural Scientific Enterprise. A System in Transition.* Boulder CO: Westview Press.

Fowler, A. (1991) 'The Role of NGOs in Changing State-Society Relationships: Perspectives from Eastern and Southern Africa', *Development Policy Review* 9(1):53–84.

Fowler, C. (1994) *Unnatural Selection. Technology, Politics, and Plant Evolution.* Yverdon, Switzerland: Gordon and Breach.

Francks, P. (1984) *Technology and Agricultural Development in Pre-War Japan.* New Haven, CT: Yale University Press.

Freeman, C. (1988) 'Preface to Part II', in G. Dosi, C. Freeman, R. Nelson, G. Silverber and L. Soete (eds) *Technical Change and Economic Theory.* London: Pinter Publishers.

Friedman, L. (1985) 'On Regulation and Legal Process', in R. Noll (ed.) *Regulatory Policy and the Social Sciences.* Berkeley, CA: University of California Press.

Friis-Hansen, E. (1989) *Seeds of Wealth, Seeds of Risk? The Vulnerability of Hybrid Maize Production in the Southern Highlands of Tanzania.* Copenhagen: Centre for Development Research.

Friis-Hansen, E. (1992) *Seeds for African Peasants. A Case Study from Zimbabwe.* Copenhagen: Centre for Development Research.

Fujisaka, S., Guino, R.A., Lubigan, R.T. and Moody, K. (1993) 'Farmers' Rice Seed Management Practices and Resulting Weed Seed Contamination in the Philippines', *Seed Science & Technology* 21:149–57.

Galt, D.L. (1989) *Joining FSR to Commodity Programme Breeding Efforts Earlier: Increasing Plant Breeding Efficiency in Nepal,* Agricultural Administration (Research and Extension) Network Paper No. 8. London: 4Overseas Development Institute.

Garay, A., Pattie, P., Landivar, J. and Rosales, J. (1988) *Setting a Seed Industry in Motion: A Non-Conventional Successful Approach in a Developing Country,* Working Document No. 57. Cali, Colombia: CIAT.

GATT (1994) *Final Act Embodying the Results of the Uruguay Round of Multilateral Trade Negotiations.* Marrakesh, 15 April 1994: GATT Secretariat.

GGDP (Ghana Grains Development Project) (1991) *A Study of Maize Technology Adoption in Ghana.* Mexico City: GGDP.

Gisselquist, D. (1994) *Import Barriers for Agricultural Inputs,* UNDP-World Bank Trade Expansion Program Occasional Paper 10. Washington, DC: World Bank.

Goldberg, V. (1976) 'Towards an Expanded Economic Theory of Contract', *Journal of Economic Issues* X(i):45–61.

Green, T. (1987) *Farmer-to-farmer Seed Exchange in the Eastern Hills of Nepal: The Case of Pokhreli Masino Rice*, Working Paper 05/87. Dhankuta, Nepal: Pakhribas Agricultural Centre.

Grindle, M. and Thomas, J. (1991) *Public Choices and Policy Change. The Political Economy of Reform in Developing Countries.* Baltimore, MD: Johns Hopkins University Press.

Grisley, W. (1993) 'Seed for Bean Production in Sub-Saharan Africa: Issues, Problems, and Possible Solutions', *Agricultural Systems* 43:19–33.

Groosman, T., Linnemann, A. and Wierema, H. (1991) *Seed Industry Development in a North-South Perspective.* Wageningen, the Netherlands: Pudoc.

Gutiérrez, M.B., with Gianni, C. and Mujica, G. (1995) *El debate y el impacto de los derechos de obtentor en los países en desarrollo. El caso Argentino.* Buenos Aires: INTA/IICA.

Gutiérrez, M.B. (1996) 'La puesta en vigor de los derechos de obtentor en la Argentina', in van Wijk and Jaffé.

Hamilton, N.D. (1996) 'Possible Effects of Recent Developments in Plant Related Intellectual Property Rights in the US', in van Wijk and Jaffé.

Hampton, J.G. and Scott, D.J. (1990) 'New Zealand Seed Certification', *Plant Varieties and Seeds* 3(3):173–80.

Harriss-White, B. (1995) 'The Changing Public Role in Services to Food and Agriculture', *Food Policy* 20:585–96.

Harriss-White, B. (1996) 'Free Market Romanticism in an Era of Deregulation', *Oxford Development Studies* 24:27–45.

Heijbroek, A., Schutter, E. and Gaasbeek, A. (1996) *The World Seed Market. Developments and Strategies.* Utrecht: Rabobank Nederland.

Heisey, P. and Brennan, J. (1991) 'An Analytical Model of Farmers' Demand for Replacement Seed', *American Journal of Agricultural Economics* 73:1 044–52.

Helfand, G. and Archibald, S. (1990) 'California's Proposition 65: A New Regulatory Trend?', in J. Braden and S. Lovejoy (eds) *Agriculture and Water Quality: International Perspectives.* Boulder, CO: Lynne Rienner.

Henderson, P.A. and Singh, R. (1990) *NGO–Government Links in Seed Production: Case Studies from The Gambia and Ethiopia*, Agricultural Administration (Research and Extension) Network Paper No. 14. London: Overseas Development Institute.

Hernandez, J.E. and Borromeo, T.H. (1996) 'Variety Testing, Selection and Release System for Rice in the Philippines', unpublished paper prepared for ODI/CAZS Seed Regulatory Project.

Hirschman, A.O. (1970) *Exit, Voice and Loyalty: Responses to Decline in Firms, Organizations, and States.* Cambridge, MA: Harvard University Press.

Hirschman, A.O. (1986) *Rival Views of Market Society.* New York: Viking.

Iglesias, C. and Hérnandez, L.A. (1994) 'Participatory Cassava Breeding', *Cassava Program Annual Report.* Palmira, Colombia: CIAT

International Service for National Agricultural Research (ISNAR) (1994) *Report of a Workshop: Strengthening the Role of Farmers' Organizations in Technology Development and Transfer*, Briefing Paper 15. The Hague: ISNAR.

Jaffé, W. and van Wijk, J. (1995) *The Impact of Plant Breeders' Rights in Developing Countries: Debate and Experience in Argentina, Chile, Colombia, Mexico, and Uruguay.* The Hague: Directorate General International Cooperation (DGIS), Ministry of Foreign Affairs.

Jaffee, S. and Srivastava, J. (1994) 'The Roles of the Private and Public Sectors in Enhancing the Performance of Seed Systems', *The World Bank Research Observer* 9:97–117.

Jaisani, B.G. (1995) 'Regulatory Framework and Seed Legislation in Gujarat', unpublished paper prepared for ODI/CAZS Seed Regulatory Project.

Jansen, H.G.P., Walker, T.S. and Barker, R. (1989) *Adoption Ceilings and Modern Coarse Cereal Cultivars in India*, Progress Report 92 of the Resource Management Program, Economics Group. Patancheru, A.P., Indra: ICRISAT.

Janssen, W., Luna, C.A. and Duque, M.C. (1992) 'Small-farmer Behaviour Towards Bean Seed: Evidence From Colombia', *Journal of Applied Seed Production* 10:43–51.

Jones, K. (1994) 'Registration and Use of Microbial Insecticides in Developing Countries', in *Proceedings of VIth International Colloquium of Invertebrate Pathology and Microbial Control*, 28 August–2 September 1994, Vol. 1. Montpelier, France: Society for Invertebrate Pathology.

Joshi, K.D. (1995) 'Participatory and Other Alternative Approaches to Seed Production and Distribution in Nepal', ODI/CAZS. Pokhara, Nepal: Lumle Agricultural Research Centre.

Joshi, A. and Witcombe, J.R. (1996a) 'Farmer Participatory Crop Improvement II: Participatory Varietal Selection, a Case Study in India', *Experimental Agriculture* 32:461–77.

Joshi, A. and Witcombe, J.R. (1996b) 'Farmer Participatory Research for the Selection of Rainfed Rice Cultivars' in *Proceedings of the Conference on Fragile Lives in Fragile Ecosystems, International Rice Research Institute*, Los Baños, Philippines.

Kahre, L. (1990) 'The History of Seed Certification in Sweden', *Plant Varieties and Seeds* 3:181–93.

Kaimowitz, D. (ed.) (1990) *Making The Link: Agricultural Research and Technology Transfer in Developing Countries.* Boulder, CO: Westview/ International Service for National Agricultural Research.

Kelly, A.F. (1989) *Seed Planning and Policy for Agricultural Production.* London: Belhaven Press.

Kelly, A.F. and Bowring, J.D.C. (1990) 'The Development of Seed Certification in England and Wales', *Plant Varieties and Seeds* 3(3):139–50.

Kelman, S. (1983) 'Regulation and Paternalism', in T.R. Machan and M.B. Johnson (eds) *Rights and Regulation: Ethical, Political and Economic Issues.* Cambridge, MA: Ballinger Publishing Company.

Kimenye, L. and Nyangito, H. (1996) 'Seed Regulatory Frameworks: Kenya', unpublished paper prepared for ODI/CAZS Seed Regulatory Project.

Klein, B. and Leffler, K.B. (1981) 'The Role of Market Forces in Assuring Contractual Performance', *Journal of Political Economy* 89(4):615–41.

Klitgaard, R. (1988) *Controlling Corruption*. Berkeley, CA: University of California Press.

Kloppenburg, J. (1988) *First The Seed*. Cambridge: Cambridge University Press.

Kloppenburg, J. and Kleinman, D. (1988) 'Seeds of Controversy: National Property Versus Common Heritage', in J. Kloppenburg (ed.) *Seeds and Sovereignty*. Durham, NC: Duke University Press.

Knudson, M. (1990) 'The Role of the Public Sector in Applied Breeding R&D', *Food Policy* 15:209–17.

Kornegay, J., Beltran, J.A. and Ashby, J. (1996) 'Farmer Selection within Segregating Populations of Common Bean in Colombia', in Eyzaguirre and Iwanaga.

Krattiger, A.F. and Rosemarin, A. (1994) *Biosafety for Sustainable Agriculture: Sharing Biotechnology Regulatory Experiences of the Western Hemisphere*. Stockholm and Ithaca, NY: Stockholm Environment Institute (SEI) and International Service for the Acquisition of Agri-Biotech Applications (ISAAA).

Kshirsagar, K. and Pandey, S. (1996) 'Diversity of Rice Cultivars in a Rainfed Village in the Orissa State of India', in L. Sperling and M. Loevinsohn (eds) *Using Diversity: Enhancing and Maintaining Genetic Resources On-Farm*. New Delhi: IDRC/SARO.

Lepiz, R., Ashby, J. and Roa, J. (1994) 'Artisanal Bean Seed Production Experiences in Latin America', paper presented at Workshop on Integrated Seed Systems, Kampala, Uganda, October.

Lewis, D. (1992) *Catalysts for Change? NGOs, Agricultural Technology and the State in Bangladesh*, ODI Agricultural Administration (Research and Extension) Network Paper No. 38. London: Overseas Development Institute.

Lipton, M. and Longhurst, R. (1989) *New Seeds and Poor People*. London: Unwin Hyman.

Lipton, M. and Paarlberg, R. (1990) *The Role of the World Bank in Agricultural Development in the 1990s*. Washington, DC: International Food Policy Research Institute.

Logroño, M.L. (1996) 'Maize Seed Regulatory Framework in the Philippines', unpublished paper prepared for ODI/CAZS Seed Regulatory Project.

Lopez-Pereira, M. and Filippello, M. (1995) *Emerging Roles of the Public and Private Sectors of Maize Industries in the Developing World*, CIMMYT Economics Working Paper 95–01. Mexico D.F.: CIMMYT.

Louwaars, N.P. (1994) 'Integrated Seed Supply: A Flexible Approach', paper presented at the ILCA/ICARDA Research Planning Workshop on Smallholder Seed Production, 13–15 June, Addis Ababa.

Louwaars, N.P. (1996) 'Policies and Strategies for Seed System Development', in H. van Amstel, J. Bottema, M. Sidik and C. van Santen (eds) *Integrating Seed Systems for Annual Food Crops*. Bogor, Indonesia: CGPRT Centre.

Louwaars, N. and Ghijsen, H. (1996) 'Plant Variety Protection. Developing Countries Should Adopt Alternative Schemes', *Prophyta Annual 1996*: 62–4.

Lowry, G. (1995) 'Task Force Studies National Variety Review Boards', *Seed World* 28 (December):28–9.

Lupton, F.G.H. (1988) 'History of Wheat Breeding', in F.G.H. Lupton (ed.) *Wheat Breeding: Its Scientific Basis*. London: Chapman and Hall.

McLaughlin, F. (1985) 'The Role of Seed Certification in the Seed Industry', in M.B. McDonald Jr. and W.D. Pardee (eds) *The Role of Seed Certification in the Seed Industry*, Crop Science Society of America Special Publication Number 10. Madison, WI: CSSA.

McMullen, N. (1987) *Seeds and World Agricultural Progress*. Washington, DC: National Planning Association.

Merrill-Sands, D., Biggs, S., Bingen, R.J., Ewell, P., McAllister, J. and Poats, S. (1991) 'Institutional Considerations in Strengthening On-Farm Client-Oriented Research in National Agricultural Research Systems: Lessons from a Nine Country Study', *Experimental Agriculture* 27:343–73.

Maredia, M. and Eicher, C. (1995) 'The Economics of Wheat Research in Developing Countries: The One Hundred Million Dollar Puzzle', *World Development* 23:401–12.

Marquand, D. (1996) 'Time to take sides', *The Guardian* (London) 26 May:11.

Marshall, D. (1977) 'The Advantages and Hazards of Genetic Homogeneity', in P. Day (ed.) *The Genetic Basis of Epidemics in Agriculture*. New York: The New York Academy of Sciences.

Mashiringwani, N.A. (1996) 'Variety Testing, Selection and Release in the Department of Research and Specialist Services', unpublished paper prepared for ODI/CAZS Seed Regulatory Project.

Maurya, D.M. (1989) 'The Innovative Approach of Indian Farmers', in R. Chambers, A. Pacey and L.A. Thrupp (eds) *Farmer First. Farmer Innovation and Agricultural Research*. London: Intermediate Technology Publications.

Miclat-Teves, A. and Lewis, D. (1993) 'NGO–government Interaction in the Philippines: Overview', in J. Farrington and D. Lewis with S. Satish and A. Miclat-Teves (eds) *Non-Governmental Organizations and the State in Asia*. London: Routledge.

Mitnick, B.M. (1980) *The Political Economy of Regulation: Creating, Designing and Removing Regulatory Forms*. New York: Columbia University Press.

Moore, M. (1995) 'Promoting Good Government by Supporting Institutional Development?' *IDS Bulletin* 26(2):89–96.

Muchow, R.C. and Bidinger, F.R. (1996) 'Targeting Selection Programs to Drought-Prone Environments', paper presented at the International Conference on Genetic Improvement of Sorghum and Pearl Millet, 23–27 September, South Lubbock, TX.

Munankami, R. and Neupane, N. (1994) 'The Marketing of Seeds in Nepal: Policy Needs for its Expansion through Private Sector Involvement', in

Proceedings of Workshop for Enhancing Private Sector Involvement on Production, Processing, Marketing and Export of Vegetable and Other Seeds in Nepal, 10–12 August, Kathmandu.

Mushita, T.A. (1993) 'Strengthening the Formal Seed System in Communal Areas of Zimbabwe', in W. de Boef, K. Amanor, K. Wellard with A.J. Bebbington (1993) *Cultivating Knowledge. Genetic Diversity, Farmer Experimentation and Crop Research*. London: Intermediate Technology Publications.

Myrdal, G. (1970) *The Challenge of World Poverty*. New York: Vintage Books.

Needham, D. (1983) *The Economics and Politics of Regulation: A Behavioural Approach*. Boston MA: Little, Brown and Company.

Njoroge, K. (1996) 'Kenya Seed Regulatory Framework: Variety Testing, Selection, and Release', unpublished paper prepared for ODI/CAZS Seed Regulatory Project.

Norskog, C. (1995) *Hybrid Seed Corn Enterprises. A Brief History*. Willmar, MN: Maracom Corp.

North, D. (1990) *Institutions, Institutional Change and Economic Performance*. Cambridge: Cambridge University Press.

ODI Seeds and Biodiversity Programme (1996) *Relief and Rehabilitation Network: Good Practice Review* No. 4: Seeds Provision After Disasters. London: Overseas Development Institute.

O'Donoghue, M. (1995) 'The Whole Family Training Program on Post-Harvest Technologies. A Program Review'. A report for the Bangladesh-Australia Wheat Improvement Project, Dhaka.

Osborn, T. (1990) *Multi-Institutional Approaches to Participatory Technology Development: A Case Study From Senegal*, Agricultural Administration (Research and Extension) Network Paper No. 13. London: Overseas Development Institute.

Ostrom, E. (1990) *Governing the Commons*. Cambridge: Cambridge University Press.

Pain, A. (1986) 'Agricultural Research in Sri Lanka: An Historical Account', *Modern Asian Studies* 20(4):755–78.

PAMU (Projet Agricole de Muganza) (1993) *Rapport Annuel 1992*, Butare, Rwanda, Février.

Pardey, P.G., Roseboom, J. and Anderson, J.R. (1991) 'Regional Perspectives on National Agricultural Research', in P.G. Pardey, J. Roseboom and J.R. Anderson (eds) *Agricultural Research Policy: International Qualitative Perspectives*. Cambridge: Cambridge University Press.

Pattie, P. and Madawanaarchchi, W. (1993) 'Factors Affecting Seed Marketing in Sri Lanka', Peradeniya, Sri Lanka: Diversified Agriculture Research Project.

Paul, S. (1992) 'Accountability in Public Services: Exit, Voice and Control', *World Development* 20:1 047–60.

Pavez, I. and Bojanic, A. (1995) 'Enfoques Participativos y Alternativos para la Producción y Distribución de Semillas. Casos La Paz y Oruro: Papa y Quinua', unpublished paper prepared for ODI/CAZS Seed Regulatory Project.

Poey, F. (1991) 'Philippines: The Development of the Rice and Corn Seed Industry', Agricultural Policy Analysis Project, Phase II, Report No. 312. Boston, MA: Abt Associates.

Pray, C. (1990) 'The Potential Impact of Liberalizing India's Seed Laws', *Food Policy* 15:193–8.

Pray, C. and Gisselquist, D. (forthcoming) 'Impact of Turkey's 1980s Seed Regulatory Reforms', in D. Gisselquist and J. Srivastava (eds) *Easing Barriers to Movement of Plant Varieties for Agricultural Development*, World Bank Discussion Paper. Washington, DC: World Bank.

Pray, C. and Ramaswami, B. (1991) *A Framework for Seed Policy Analysis in Developing Countries*. Washington, DC: International Food Policy Research Institute.

Primo Braga, C. (1990) 'Guidance from Economic Theory', in E.W. Siebeck (ed) *Strengthening Protection of Intellectual Property in Developing Countries. A Survey of the Literature*, World Bank Discussion Papers, No. 112. Washington, DC: World Bank.

RAFI (1995) 'Utility Plant Patents: A Review of the US Experience (1985–July 1995)', *RAFI Communique*, July/August.

Rajbhandary, K.L. (1994) 'The Regulatory Frameworks for Seed Production, Purity and Sale in Nepal', ODI/CAZS. Pokhara, Nepal: Lumle Agricultural Research Centre.

Rao, A. (1996) 'The Regulatory Framework of Wheat and Rice in the Punjab, Pakistan', unpublished paper prepared for ODI/CAZS Seed Regulatory Project.

Rhoades, R.E. (1985) 'Traditional Potato Production and Farmers' Selection of Varieties in Eastern Nepal', *Potatoes in Food Systems Research Series No. 2*. Lima: International Potato Center.

Richards, P. (1985) *Indigenous Agricultural Revolution. Ecology and Food Production in West Africa*. London and Boulder, CO: Hutchinson and Westview Press.

Richards, P. (1986) *Coping with Hunger: Hazard and Experiment in an African Rice Farming System*. London: Allen and Unwin.

Romero, G.A. (1995) 'Generación y Liberación de Variedades de Tres Cultivos de Importancia Alimenticia en Bolivia: Maiz, Papa, Trigo', unpublished paper prepared for ODI/CAZS Seed Regulatory Project.

Rosales, J. (1995a) 'Informe Sobre Marcos Regulatorios para Semillas en Bolivia', unpublished paper prepared for ODI/CAZS Seed Regulatory Project.

Rosales, J. (1995b) 'Informe Sobre Enfoques Participativos y Alternativos para la Producción y Distribución de Semillas en Santa Cruz', unpublished paper prepared for ODI/CAZS Seed Regulatory Project.

Rose-Ackerman, S. (1978) *Corruption: A Study in Political Economy*. New York: Academic Press.

Rusike, J. (1995) 'An Institutional Analysis of the Maize Seed Industry in Southern Africa', unpublished PhD thesis, Dept. of Agricultural Economics, Michigan State University, Lansing, MI.

Rusike, J. and Musa, T.M. (1996) 'Seed Regulatory Frameworks: Zimbabwe', unpublished paper prepared for ODI/CAZS Seed Regulatory Project.

Rutz, H.W. (1990) 'Seed Certification in the Federal Republic of Germany', *Plant Varieties and Seeds* 3(3):157–63.

Sadowski, Y. (1991) *Political Vegetables? Businessman and Bureaucrat in the Development of Egyptian Agriculture.* Washington, DC: The Brookings Institition.

Salazar, R. (1992) 'Community Plant Genetic Resources Management: Experiences in Southeast Asia, in D. Cooper, R. Vellvé and H. Hobbelink (eds) *Growing Diversity: Genetic Resources and Local Food Security.* London: Intermediate Technology Publications.

Scheidegger, U. (1993) 'Genetic Diversity of Bean Production in Rwanda', in *Bean Program Annual Report 1993.* Cali, Colombia: CIAT.

Scheidegger, U., Prain, G., Ezeta, F. and Vittorelli, C. (1989) *Linking Formal R&D to Indigenous Systems: A User-Oriented Potato Seed Programme for Peru,* Agricultural Administration (Research and Extension) Network Paper No. 10. London: Overseas Development Institute.

Seghal, S. (1994) 'Opportunities in Hybrid Rice Development', *Patent World,* December.

Sharma, D. (1995) 'Food Will Be Used as a Weapon Against India', *Ceres* 151:38–41.

Simmonds, N.W. (1979) *Principles of Crop Improvement.* Harlow, UK: Longman.

Simmonds, N.W. (1984) 'Decentralized Selection', *Sugarcane* 6:8–10.

Simmonds, N.W. (1991) 'Selection for Local Adaptation in a Plant Breeding Programme', *Theoretical and Applied Genetics* 82:363–7.

Singh, R.P., Pal, S. and Morris, M. (1995) *'Maize Research, Development, and Seed Production in India: Contributions of the Public and Private Sectors',* CIMMYT Economics Working Paper 95–03. Mexico D.F.: CIMMYT.

Singh, S. (1992) 'Role of On-Farm Testing and Minikit in Varietal Releases', in *Proceedings of the Group Discussion on Management of Change in All India Co-ordinated Crop Improvement Projects.* New Delhi: Indian Council of Agricultural Research.

Smale, M. with Kaunda, Z., Makina, H., Mkandawire, M., Msowoya, M., Mwale, D. and Heisey, P. (1991) *Chimanga Cha Makolo, Hybrids, and Composites: An Analysis of Farmers' Adoption of Maize Technology in Malawi, 1988–91,* CIMMYT Economics Working Paper 91/04. Mexico D.F.: CIMMYT.

Smith, J.S.C. (1992) 'Plant Breeders' Rights in the USA; Changing Approaches and Appropriate Technologies in Support of Germplasm Enhancement', in *Plant Varieties and Seeds* 5(3):183–99.

Smith L. and Thomson, A. (1991) *The Role of Public and Private Agents in the Food and Agricultural Sectors of Developing Countries,* FAO Economic and Social Development Paper 105. Rome: FAO.

Smith, M.E., Coffman, W.R. and Barker, T.C. (1990) 'Environmental Effects of Selection Under High and Low Input Conditions', in M.S. Kang (ed.) *Genotype-by-Environment Interaction and Plant Breeding.* Baton Rouge, LA: Department of Agronomy, Louisiana Agricultural Experiment Station.

Smith, S. (1996) 'Farmers' Privilege, Breeders' Exemption and the Essentially Derived Varieties Concept: Status Report on Current Developments', in van Wijk and Jaffé.

Sperling, L. and Scheidegger, U. (1995) *Participatory Selection of Beans in Rwanda: Results, Methods and Institutional Issues*, Gatekeeper Series No. 51. London: International Institute for Environment and Development.

Sperling, L. (1992) 'Farmer Participation and the Development of Bean Varieties in Rwanda', in J. Moock and R. Rhoades (eds) *Diversity, Farmer Knowledge, and Sustainability*. Ithaca, NY and London: Cornell University Press.

Sperling, L. and Loevinsohn, M. (1992) 'The Dynamics of Adoption: Distribution and Mortality of Bean Varieties among Small Farmers in Rwanda', *Agricultural Systems* 41:441–53.

Sperling, L. and Berkowitz, P. (1994) *Partners in Selection. Bean Breeders and Women Bean Experts in Rwanda*. Washington, DC: CGIAR Gender Program.

Sperling, L., Loevinsohn, M. and Ntabomvura, B. (1993) 'Rethinking the Farmer's Role in Plant Breeding: Local Bean Experts and On-Station Selection in Rwanda' in *Experimental Agriculture* 29:509–19.

Sperling, L., Scheidegger, U. and Buruchara, R. (1996) *Designing Seed Systems with Small Farmers: Principles Derived from Bean Research in the Great Lakes Region of Africa*, Agricultural Administration (Research and Extension) Network Paper No. 60. London: Overseas Development Institute.

Srivastava, J.P. and Jaffee, S. (1993) *Best Practices for Moving Seed Technology. New Approaches to Doing Business*, World Bank Technical Paper No. 213. Washington, DC: World Bank.

Stallman, J.I. and Schmidt, A.A. (1987) 'Property Rights in Plants: Implications for Biotechnology Research and Extension', *American Journal of Agricultural Economics* 69(2):432–7.

Sthapit, B.R. (1995) 'Variety Testing, Selection and Release System for Rice and Wheat Crops in Nepal', ODI/CAZS. Pokhara, Nepal: Lumle Agricultural Research Centre.

Sthapit, B.R., Joshi, K.D. and Witcombe, J.R. (1996) 'Farmers' Participatory High Altitude Rice Breeding in Nepal: Providing Choice and Utilizing Farmers' Expertise', in L. Sperling and M. Loevinsohn (eds) *Using Diversity: Enhancing and Maintaining Genetic Resources On-farm*, Proceedings of a workshop 19–21 June 1995. New Delhi: IDRC/SARO.

Stigler, G. (1971) 'The Theory of Economic Regulation', *The Bell Journal of Economics and Management Science* 2:3–21.

Streeten, P. (1995) 'Markets and States: Against Minimalism and Dichotomy', in A. de Janvry, S. Radwan, E. Sadoulet and E. Thorbecke (eds) *State, Market and Civil Organizations*. Geneva: ILO.

Systemwide Programme on Participatory Research and Gender Analysis (1997) *A Global Programme on Participatory Research and Gender Analysis for Technology Development and Organizational Innovation*, Agricultural Administration (Research and Extension) Network Paper No. 72. London: Overseas Development Institute.

Tanzi, V. (1995) 'Corruption, Governmental Activities, and Markets', *Finance and Development* (December):24–6.

Tetlay, K., Heisey, P., Ahmed, Z. and Ahmad, M. (1990) 'Farmers' Seed Sources and Seed Management', in P. Heisey (ed.) *Accelerating the Transfer of Wheat Breeding Gains to Farmers: A Study of the Dynamics of Varietal Replacement in Pakistan.* Mexico, D.F.: CIMMYT.

Thakur, R. (1995) 'Prioritization and Development of Breeding Strategies for Rainfed Lowlands: a Critical Appraisal', in *Proceedings of the Conference 'Fragile Lives in Fragile Ecosystems'*, International Rice Research Institute, Los Baños: IRRI.

Thirtle, C. and Echeverria, R. (1994) 'Privatization and the Roles of Public and Private Institutions in Agricultural Research in Sub-Saharan Africa', *Food Policy* 19:31–44.

Tiedje, J. (1996) 'Possible Effects of Recent Developments in Plant-related Intellectual Property Protection in Europe', in van Wijk and Jaffé.

Trutmann, P. and Kayitare, E. (1991) 'Disease Control and Small Multiplication Plots Improve Seed Quality and Small Farm Dry Bean Yields in Central Africa', *Journal of Applied Seed Production* 9:36–40.

Turner, M. (1990) 'Republic of the Philippines. Policy Review of the National Seed Industry', paper prepared for FAO/DANIDA Regional Seed Improvement Project, Bangkok, Thailand.

Turner, M.R. (1994) 'Trends in India's Seed Sector', paper presented at Asian Seed 94, Chiang Mai, Thailand, 27–29 September.

Turton, C. and Baumann, P. (1996) 'Fodder Seed Systems in India: Meeting Future Demands?', unpublished paper. London: Indian Grasslands and Fodder Research Institute and Overseas Development Institute.

Ulrich, A., Furtan, W.H. and Schmitz, A. (1987) 'The Cost of a Licensing System Regulation: An Example from Canadian Prairie Agriculture', *Journal of Political Economy* 95(1): 160–78.

Upadhyaya, Y.M. (1995) 'ODA-CAZS-KRIBP Regulatory Framework Project: Report on Madhya Pradesh', unpublished paper prepared for ODI/CAZS Seed Regulatory Project.

Uphoff, N. (1994) 'Revisiting Institution Building', in N. Uphoff (ed.) *Puzzles of Productivity in Public Organizations.* San Francisco: ICS Press.

UPOV (1991a) *International Convention for the Protection of New Varieties of Plants of December 2, 1961, as Revised at Geneva on November 10, 1972, and on October 23, 1978*, Publication No. 295 (FEG). Geneva: UPOV.

UPOV (1991b) *International Convention for the Protection of New Varieties of Plants of December 2, 1961, as Revised at Geneva on November 10, 1972, on October 23, 1978, and on March 19, 1991*, Publication No. 221 (E). Geneva: UPOV.

UPOV (1992) *Records of the Diplomatic Conference for the Revision of the International Convention for the Protection of New Varieties of Plants, Geneva 1991.* Geneva: UPOV.

Van der Heide, W.M., Tripp, R. and de Boef, W.S. (compilers) (1996) *Local Crop Development: An Annotated Bibliography.* Rome: IPGRI, Wageningen, the Netherlands: CPRO-DLO(CGN) and London: ODI.

Van der Kooij, P.A.C.E. (1990) *Kwekersrecht in Ontwikkeling* (Plant Breeders' Rights in Development). Zwolle: Tjeenk Willink.

Van Santen, C. and Heriyanto (1996) 'The Source of Farmers' Soybean Seed in Indonesia', in H. van Amstel, J. Bottema, M. Sidik and C. van Santen (eds) *Integrating Seed Systems for Annual Food Crops*. Bogor, Indonesia: CGPRT Centre.

Van Wijk J. and Jaffé, W. (eds) (1996) *Intellectual Property Rights and Agriculture in Developing Countries*, Proceedings of a Seminar on the Impact of Plant Breeders' Rights in Developing Countries, March 7–8, 1995, Santa Fé de Bogotá, Colombia. Amsterdam: University of Amsterdam.

Van Wijk, J. and Junne, G. (1993) *Intellectual Property Protection of Advanced Technology. Changes in the Global Technology System: Implications and Options for Developing Countries*, Working Paper No. 10. Maastrict, The Netherlands: United Nations University, Institute for New Technologies.

Virk, D.S., Packwood, A.J. and Witcombe, J.R. (1996) *Varietal Testing and Popularisation and Research Linkages*, Centre for Arid Zone Studies Discussion Paper No. 2. Bangor, UK: CAZS.

Voss, J. (1992) 'Conserving and Increasing On-farm Genetic Diversity: Farmer Management of Varietal Bean Mixtures in Central Africa', in J.L. Moock and R.E. Rhoades (eds) *Diversity, Farmer Knowledge and Sustainability*. Ithaca, NY and London: Cornell University Press.

Voss, J. (1996) 'Participatory Breeding and IDRC's Biodiversity Programme', in Eyzaguirre and Iwanaga.

Vyas, K.L. (1995) 'Regulatory Framework and Seed Legislation in Rajasthan', unpublished paper prepared for ODI/CAZS Seed Regulatory Project.

Weltzein, E., Whitaker, M.L. and Anders, M.M. (1996a) 'Farmer Participation in Pearl Millet Breeding for Marginal environments', in *Participatory Plant Breeding: Proceedings of a Workshop on Participatory Plant Breeding*, Wageningen, The Netherlands, 26–29 July 1995. Rome:IPGRI.

Weltzein, E., Whitaker, M.L. and Dhamotharan, M. (1996b) 'Diagnostic Methods for Breeding Pearl Millet with Farmers in Rajasthan', in L. Sperling and M. Loevinsohn (eds) *Using Diversity: Enhancing and Maintaining Genetic Resources On-farm*, proceedings of a workshop held on 19–21 June 1995. New Delhi: IDRC/SARO.

Wilson, J.Q. (1980) 'The Politics of Regulation', in J.Q. Wilson (ed.) *The Politics of Regulation*. New York: Basic Books.

Witcombe, J.R. (1989) 'Variability in the Yields of Pearl Millet Varieties in India and Pakistan', in J.R. Anderson and P.B.R. Hazell (eds) *Variability in Grain Yields. Implications for Agricultural Research and Policy in Developing Countries*. Baltimore, MD and London: International Food Policy Research Institute and Johns Hopkins University Press.

Witcombe, J.R., Joshi, A., Joshi, K.D. and Sthapit, B.R. (1996) 'Farmer Participatory Crop Improvement I: Varietal Selection and Plant Breeding Methods and their Impact on Biodiversity'. *Experimental Agriculture*, 32:445–60.

246

Witcombe, J.R. and Joshi, A. (1996a) 'The Impact of Farmer Participatory Research on Biodiversity of Crops', in L. Sperling and M. Loevinsohn (eds) *Using Diversity: Enhancing and Maintaining Genetic Resources On-farm*, proceedings of a workshop held on 19–21 June 1995. New Delhi: IDRC/SARO.

Witcombe, J.R. and Joshi, A. (1996b) 'Farmer Participatory Approaches for Varietal Breeding and Selection and Linkages to the Formal Seed Sector', in Eyzaguirre and Iwanaga.

Worede, M. and Mekbib, H. (1993) 'Linking genetic resource conservation for farmers in Ethiopia', in W. de Boef, K. Amanor, K. Wellard with A. Bebbington (eds) *Cultivating Knowledge. Genetic Diversity, Farmer Experimentation and Crop Research.* London: Intermediate Technology Publications.

Wright, M., Donaldson, T., Cromwell, E. and New, J. (1994) *The Retention and Care of Seeds by Small-scale Farmers.* Chatham, UK: Natural Resources Institute.

Young, N. (1990) *Seed Potato Systems in Developed Countries: Canada, The Netherlands and Great Britain.* Lima, Peru: International Potato Center.

Ziegler, R. (1986) 'Application of a Systems Approach in a Commodity Research Programme: Evaluating Burundi Highland Maize', *Experimental Agriculture* 22:319–28.

Zimmerer, K.S. (1991) 'Managing Diversity in Potato and Maize Fields of the Peruvian Andes', *Journal of Ethnobiology* 11(1):23–49.

Zimmerman, M.J. de O. (1996) 'Breeding for Marginal/Drought-prone Areas in Northeastern Brazil', in *Participatory Plant Breeding, Proceedings of a Workshop on Participatory Plant Breeding*, Wageningen, The Netherlands, 26–29 July 1995. Rome: IPGRI.

Zulauf, C.R. and King, K.F. (1985) 'Farm Operators Who Sell Crop Production Inputs: The Case of Ohio Farmers Who Sell Seed', *Agribusiness* 1(2):193–9.

Appendix 1

Participants in the workshop

'REFORMING REGULATORY FRAMEWORKS FOR SMALL FARMER SEED SUPPLY'

London, 29–31 May 1996

Paul Balogun
Bedford, UK

M.P. Bharati
Koshi Hills Seed & Vegetable Project
Kathmandu, Nepal

L.J. (Bees) Butler
Department of Agricultural Economics
University of California
Davis, California

S. Ceccarelli
Acting Leader, Germplasm Programme
ICARDA (International Centre for Agricultural Research in the Dry Areas)
Aleppo, Syria

Elizabeth Cromwell
Overseas Development Institute
London

Soniia David
CIAT (International Center for Tropical Agriculture)
Kampala, Uganda

John Farrington
Overseas Development Institute
London

David Gisselquist
World Bank
Washington, DC

C.T. Hash
International Crops Research Institute for the Semi-arid Tropics
Andhra Pradesh, India

M.D. Hayward
Department of Plant Genetics and Plant Breeding
Institute of Grassland and Environment Research
Aberystwyth, UK

Shakeel Khan
Deputy Director
Federal Seed Certification Department
Islamabad, Pakistan

Mogens Lemonius
Regional Seed Programme Manager
FAO Regional Office for Asia and the Pacific
Bangkok, Thailand

Niels Louwaars
Centre for Plant Breeding and Reproduction Research
Wageningen, The Netherlands

J. Luhanga
Deputy Chief Agriculture
Research Officer
Department of Agricultural
Research
Lilongwe, Malawi

A.K.M. Giasuddin Milki
Director General, Seed Wing
Ministry of Agriculture
Dhaka, Bangladesh

Stephen Muliokela
Director
Seed Control and Certification
Institute
Chilanga, Zambia

John Nelson
Overseas Development Institute
London

V.K. Ocran
Head, National Seed Service
Department of Crop Services
Accra, Ghana

Mangala Rai
Assistant Director General
(Policy and Planning)
Indian Council of Agricultural
Research
New Delhi, India

Cadmo Rosell
Senior Officer
Seed and Plant Genetic
Resources Service
Plant Production and Protection
Division, FAO
Rome, Italy

J.M. Scott
Head
Natural Resources Policy and
Advisory Department
Overseas Development
Administration
London

Rajendra Shrestha
President
Seed Entrepreneurs Association
of Nepal
Kathmandu, Nepal

Louise Sperling
Overseas Development Institute
London

Jitendra Srivastava
Principal Agriculturalist
World Bank
Washington, DC

Bhuwon Sthapit
Nepal Agricultural Research
Council
Pokhara, Nepal

S.P. Tiwari
Assistant Director General
(Seeds)
Indian Council of Agricultural
Research
New Delhi, India

Robert Tripp
Overseas Development Institute
London

Michael Turner
Course Director (Seed
Technology)
University of Edinburgh
Edinburgh, UK

M.P. Upadhyay
Nepal Agricultural Research
Council
Kathmandu, Nepal

A. van Gastel
Team Leader,
IITA/GTZ Seed Promotion and
Marketing Project
Accra, Ghana

Jeroen van Wijk
  Department of Political Science
  University of Amsterdam
  The Netherlands

W.J. van der Burg
  Centre for Plant Breeding and
  Reproduction Research
  Wageningen, The Netherlands

D.S. Virk
  Centre for Arid Zone Studies
  University of Wales
  Bangor, UK

John R. Witcombe
  Centre for Arid Zone Studies
  University of Wales
  Bangor, UK

Index

ENDA 219
enforcement 12, 45, 52–3, 116, 126, 135, 146, 148–56 *passim*, 170, 180, 182
Eritrea 221
Ethiopia 22–3, 26
Europe 14, 16, 17, 89, 149, 160–3 *passim*, 188, 193, 196
European Union 50, 89, 90, 92, 100, 107, 124, 125, 161, 176–7, 194, 194n9, 197
   Common Catalogue 100, 107, 177
   Parliament 108
Evans, L. 14, 15
exchange 7, 10, 14, 59, 81, 87, 116, 220, 222
'exit' 53, 159–60, 172
experimental stations 36, 71, 112, 147, 200, 204, 209
exports 89, 105, 140, 162, 165, 179, 183, 185
extension 4, 13, 18, 20, 34, 35, 37, 61, 62, 64, 76, 77, 79, 81, 87, 93, 95, 96, 98, 104, 109, 114, 132, 138, 150, 153, 154, 169, 171–3, 200, 224
Eyzaguirre, P. 211n2

FAO 28, 125, 134, 137, 144, 145, 218
   Seed Improvement Project 217
farmers group, 26, 114, 119, 120, 151, 160, 200, 206–12 *passim*, 220, 221
'farmers' privilege' 21, 193–5, 197
farmers, resource-poor 3, 4, 7, 9, 12, 26, 41, 54, 74, 85, 87, 98, 112, 131–2, 160, 162, 168, 194n9, 198, 215–30 *passim*
Farrington, J. 211, 222
fees 95, 109, 113, 128, 151, 177, 178
Ferguson, J. 102
fertilizers 71–2, 174, 179
Filippello, M. 21, 31, 34
Finney, D.J. 67
FIS 193
Fitzgerald, D. 115, 149
Flora, J. 165
fodder 20, 22, 64, 73, 78, 105, 150, 194n9
food security 46, 105, 117
foundation seed 34, 37, 95, 132, 136, 137, 154, 170, 175, 226
Fowler, A. 223
Fowler, C. 21, 149, 163, 164
France 16, 17, 29, 161

Francks, P. 16
Freeman, C. 185
Friedman, L. 44
Friis-Hansen, E., 27, 98, 130
Fujisaka, S. 22

Galt, D.L. 83
Gambia, The 34, 220, 222, 225
Garay, A. 136, 167
GATT 40, 105, 185
   Uruguay Round 105, 186nl
Germany 89, 123, 124, 161, 162
germination capacity 37, 121, 123, 129–31 *passim*, 136, 181
germplasm 14, 15, 19, 24–6 *passim*, 33, 41, 59, 171, 198, 199, 201, 202
GGDP 19
Ghana 19, 27, 151, 167, 177, 221, 227
Ghijsen, H. 108
GIS 77
Gisselquist, D. 174–84
Goldberg, V. 43
grain/seed swaps 30–1, 127, 138, 191, 192, 195
Green, T. 99, 223
Grindle, M. 157, 163, 164, 167
Grisley, W. 28
groundnut 14, 63, 69, 70, 72, 128, 130, 181
Groosman, T. 27
Gutiérrez, M.B. 188, 192

Hamilton, N.D. 194, 197
Hampton, J.G. 90, 92, 110
Harriss-White, B. 52, 55, 165, 170
Heijbroek, A. 191
Heisey, P. 66
Helfand, G. 51
Henderson, P.A. 23
Heriyanto 31, 127
Hernandez, J.E. 66, 68, 73, 99
Hérnandez, L.A. 213
Hirschman, A.O. 159, 160
hybrids/hybridization 15, 16, 20, 21, 24, 25, 27, 39, 46, 66, 82, 124, 183, 184, 196, 197

ICARDA 210
ICRISAT 210
ideology 44, 157, 162
Iglesias, C. 213
imitation 189–90

technology 3, 5, 176–9 *passim*, 185, 200, 211, 226
testing 12, 20, 26, 30, 33, 36–8, 40, 59–123, 151, 171, 176–9, 199, 200, 206–11, 223, 230 *see also* certification
cost/funding 93–5, 109, 115–16, 120
DUS 92, 94, 100, 109, 113, 130, 176
efficiency 63, 64, 67–9 *passim*, 76–8, 92–6
ISTA 123
performance 8, 12, 39, 88–92, 98–100, 106, 108, 109, 111–19, 164, 176, 177, 181
reform of 76–84
Tetlay, K. 19
Thailand 134, 167, 180
Thakur, R. 83
Thirtle, C. 32
Thomas, J. 157, 163, 164, 167
Thomson, A. 54
Tiedje, J. 194
trade 6, 7, 13, 14, 29, 30, 138, 180, 185, 191–5, 197, 230
training 30, 34, 132, 147, 150, 151, 168, 169, 171–2, 221
transparency 64, 92, 93, 102, 105, 106, 126, 133, 163
trials 37, 59–87, 98–100, 102
multi-locational 61, 70–3, 77, 112
on-farm 75, 76, 82, 96, 112, 114, 120, 130, 180, 201–4 *passim*, 207, 209; farmer managed 82–3, 114, 120
Tripp, R. 3–58, 88–154, 157–73, 221
TRIPs 185–7 *passim*, 186n1
truthful labelling 74, 123–5, 131–3 *passim*, 136, 139, 144, 148–50, 152–4, 180–3 *passim*
Trutmann, P. 130, 131
Tunwar, N.S. 124, 131, 135
Turkey 179, 183
Turner, M.R. 18, 27, 91, 102, 107, 142, 152
Turton, C. 150

Ulrich, A. 105, 165
UK 26, 47–8, 50, 89, 97, 109, 115, 124, 144, 147, 161, 162, 167
ODA 147
uniformity 39, 97, 130, 138, 212

universities 25, 59, 60, 75, 79, 123, 169, 221, 226
Upadhyaya, Y.M. 65, 75
Uphoff, N. 158
UPOV 96, 97, 108, 193–5, 197
Uquillas, J.E. 130, 133
Uruguay 187–9 *passim*, 194
US 14–15, 17, 19, 21, 25, 28, 90, 97, 115, 125, 138, 148–9, 176, 177, 188, 190, 193–4, 197
certification in 123, 124, 127, 144, 181
regulation in 44, 47, 48, 50–2, 89, 100, 160–5

value, market 74, 78
van der Burg, W. Joost 121–54
van der Heide, W.M. 198
van der Kooij, P.A.C.E. 193
van Ree, M.C. 188
van Santen, C. 31, 127
van Wijk, J. 41, 90, 108, 125, 128, 131, 162, 185–97
VCU 92, 100, 177
vegetables 19, 22, 30, 34, 100, 107–8, 117, 124, 134, 147–9 *passim*, 175, 180, 183, 184, 196
Venezuela 187–9 *passim*
Virk, D.S. 59–87, 96
'voice' 53–4, 159–60, 172
voluntary sector 4, 10, 11, 13, 32, 41, 81–2, 159, 169, 173, 217–19, 222–30 *see also* NGOs
Voss, J. 97, 198, 206
Vyas, K.L. 65, 75

weeds 22, 46, 123, 137
Weltzein, R.E. 200, 210
wheat 14, 16–19 *passim*, 22, 25–7 *passim*, 37, 63, 65–8 *passim*, 70, 71, 97, 99, 124, 128, 144, 165, 174, 177, 178, 181, 183, 190–2, 195, 196 *see aso* India
Wilson, J.Q. 44
Witcombe, J.R. 59–87, 198, 199, 202
women 15, 204, 208–9
Worede, M. 25
World Bank 189
WTO 21, 40, 108, 171, 187
Wright, M. 150, 222